Illustrated Editions

of the Works

of

William Morris

in

English

BARRY BURMAN
["I . . . slew Guy of the dolorous blast"]
Shameful Death, p. 4 (2.20)

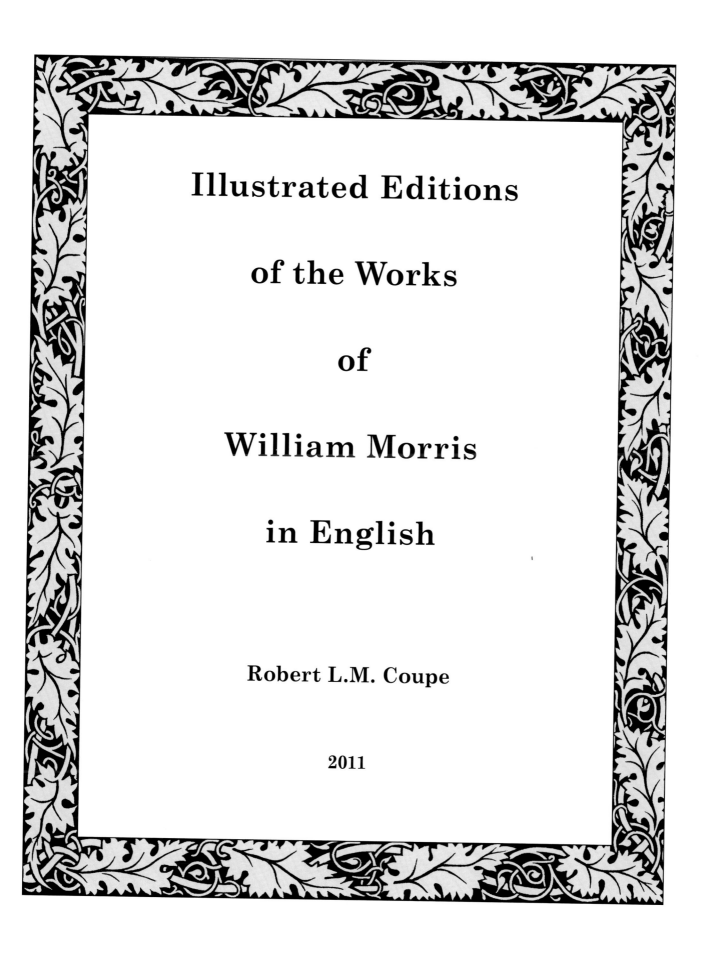

Illustrated Editions

of the Works

of

William Morris

in English

Robert L.M. Coupe

2011

Second edition, 2011
First edition 2002, published jointly by Oak Knoll Press and the British Library.

Published by
Lonsdale and Young Publishers
4916 Rowan, Burnaby, BC V5G 3T1
Canada

ISBN: 978-0-9867535-0-3

Title: Illustrated Editions of the Works of William Morris in English
Author: Robert L.M. Coupe
Layout and design: Mary Lee Shelley

Library and Archives Canada Cataloguing in Publication

Coupe, Robert L.M.
Illustrated editions of the works of William Morris in English / Robert L.M.
Coupe. -- 2nd ed.

Includes bibliographical references.
ISBN 978-0-9867535-0-3

1. Morris, William, 1834-1896--Bibliography. 2. Morris, William,
1834-1896--Illustrations--Bibliography. 3. Illustrated books--Bibliography.
I. Title.

Z8595.C68 2011   016.821'8   C2010-906670-7

This work was printed in Canada.

Contents

List of Illustrations

Where an illustration has a caption or a title I have used it. If it lacks one or the other, an appropriate caption appears in brackets.

Abbreviations

AIC	Art Institute of Chicago
BF	H. Buxton Forman, *The Books of William Morris*
BOD	The Bodleian Library, Oxford
BL	The British Library
ECR	English Civil Registers
GSA	Glasgow School of Art
HL	The Huntington Library, San Marino, California
HLH	Houghton Library, Harvard University, Cambridge, Massachusetts
KP	Kelmscott Press
NATS	National Arts Training School, South Kensington, London
n.d.	No date
NIF	No information found
NLS	The National Library of Scotland
NYPL	New York Public Library
PRB	Pre-Raphaelite Brotherhood
RA	Royal Academy
RCA	Royal College of Art, London
RSA	Royal Scottish Academy
RSBA	Royal Society of British Artists
TS	Temple Scott, *A Bibliography of the Works of William Morris*
UBC	University of British Columbia Library
WAL	J.J. Walsdorf, *William Morris in Private Press and Limited Editions*

Preface

This book appeared in 2002 under the title
*Illustrated Editions of the Works of William
Morris: A Descriptive Bibliography*, published by
Oak Knoll Press. In this book I sought to describe
the visual interpretation of texts by Morris as
seen in the illustrated books published during his
lifetime and subsequently to the present day. In
spite of the title, I made no attempt to provide the
level of bibliographical description advocated by
such modern writers as Fredson Bowers. Instead
I presented a description in a form accessible to
general readers and detailed enough for them to
visualise the physical form of the book. The main
focus was the art work and its success or otherwise
in complementing the text.

Since the publication of this original edition I have
become dissatisfied with many aspects of it. Most
importantly it lacks several entries found only after
publication. It has some factual errors, which do not
invalidate the main body of information, but do vitiate
it. Furthermore, presentation of information seems
unnecessarily wordy in some respects and too sparse
in others. I have sought to amend these problems in
this new edition, retaining the previous framework,
but largely re-writing the text. Naturally, I have
corrected the factual errors, taken out two items
which I decided do not qualify as illustrated, added
many more that do, reorganised the arrangement of
chapters, renumbered entries as necessary, made the
descriptions of the physical aspects of the books more
concise, discussed and described their decoration and
illustration at much greater length, relegated the
chapter on unique copies to an appendix, and deleted
the irrelevant parts of the appendix on paperback
books. Finally, I have emphasised the main thrust of

the book with a more appropriate title, which draws attention to its object, the description of the art work.

Bibliographers of Morris's published work have documented various parts of it, from the year of his death to contemporary times. Buxton Forman and Scott Temple separately aimed at a complete listing when their books appeared in 1896. Indeed, the former has remained the standard reference up to recent times, in spite of the revelation by Carter and Pollard in 1934 that Buxton Forman himself fraudulently created some of the entries. In 1981 Walsdorf supplemented the earlier books with a bibliography of works "by and about Morris" published "by private presses and [in] limited editions." Peterson wrote a bibliography in 1984 dealing with the output of the Kelmscott Press. Pye performed a similar service in 1990 with a detailed listing of the American editions of Morris's work published by Roberts Brothers of Boston. Bishop's bibliography of the Mosher Press, which Oak Knoll published in 1996, includes those works of Morris which Mosher put out. The closest we have to a comprehensive bibliography of the various editions of Morris's writing came from LeMire in 2006. LeMire aimed to document all first editions of Morris to the time of publication of his bibliography, and all editions, including later ones, published up to 1915. Thus later editions published after 1915 do not appear. In recent years the William Morris Society has recorded new editions of books by and about Morris in a centrefold in *The Journal of William Morris Studies* and its predecessor *The Journal of the William Morris Society*, at roughly two-year intervals. These sources contain many of the entries which appear in my own book, and those readers seeking detailed bibliographical information may find it there. They will obtain from my book more information about the illustrations and about the artists who created them.

I see this book as of value to academic libraries, book dealers, and collectors of Morris's printed works.

Acknowledgements

The author of any book which presents information depends on others for some or even much of his data. I am no exception, and recognise with pleasure the help received from the staffs of the libraries which gave me access to items in their collections. Where the description of a book derives from a copy held in one of these libraries, I have indicated it after the title of the work concerned. These libraries comprise the Bodleian Library, Oxford; British Library, London; Fisher Rare Book Library, Toronto; Houghton Library, Harvard University; Huntington Library, San Marino, California; New York Public Library; and Pierpont Morgan Library, New York. In addition to my visits there, Alan Jutzi of the Huntington Library and Jenny Rathbun of the Houghton Library sent further information about items in their collections. Some publishers supplied information about their books directly. They comprise James Jasek of the Library Binding Company of Waco, Texas, and Douglas Menville of Newcastle Publishing, Hollywood, California. I am also grateful to the many booksellers, too numerous to list individually, who drew my attention to illustrated editions included herein of which I had been previously unaware. Mark James of Christie's Auctioneers was generous with his time when he gave me an unequalled opportunity to examine a unique copy of *The Roots of the Mountains* (see Appendix 3) prior to its auction in July 2000, and subsequently corresponded with me about this book.

Information about artists came from many sources. Michael Felmingham and Mike Goldmark gave biographical details of the artist Barry Burman. Edward Maggs of Maggs Brothers, London, and Richard Swift of Sheffield Hallam University supplied similar information about Edmond Reuter

and William Northend respectively. John De Pol sent biographical information about himself, and Elspeth Lamb directed me to information relating to herself. I owe a particular debt of gratitude to Philip Bishop of Mosher Books for putting me in contact with James O'Kane Conwell Jr., who wrote a vivid account of his grandmother, Helen Marguerite O'Kane. Without his help virtually no information about her would have been available, and my deepest thanks go to him. Philip Bishop has also provided me with ongoing support and encouragement in general, and specifically in putting me in contact with Dr. Terence Day of Okanagan College, Kelowna, British Columbia; Dr. Kurt Bodling of the Office of Commonwealth Libraries, Harrisburg, Pennsylvania; and Mr. Steven Beare of Wilmington, Delaware. These three individuals provided much of the information about the artist John Gretzer in the biographical sketch in this book. The staff of the Fine Arts Library of the University of British Columbia were most helpful in directing me to much of the biographical information on other artists. I am further indebted to Michael Felmingham for information about his Gazebo Press and have a similar debt to Asa Peavy of the Bullnettle Press.

My heartfelt thanks go to all these individuals and institutions. Their help has provided considerable pleasure in the otherwise arduous task of compiling this book. My deep thanks go to my wife, Rosemary, who proofread and edited the manuscript and pulled the crop of typographical weeds which had choked the text.

Various illustrations are reproduced by gracious permission of the copyright holders. They comprise Michael Felmingham and the late Barry Burman (*Shameful Death* [2.20]), Clover Hill Editions (*Cupid and Psyche* [4.7]); Stephen Gretzer, the son of the artist (*Grettir the Strong* [5.3]); Owen Legg (*On First Seeing Iceland* [12.1]), Elspeth Lamb (*The Well at the World's End* [17.2]) and Greg Suriano (for re-use of many of the decorations throughout the text). My thanks go to all of these individuals.

Introduction

William Morris was born in Walthamstow, northeast of London, in 1834 into an affluent family. His parents sent him to school at Marlborough in 1848. On leaving there he had a short period of private tutoring and then proceeded to Exeter College, Oxford University, in 1852. Shortly after he arrived he met Edward Jones, later Burne-Jones (see 3.1), who, like himself, planned to take holy orders. They became life-long friends and collaborators, with incalculable effects on the future of the Arts and Crafts movement in Britain. Their joint reading brought them under the influence of John Ruskin and, a little later, of Dante Gabriel Rossetti (see 2.4). The precepts of these two men fired them with enthusiasm for a career in the arts. Acting on this conviction, Morris articled himself to an architect in Oxford in early 1856 after graduating late the previous year. Meanwhile, he had started the *Oxford and Cambridge Magazine*, to which he contributed his first significant prose and poetry. In mid-1856 he finally met Rossetti, who persuaded Morris to devote himself to fine art. Morris abandoned architecture after his first twelve months of articles to follow Rossetti's advice. Throughout 1857 he worked in a range of artistic media. That summer Rossetti conscripted him and a group of young artists to paint murals on the ceiling of the Oxford Union Debating Hall. This project eventually extended over nine months. During this time Morris published his first book of poetry, *The Defence of Guenevere*, which appeared early in 1858. While he was engaged in painting the murals, Morris met Jane Burden, whom he married in 1859. He promptly commissioned the building of his first home, Red House in Kent. To accomplish this he turned to Philip Webb, the architect who had supervised Morris during his year of articling. Morris employed the contractor William

Kent for the actual construction. The Morrises lived at Red House for the following five years.

By 1860 Morris had settled on interior decoration as his chosen field and set up a company to execute his plans. It had a slow start but eventually became enormously successful, largely due to the artistic gifts, energy, and application of Morris himself. In particular, he sought personal proficiency in the techniques of manufacture, as the best way to ensure a high quality of the finished item. Over a period of years his company became a major supplier of fabrics, wallpapers, carpets, tapestries, stained glass, tiles, and furniture. He continued to write poetry and achieved fame with the Victorian public as the author of *The Earthly Paradise*, published in instalments between 1868 and 1870. Meanwhile, he had become interested in the Norse sagas and began a long and fruitful collaboration with Eirikr Magnusson, translating the sagas into English and rendering some in verse. Another artistic activity not connected with his business was calligraphy. He produced numerous manuscripts in his own hand through the 1860s until the mid-1870s (see Appendix 3).

As Morris's firm grew, he found it increasingly hard to travel from Kent to London to manage it. He therefore sold Red House late in 1865 and moved his family, which now included two daughters, Jane Alice (Jenny) and Mary (May), born in 1861 and 1862 respectively, back to London. The second half of the 1860s saw his wife's growing disaffection towards their marriage, eventuating in her liaison with Rossetti. However, Morris and Jane maintained the form of a relationship. In 1871, Morris, helped by Fairfax Murray (see 6.1), found Kelmscott Manor in Oxfordshire, which became Morris's much-loved country home for the rest of his life. It was this year too that Morris undertook the first of his two visits to Iceland, which made a great impression on him. Its landscapes were later to loom large in his prose fiction, and they undoubtedly enhanced the imagery of his translations of the Icelandic sagas and stories.

Morris's activities took a new turn in the late 1870s when he involved himself in politics, becoming an active and committed socialist by the early 1880s. He put enormous effort into promoting the socialist cause throughout the decade, lecturing up and down the country, organising the often fractious socialist movement, writing prolifically on the subject of social justice, and editing and publishing the socialist periodical *Justice*. He broke with the main socialist body, the socialist Democratic Federation, at the end of 1884, and set up his own group, the Socialist League. He edited and financed the League's journal, *Commonweal*, from 1885 to 1890. By this time, in spite of Morris's efforts, the League had split into factions. He continued to support Socialism through a local Hammersmith branch, but resigned from the League and ceased taking a significant part in political activity at the national level. Instead he became absorbed by the last great interest in his life, the production of beautiful books.

Morris had had a long-standing interest in books and especially in the form a book should have. This interest found expression in the large collection of early printed books which he amassed, but more importantly in his writings and lectures on the subject. William Peterson gathered this material into a single volume in 1982 (see bibliography). Morris found the opportunity to put his ideas into practice when he came into contact with Emery Walker, an expert in printing and types. Between them they set up the Kelmscott Press that year. Morris had continued to write since the success of *The Earthly Paradise*. He put out verse translations of classical epics, *The Aeneids of Virgil* in 1876 and *The Odyssey of Homer* in 1887, and poems in periodicals. Starting in 1886 he began to write full-length works of fiction. He continued to reprint many of these and most of his earlier works at the Kelmscott Press until his death in 1896.

MacKail, Morris's first biographer, quotes one of Morris's doctors, who famously remarked, "He died of being William Morris, and has done more work than most ten men." The doctor erred if he implied that overwork caused Morris's death. More likely he had in mind the true state of affairs: the very attributes which endowed Morris with his abundant gifts, and enabled him to play so many parts, also determined his physical make-up, one prone to the illnesses that killed him. The doctor might have added that Morris did the work of ten men *better* than most men could have done a tenth of it. Morris's legacy of fine design in all his fields of activity still influences artists and craftsmen today, just as his political writings still influence current socialist thought.

Advances in technology in the nineteenth and early twentieth centuries made it increasingly easy to print illustrations of good quality in colour. This resulted in an outpouring of illustrated books in the period preceding World War I. Most of the significant illustrated editions of works by Morris date from this time. The last commercial edition with art work commissioned specially for the book appeared in 1968 (see 5.3). In modern publishing, illustration accompanying the text has become uncommon. If present at all one finds it limited to the dust jacket or, in the case of paperback books, to the cover. However, one does see textual illustration occasionally in science fiction and fantasy writing, as in a reprint of "The Hollow Land" which appeared in 1971 included in a magazine (see 1.4). In the last three decades readers of Morris have seen the trend, now commonplace, of pictures originally created for another purpose used to illustrate the text of a new edition, rather than the commissioning of contemporary art work with the potential of fresh insight. The phenomenon probably goes back to 1888 (see 4.3) among the group of works described in this book, but from an aberration in the nineteenth century it has become the norm by the twenty-first. I include editions of this kind, mostly anthologies, with distaste, since the illustration generally reflects not the response of an artist to a text, but the cunning of a designer in choosing a good match between picture and written word. In recent years new illustration of Morris texts has come from private presses, notable among recent ones being *Masters in This Hall* from The Poole Press in 1996 (see 2.22) and *The Story of the*

Unknown Church from The Hill Press of Steven Heaver Jr. in 2001 (see 1.5).

After his centenary year in 1934, interest in Morris waned judging by the decline in the number of new editions of books by and about him. Beginning about 1960, interest in him revived, and he and his work are once again the focus of intense attention. This likely stems in part from the activity of the William Morris Society, founded in 1955, but more from the recognition that his thinking, as expressed in his writing, addresses many of the social problems we face today. The output of new editions has paralleled this renewed interest. Illustrated editions have participated both in this nadir and subsequent renaissance. This book contains no entries for new editions, as distinct from reprints of earlier ones, between 1932 and 1961. The earlier year saw MacMillan's *Sons of the Volsungs* (see 7.3P) while the later one produced *The Story of Grettir the Strong* from The Bodley Head (see 5.2P). More dispiritingly still, both of these editions are paraphrases, in which the artist responds to Morris's story but not to his original text. Since 1960 a steady trickle of illustrated editions has appeared, though with the limitations noted above.

The present text looks at the response which Morris's writing elicited from the artists who illustrated his works. In art, as in many other things, the work of one individual often shapes that of another expressing him or herself in a different medium. Given the lifelong friendship and artistic collaboration between William Morris and Edward Burne-Jones, there can be no doubt of the influence each had on the other. Morris also had a direct influence on the illustrations of other artists from whom he commissioned work, as is documented by letters in which he discusses the concepts he had in mind. Scholars of Morris have paid less attention to the influence Morris has exerted on other artists purely through his artistic creations, at least as far as the written word is concerned. However, some of the finest illustrated editions of Morris's writings were published after his death. While some are well known, others have been neglected and should receive recognition. This book seeks to describe the editions in which these illustrations appear and to discuss the success of the illustrators in interpreting Morris's text. Naturally these descriptions include the illustrated editions of his work in which Morris himself collaborated.

The Victorian public at large, as distinct from the minority who could afford his decorations and furnishings, knew William Morris principally through his poetry, to the point that he was offered the post of Poet Laureate in 1892. Indeed, the catalogue of the British Library still identifies him as "William Morris, Poet." The many editions of his works attest to his immense popularity. No doubt school teachers shared in this enthusiasm and would have transmitted it to their pupils. In fact, Ticknor and Company's edition of parts of *The Earthly Paradise* was published for school use as early as 1888. It therefore comes as no surprise to find his work, particularly his poetry, republished often in the decades after his death. These new editions include an appreciable

number with illustration. Except for some of the translations, publishers put out at least one illustrated edition, in whole or in part, of all of Morris's major poems and collections of poetry. His prose works attracted less interest from artists, and Morris himself published most of their illustrated editions. Some of the illustrated editions of his poetry were brought out by commercial publishers and some by private presses, for whom the primary consideration is the beauty of the book. Whereas one would expect considerations of profit to constrain commercial publishers, in actuality they produced some of the more attractive works during the heyday of illustrated books.

What constitutes an illustrated book? A broad definition would include any printed material with at least one picture relating to the text. A more narrow view requires a series of such pictures, specially commissioned for the particular edition. I incline to the second interpretation, but shall describe and discuss all the editions which can lay claim to be illustrated. Most attention goes to those in the second group, with comments on the layout of the text and the artist's visual interpretation of it.

I have also omitted one or two items which some might regard as illustrated. For example, in 1996 Gwasg Gregynog printed a sheet in an edition "of about 150 copies" [personal communication from David Esselmont, the printer] and reprinted it a year later with a different layout. It contains a linocut by Peter Allen and the well-known lines by Morris extolling the importance of a beautiful house and a beautiful book. Exquisitely produced as it is, one cannot accept a fragment like this quotation as an independent work.

A related but more difficult decision arises from books which contain decoration, such as *The Earthly Paradise of William Morris*, published by Dove Tail Books in 1996. This small anthology contains excerpts of Morris's writing on the decorative arts, architecture, literature, and social issues. It has numerous floral tailpieces and marginal decoration, some full-page designs by Burne-Jones for tapestries and stained glass, and a picture of a church window with Morris and Company's glass in place. However, these designs do not illustrate the text as such. The same objection applies to *Notes on His Aims in Founding the Kelmscott Press*. While it contains a frontispiece woodcut engraving, the picture was originally drawn by Burne-Jones to illustrate an abortive edition of *Cupid and Psyche*, and it does not illustrate the text of *Notes on His Aims* itself. Some books, such as the Morris titles which Pryor published in 1979-80 in their *Fiction in English* series, have illustration limited to the dust jacket. Since the jacket is ephemeral, these books also do not find a place in these pages. Finally, I have not included the many works which have only a frontispiece picture of Morris himself, and the smaller number which contain a series of pictures of his family and his associates, such as most volumes of *The Collected Works of William Morris*, published between 1910 and 1915, or Douglas Wilson's *Two Sides of the River* (WAL #179).

In the books selected for description, I shall consider the work of an illustrator from the standpoint of choice of subject, technical ability, artistic creativity, and degree of success in unifying the illustration with the text and layout of the book. The artist can choose any subject the work suggests. However, pictures which portray the central theme, the dominant action, climactic event or a combination of all three are the most appropriate focus for the artist's attention. Technical competence and artistic creativity need little elaboration; one expects competence and if it is deficient one may not fully appreciate the artist's creative vision. Conversely, the artist may have high technical skill but lack something which seizes and holds the attention of the viewer. Ideally, the illustrated book is a creation which includes binding, type of paper, layout, text, and pictures, all combined to form a unified whole. Much of the success of such a book therefore rests with the editor and publisher, unless the artist has a measure of control over its final form, as did Morris himself with books from the KP.

Those KP editions of his writing for which Morris obtained illustration figure prominently in the present book. In describing them, I emphasise their pictorial and decorative qualities, with less attention to purely mechanical features of publication, though these are outlined as well. Peterson supplies full details of these features in his bibliography of the KP.

Each description of a book includes a biographical sketch of the artist[s]. Where the bulk of the information comes from one source, a brief reference appears at the end of the sketch. The bibliography at the end of the book provides the full reference. However, in some cases I could discover little or nothing about an artist and have had to leave a section with fragmentary data or completely blank. In a few books the artist signed himself only by his initials. This practice is so widespread that publishers have issued several dictionaries devoted solely to identifying artists from initials or monograms. These dictionaries helped only in a few instances.

If the date of publication of a book does not appear on the title page or in the colophon, I have given it where the publisher states it elsewhere in the book. If internal evidence is lacking, I have supplied the date, when it is available, from external sources, or failing that resorted to informed conjecture.

Finally, some of the entries come from relatively obscure private presses. The older presses are well documented in such standard references as those of Ransom and of Franklin (1969). For more modern private presses I have supplied information in the introduction to the chapter in which the entry appears.

In the first version of this book entries are arranged chronologically, with each work assigned its own chapter, and each edition of the work a separate number within the chapter. This results in several chapters with only one entry. In the current book some of these chapters are

consolidated; for example the socialist pamphlets now appear together, as do *A Book of Verse* and *Love Is Enough*. I perceive these last two works as having a common origin (see introduction to Chapter 6). Thus the numeration of entries differs in many cases from that of the old edition. It also differs within a chapter where I have inserted additional entries. When referring to an entry in future one will need to specify the edition. This seems preferable to the alternative of maintaining the old numeration with an ever-lengthening tail of suffix letters or numbers or both. The previous framework still exists, summarised on the following page.

The popularity of Morris's poetry during his life and in the first decades after he died ensured the attention of composers who provided musical settings for some of his work. I am unaware of any list of these composers or of the poems they set and make no claim that the following compilation is complete. However the list does include Sir Edward Bax ("Golden Guendolen" and a fragment from *Sigurd the Volsung*) and Gustav Holst ("several songs"). Holst was acquainted with Morris. His setting of *Masters in this Hall* is discussed more fully in the introduction to Chapter 2. Other composers comprise Julius Harrison (four poems from *The Defence of Guenevere* and "Golden Guendolen"), A. Jaimare (a fragment from *The Earthly Paradise*), and Vincent Thomas (a fragment from "The Eve of Crecy"). I have seen Jaimare's piece only in manuscript, and do not know whether it was ever published. Most of the sheet music I have seen which presents these settings is not illustrated. The last in the list just given provides an exception. On the cover a rectangular headpiece in black and white depicts two knights charging each other. The banner of the one on the left carries the fleur de lys, the one on the right the running lion of England. I have not included this item in the present book, since the whole emphasis is on the musical score and it contains only a small fragment of the poem. An illustrated score which does appear is *A Death Song for Alfred Linnell* (see 8.3). The composer for this song was Malcolm Lawson. Poems with a political message lend themselves to music. Communal singing has a unifying effect on a group, as every religious organisation, past and present, knows very well. However, I have come across only two other such poems set to music, *The March of the Workers* set by Alan Bush, and *Down among the Dead Men*. Morris published both in *Chants for Socialists*. The melody for *Down among the Dead Men* was published in *People's Songs*, volume III, number 8, in September 1948, but I have been unable to locate its source. While this pamphlet contains illustration, none relates directly to Morris's text. The single folded sheet of Bush's setting of "The March of the Workers" has an illustration on the top half of the front page showing a group of roughly-dressed marching men, the foremost carrying a flag on a pole, presumably the red flag of the International. The sheet is dated 1950.

Conventions Used
in Describing the Illustrated Books

Copies examined: I have examined at least one copy of every book described. Where a publisher issued multiple reprints, underlined dates designate those reprints examined.

Order of entries: The date on which Morris published his work determines the order of chapters, the earliest first.

All illustrated editions of any given text are grouped together in their own chapter and arranged chronologically by the date of their publication.

Editions which contain the entire text of the original precede any which contain only a part. Thus the complete illustrated *Earthly Paradise* (see 4.1), though published only in 2002, comes before all the editions of a part of it, going back to 1870.

If a publisher issues a full edition and later an offprint containing only a part, then the offprint is listed directly after the full text, and precedes any later full texts.

In a few instances more than one text appears in one chapter, this where the number of entries is so small as not to justify a separate chapter for each.

Numbering of entries: The first number comes from the chapter in which the entry appears, and the second designates its order in that chapter. The suffix of a capital "P" indicates that the entry represents a paraphrase of Morris's text. In Chapter 18 the suffixes of "o" (only) and "p" (partly) respectively denote a collection or anthology containing only writing by Morris or his writing mingled with that of others.

Order of description: 1. Wording of title page. 2. Colophon if present. 3. Date of publication (if not given in sections 1 or 2). 4. Binding. 5. Pagination and size. 6. Contents. 7. Illustrator[s]. 8. Illustrations and decoration.

Numbered copies: If each copy of a limited edition has a unique number, it is usually hand-written. Where present, this hand-writing is so indicated by italicisation.

Pagination: As supplied by the publisher. Pages un-numbered by the publisher are listed in brackets, using Roman numerals for preliminary pages and Arabic for all others.

Size: Dimensions refer to the gatherings and exclude the binding, with vertical dimension given first. In untrimmed books size varies from page to page, so size given will vary from copy to copy as well.

Binding: No mention is made of the endpapers if they are blank and white.

Multiple forms of a single edition: Deluxe version is described first, unless evidence indicates that the publisher issued a standard edition earlier.

Differing features of the various forms of one edition: All features peculiar to the first form are given before listing features of the other form[s].

Comments: Comments on anomalies are given as needed, immediately following the relevant section.

The reader will find occasional deviations and variations from this format where such variation clarifies the description.

The
Illustrated
Works

Chapter 1

Oxford and Cambridge Magazine

Morris's first published writing appeared in the *Oxford and Cambridge Magazine* in 1856. (Morris's earlier writing, edited by Florence Boos, was published by the William Morris Society in 1983 as *Juvenilia*, but this book lacks illustration.) In *The Oxford and Cambridge Magazine* the authors remained anonymous. However, Morris and others later identified the pieces he had written, and the Chiswick Press republished them in 1903 as *The Hollow Land*, the title of the first story in the collection. Even before this, the Mosher Press had put out all of the pieces as separate works. None of these reprints is illustrated. Stories which did later appear as illustrated editions form the subject matter of this chapter.

Unquestionably, the most commanding of these books is 1.5, *The Story of the Unknown Church*. Its size alone demands respect, but more importantly it displays excellence of materials, good layout, and pleasing typography. *The Hollow Land* (1.2) as an octavo also has distinct presence, but *A Dream, Being a Romance* (1.3) is more satisfying in its unity of text, decoration, and illustration. A further republication of the story "The Hollow Land" (1.4) appeared in *Forgotten Fantasy*, a short-lived magazine published by the Newcastle Publishing Company. The first issue appeared in October 1970 and subsequent ones every two months. I have found no record of any after April 1971, in which the story by Morris appeared. Newcastle later published separate books in the same field, including several by Morris (see 11.3 and Appendix 1).

Foreign-language editions fall outside the purview of this book. However, those interested in the subject should be aware of German editions of

works by Morris published in the early to mid-1980s by Bastei-Lübbe as paperbacks. The designer obtained illustrations for two of these paperbacks, one of them an anthology *Die goldene Maid*. The title is that of the first story, the publisher's translation of "Golden Wings." The cover illustration reproduces in colour a detail from the painting *Astarte Syriaca* by Rossetti (see 2.4). Johann Peterka drew a frontispiece for each story in the form of a line drawing. With one exception, each portrays a man in armour and a woman in a stage of undress which varies from one picture to another. In these illustrations the influence of Morris persists, evident in the Kelmscott-like border around the picture, the one border serving repeatedly throughout the book. The artist even seems to have borrowed part of a Morris border to portray a flowery meadow in one of his illustrations. See also the introductions to Chapters 11 and 14.

1.1a
Golden Wings/ A Prose Romance/ and a Poem/
William/ Morris/
George G. Harrap & Co./ London: 15 York Street, Covent Garden

1.1b
Golden Wings/ A Prose Romance/ and a Poem/
William/ Morris/
H.M. Caldwell Co./ New York and Boston

Date of publication: n.d. (British edition). The Caldwell Company claims "copyright 1904." Harrap's edition probably came out at the same time.

1.1a Binding: Bright red limp suede. Single rule around edges of front cover. Vertical central rectangle contains title at top and author at bottom, both in gilt, separated by blind-stamped heraldic pattern. Top edge gilt. Decorative foliate endpapers in brown with a horizontal central rectangle containing the words " 'Volumes that I prize above my Dukedom.' Shakespeare, The Tempest."

1.1b Binding: No copy with unequivocally original binding examined.

Pagination/Size: (vi) 66 / 140 x 97 mm.

Contents: P. i series designation "The King's Treasury Literary Masterpieces" (1.1a only; 1.1b blank), p. ii blank, inserted frontispiece, p. iii title page, p. iv blank, p. v half-title, p. vi blank in 1.1a, statement of copyright in 1.1b, pp. 1-66 text.

Comment: A three-page list bound in with one of my rebound copies of 1.1b indicates that Caldwell includes the book as No. 33 in the series *The Remarque Editions of Literary Masterpieces.* Titles in this series do not always correspond with those in Harrap's *King's Treasury* series. Like several books discussed in this bibliography, one publisher issued an identical edition under licence from another. Harrap and Caldwell clearly had such an arrangement with this book. The rebound copies of 1.1b lack the series designation present on page i of 1.1a, but one can draw no conclusions from this. The page may have been removed during the rebinding. The text includes both the prose story which Morris published in *The Oxford and Cambridge Magazine* in 1856, and the textually unrelated poem which he included in *The Defence of Guenevere* two years later.

Illustrator: A.D. MARCEL. The name on the engraving may be that of the artist or of the engraver. Most likely, he was the former, possibly Alexandre Marcel, active in France in the 1830s and known for historical and portrait paintings.

Illustration: The decorative rectangle on the cover of 1.1a reappears on page i of the Harrap edition, this time enclosing the series designation in red. Halfway down the title page is a flaming brazier held up by an arm which rises from an open book supported by crossed laurel branches. This decoration, all in red, carries a quotation from Kant, "Sapere aude" (Dare to know). Below it is the author's name, also in red. The title, at the top of each page of text, is flanked by a small ornament at the outer edge, the whole separated from the text by a ruled line. The frontispiece, the only illustration, demonstrates a high level of technical competence. It purports to show the final climactic episode. A lady in flowing dress has placed her hands on the chest of a man in armour with drawn sword, while another man lies prostrate at their feet. We can expect the scene once in any romantic novel with a medieval setting, two or three times if we are in luck. Most likely, the picture was not drawn specifically for this story, certainly not if Alexandre Marcel did it. The lady's attitude conveys relief rather than the horror one expects of a woman who has just seen her lover's head cloven to the chin (cf. 2.11, Harrison's picture for "The Haystack in the Floods").

1.2
The/ Hollow/ Land/
By William/ Morris

Colophon/Limitation: Here ends *The Hollow Land, A Tale,* by William Morris. Reprinted from the *Oxford & Cambridge Magazine.* Printed by hand at The Village Press Hingham, Massachusetts, by Frederic W. & Bertha M. Goudy, from the Village type, and finished this second day of October, 1905. Frontispiece illustration from drawing by Walter J. Enright; illustration on page 43 from drawing by Bror. J. Olsson Nordfeldt; the Note by Cyrus Lauron Hooper; and double border, title and initial by Mr. Goudy, the designer of the fount. Composition by Mrs. Goudy. Two hundred and twenty copies. Sold at The Village Press.

Binding: Grey-beige paper over boards with linen spine. Title on upper left in a red Gothic type. Deckle edges retained. Endpapers of same paper as rest of book.

Pagination/Size: (4) 68 (4) / 216 x 175 mm.

Contents: Pp. 1-4 blank, p. 1 half-title, pp. 2-3 blank, pp. 4-5 frontispiece and title page double spread, p. 6 blank, pp. 7-8 note by Cyrus Hooper, pp. 9-67 text, p. 68 colophon, pp. 1-4 blank.

Illustrators: WALTER J. ENRIGHT. Born in Chicago in 1879 and trained at the AIC. He married Maginel Wright, the sister of Frank Lloyd Wright, in 1904. Both she and their only child, Elizabeth, born in 1910, were also artists. The family moved to New York City during Elizabeth's early childhood. The couple divorced in 1921. Enright remained in New York for several more years. He was best known during this period as a cartoonist, work for which he received the Harmony Cartoon award in 1929. However, he was also a genre painter of Western and Native American scenes, and did some book illustration. He later left New York and by 1950 had established himself in Florida as a cartoonist for *The Miami Herald*. During this time he wrote two books, *Sailor Jim's Cave* and *AI Alligator*.

BROR JULIUS OLSSON NORDFELDT. Born in Tunneberga, Sweden, in 1878. The family moved to America in 1891. He attended the AIC and studied as well in New York and Paris. He lived in Provincetown, Massachusetts, between 1914 and 1921 and while there invented the technique of printing a block with more than one colour using only one impression. He was known for his paintings and etchings, and also as a teacher. After he married Emily Abbott, also a painter, he lived in Santa Fe for some years, but moved to New Jersey in 1940. He died in Texas in 1955.

Illustrations and decoration: A Kelmscott-like border of vine stems and leaves surrounds the double spread of frontispiece and title page. The first letter of the text is a large, dropped capital, decorated in black and red, the only use of red anywhere in the book. The frontispiece wood engraving shows two mounted knights fighting. The caption, "a ringing and glittering of steel," refers to a state of affairs rather than an actual combat. Thus this picture seeks to capture the spirit of the story, instead of rendering a particular scene. Enright executed the picture with competence and verve. The second picture, occupying two-thirds of page 43, also displays technical competence. It shows a rural scene as a backdrop to a reclining knight with head and shoulders resting on the back of his horse, which is also lying on the ground. Possibly it seeks to illustrate the situation of the protagonist's brother after he and his horse have leapt off the cliff into the Hollow Land. If so, they both look remarkably comfortable.

I DREAMED once, that four men sat by the winter fire talking and telling tales, in a house that the wind howled round.

¶ And one of them, the eldest, said: "When I was a boy, before you came to this land, that bar of red sand rock which makes a fall in our river, had only just been formed; for it used to stand above the river in a great cliff, tunnelled by a cave about midway between the green-growing grass and the green-flowing river; and it fell one night, when you had not yet come to this land, no nor your fathers. ¶ "Now concerning this cliff or pike rather (for it was a tall slip of rock and not part of a range), many strange tales were told; and my

WILLIAM F. NORTHEND
["Four men sat . . . telling tales"]
A Dream, Being a Romance, frontispiece

1.3
A Dream, Being a Romance/
by William Morris,
Contri-/ buted to the *Oxford and/ Cambridge Magazine*, 1856

Colophon: Here ends *A Dream*, written by William Morris, with a frontispiece and ornaments designed by William F. Northend. Printed by the same at the School of Art Press, Sheffield, and finished this 14th day of March 1908.

Limitation: This edition is limited to 20 copies of which this is number *4*.

Binding: Blue paper over boards and linen spine. Title in black on front cover above a design of grapes and vine leaves. Deckle edges untrimmed.

Pagination/Size: (2) (vi) 50 (6) / 144 x 115 mm.

Contents: Pp. 1-2 blank, p. i statement of limitation, p. ii blank, p. iii title page, pp. iv-v blank, p. vi frontispiece, pp. 1-49 text, p. 50 colophon, pp. 1-6 blank.

Illustrator: WILLIAM FREDERICK NORTHEND. Born in Sheffield in 1887, the son of a local printer. He was a student at the Sheffield School of Art when he produced this book, and later he studied at the RCA. He returned to the Sheffield School of Art as a teacher. A special autumn 1916 edition of *The Studio* describing the various British schools of art mentions Northend and reproduces another book illustration by him, suggesting that he worked in this field on a regular basis. However, he was especially skilled and recognised for producing fine illuminated addresses for presentation. In addition he worked in pencil, drawing many scenes in the Sheffield area. He married Phyllis Lawton, who also studied at the Sheffield School. He gave up teaching and in 1919 joined the family printing firm, of which he eventually became the managing director. He died in 1968. (See Wills.)

Illustration and decoration: Northend took the small books of the Kelmscott Press as his model in making his own book. One finds the same covers, the same hand-made paper with deckle edges, and much the same layout. He did not have access to a font to emulate those of Morris, and his type looks commonplace, not contributing to the overall effect. Nevertheless, Northend is generally successful. The story begins with a double spread, the frontispiece facing the first page of the text, the two placed in symmetry on the apposed pages. A decorative border surrounds each. While Northend produces the effect seen in a Kelmscott book, the actual pattern owes something to Art Nouveau influences, being more angular and edgy, while retaining components similar to those Morris uses. In Northend's border we find bunches of grapes, leaves, and stems. The frontispiece illustrates the opening scene as "four men sat . . . telling tales." Northend demonstrates technical competence in his picture without being alarmingly original. Marginal floral decoration adorns the verso of most double page of text. Each paragraph begins with a large decorated capital, and the text ends with a tailpiece.

This book is an impressive and ambitious undertaking for a twenty-one year old. In its unity and completeness it remains a more satisfying work than the comparable student production of *The Well at the World's End,* while lacking the boldness of the latter (see 17.2).

Note: Northend inscribed copy number *11* for Edwena Curwen. It now forms part of the collection of the Huntington Library in San Marino, California. He inscribed copy number *18* to Miss Grace Rewis. Someone rebound this latter copy in olive-green leather with the title and author in gilt on the front cover.

1.4
The Hollow Land/
A Tale/ by/ William Morris/
Illustrated by Charles Robinson and Tim Kirk
[In] Forgotten/ Fantasy/ Classics of Science Fiction and Fantasy/
Vol. 1, No. 4 April, 1971

Binding: Glossy paper cover, same thickness as the matte paper of the interior, of newsprint quality.

Pagination/Size: 6-44 / 191 x 136 mm.

Contents: P. 6 frontispiece, pp. 7-44 text.

Comment: The story follows a one-page description of Morris's life and work.

Illustrators: TIM KIRK. Kirk trained in fine art, taking both bachelor and master's degrees in the subject. His thesis for the latter comprised a series of illustrations for *The Lord of the Rings.* This launched him on the first phase of his career, that of illustrator for science fiction and fantasy novels, an area with which he remains in touch to the present day. He received five Hugo awards for his work in this field during the first half of the 1970s. However, by the end of the decade his main activity had shifted to commercial work as a designer with both Hallmark Cards and Walt Disney Productions. He stayed with Disney for twenty-two years. At present he runs his own company, Kirk Designs of Los Angeles.

CHARLES ROBINSON. Born in 1870 in Islington, a suburb of London, into a family which had obtained its livelihood from art in one form or another for the two preceding generations. His grandfather had worked as a bookbinder and later a wood engraver, and his father as an engraver and illustrator. His uncle and namesake showed early talent as an illustrator, winning a Silver Medal in the National Competitions, but died before he could fulfil his promise. Robinson was one of three artist brothers, the best known of whom is [William] Heath Robinson, the third being Thomas Heath Robinson (see 4.16P). Robinson briefly attended the Highbury School of Art but had to leave for lack of money. Instead he served a seven-year apprenticeship as a lithographer until 1892. Beyond this point he was largely self-taught. He led a precarious existence, subsisting on odd jobs, illustrating advertisements, ephemera, publicity for charities, and the like until 1895. In that year the editor of *The Studio* brought him to the attention of John Lane, who commissioned him to illustrate Stevenson's *A Child's Garden of Verses*. This book achieved immediate and lasting success and led to further work which established him as a book illustrator of the first rank. He married Edith Favatt in 1897 and settled in Hampstead, eventually having a family of four daughters and two sons. He continued illustration, mainly of children's books, until the start of World War I. The publication of illustrated books declined at this time and never regained the level of the earlier period. This shift created hardship for Robinson and his family. During the war he served in the reserve forces. After it he obtained most of his work from magazine illustration and did book illustration as it presented itself, his last commission in 1932. Some time after the end of the war, he moved to Buckinghamshire. He was an especially gregarious man, who revelled in the company of his fellow artists and was a member of numerous art societies and clubs. To move to the quiet of the country must therefore have been difficult for him. At this point he turned to watercolour painting as his main activity, and was recognised for his excellence in this medium by election to the Royal Institute in 1932. He died suddenly in Buckinghamshire in 1937. (See de Freitas.)

Illustrations: Kirk's cover depicts the scene when Florian is in mid-air after falling from the cliff to which he has been clinging. The artist has done a competent and spirited rendering, the latter perhaps not difficult, given the subject matter. The picture is inaccurate in small details of the text, but does capture the green light of the Hollow Land; Kirk painted it almost entirely in an emerald shade, with a hazy background of mountains, lakes and coniferous forests picked out in darker hues. The editor borrowed the frontispiece from an illustration done by Robinson. It shows the influence of Morris and the KP, with a leafy, twining border, and depicts the villainous Swanhilda, whose murder sets in train the action of the story. The second picture, by Kirk, is a rather static but accurate rendering of the entrance of Florian, naked except for his sword, into his ancestral castle. While both pictures are well done, the difference in style and layout creates discordance, such that the piece loses its sense of unity. The story ends with a tailpiece in the style Aubrey Beardsley used for *Le Morte d'Arthur*.

1.5a & b
The/ Story/ of/ the Unknown/ Church/
by William Morris/
The Hill Press. At Gravelly Hill. Baltimore. MMI

Colophon: The text was hand-set in Cloister Old Style No. 2 cast by the Dale Guild and printed with an Albion hand press on paper made by Twinrocker for this book. The engravings by Simon Brett were printed from the blocks. The title page lettering by Sheila Waters was printed from an electroplate. The tissue overlay was made by Hiromi; the Mulberry endpaper by machine in Thailand. The binding was done by the Florentine Bookbindery. Numbers I-IV were printed by reserve order on parchment prepared by Cowley and bound in limp vellum. Numbers 1-40 were bound in half leather over boards. The press mark, appearing here for the first time, was engraved by Wesley Bates. The Hill Press. 2001 Stephen Heaver, proprietor. D.S.G.

1.5a Binding: In slip case of beige linen over boards with title on paper label on spine. Bound in full limp vellum with single short tie of white leather. Vellum folded over all sides of stiff parchment, secured by interlocking notches. Gilt stamped picture with title beneath top left front cover. Binding and gathering joined by five loops of white leather. No endpapers.

1.5b Binding: In slipcase of grey linen over boards. Book bound in beige paper over boards, paper with Morris's willow pattern. Spine of black leather, title vertically in gilt. Picture in gilt stamped on top left of front cover. Fixed endpapers plain black paper, free endpapers Mulberry paper (see colophon).

1.5a Pagination/Size: (4) (x) (10) (2) (2) / 296 x 251 mm.

1.5b Pagination/Size: (4) (x) (10) (2) (4) / 280 x 238 mm.

Comment: The difference in size reflects the larger margins of the deluxe version.

1.5a & b Contents: Pp. 1-4 blank, p. i half-title, pp. ii-iii précis (one line of capitals spread over the two pages), p. iv frontispiece, p. v title page in striking Gothic calligraphy, p. vi artist's statement of copyright, pp. vii-viii introduction, pp. ix-x blank, pp. 1-9 text, p. 10 blank, p. 1 list of

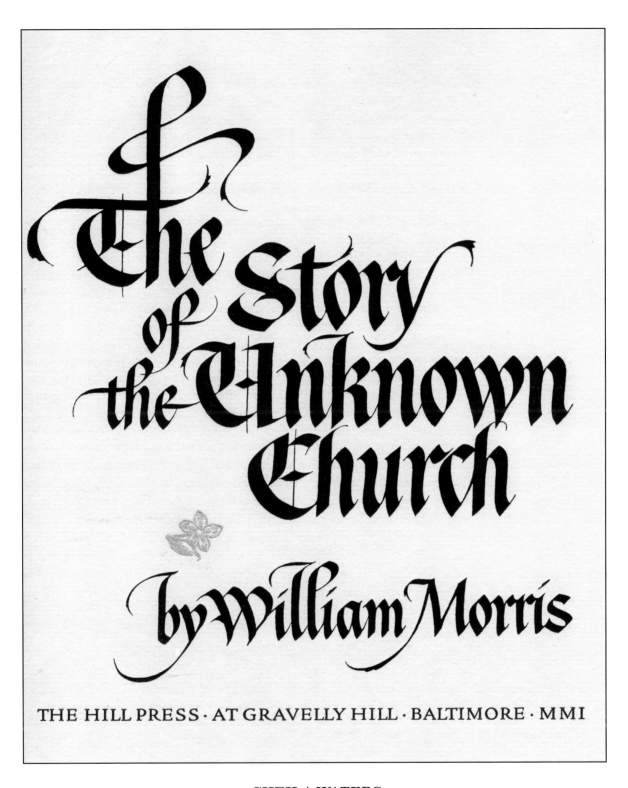

SHEILA WATERS
The Story of the Unknown Church, title page

subscribers, p. 2 colophon (signed by Heaver), pp. 1-2 blank (1.5a), pp. 1-4 blank (1.5b).

Illustrator: SIMON BRETT. Born in Windsor, England, in 1943. He studied wood engraving in London under Clifford Webb between 1961 and 1964, and subsequently he himself taught at the Marlborough College of Art for nearly two decades from 1971. During this time his work became recognised by the award of the Francis Williams prize from the National Book League in 1981, and by his admission as an Associate of the Society of Painter-Printmakers in 1986. He became a Fellow of this body in 1991. His artistic activities comprise mainly the design of bookplates, wood engraving, and book illustration.

Illustration and decoration: A design on the top left of the front cover, stamped in gilt, depicts a priest standing by a pillar, all enclosed in the outline of a Gothic window. Heaver uses the same design in black and without the outline as the initial dropped capital of the text, the pillar becoming the letter "I." A small floral decoration in gilt appears above the lettering of the half-title and also on the title page and near the bottom outer edge of pages 3, 5 and 7 of the text. The frontispiece depicts the interior of a huge Gothic cathedral, looking westwards along the length of the north side of the nave from the transept. The columns of the nave soar to pointed arches, while the west end of the building has a rose window above a row of lancet windows. A large figure bearing a lance appears below them, and at the base the heads and shoulders of five cowled monks. A glassine cover protects the frontispiece, and carries a picture of a stand of wheat in gold, with wild flowers, possibly poppies, growing at the base of the crop. The frontispiece is the only picture which illustrates the text. The other engravings portray ecclesiastical symbols and enhance the overall design, but are not illustrative as such.

SIMON BRETT
The Story of the Unknown Church, frontispiece

Chapter 2

Early Poems:
The Defence of Guenevere
Masters in This Hall

The first edition of *The Defence of Guenevere* appeared in 1858, and others followed during Morris's lifetime, most notably the one he himself published at the KP. None of these editions has illustration. Some of the poems were illustrated and published separately from 1900 on. However, no one brought out the entire selection as an illustrated edition until John Lane at the Bodley Head did so in 1904 (claimed by White to be November, 1903). Eventually, four illustrated editions appeared, all in the decade before World War I, a period when illustrated books had a wide appeal. Some later illustrated editions of *Guenevere* carry a title emphasising the authorship of Morris. Examples include *Poems of William Morris* (2.6), *Gems from Morris* (2.8), and *Early Poems of William Morris* (2.11). Possibly the publishers hoped to capitalise on Morris's name, on the assumption that the public knew it better than the title of a particular work.

Two of the four editions containing all the poems in the 1858 original have offprints with only a selection. Following the convention adopted in this book, I have grouped the offprints immediately after the listing of the main edition. The most notable is the Collins edition illustrated by Percy Hickling, which grew a tail of five offprints, six if one counts a collection which combines *Guenevere* with *The Life and Death of Jason* (see 18.4). Collins did not date any one of these books and very likely reprinted some or all at intervals. After *The Defence of Guenevere*, with all thirty poems, the offprints straggled out containing from five to eighteen poems, and including some or all of the illustrations in the main edition. All these Collins books are pocket-sized, but strangely, for pocket books, the publisher bound some of them in suede. The roughness of this material makes it

more awkward to slip into a pocket. This constitutes one example of a certain eccentricity of these offprints. In addition, most of the five are rather scarce, and some are strange in their binding or layout (see text). This eccentricity raises the possibility that they were produced in small numbers as training exercises for Collins employees.

Collins issued *Guenevere* as one in the series *The Cameo Poets*. The firm put out an edition identical in type and layout in another series, *The Hyperion Books*. The latter is a few millimetres larger and bound in reddish-brown cloth with a picture, stamped in gilt, of a farmer ploughing behind two horses, on the top half of the front cover. The frontispiece comprises a reproduction of the portrait of Morris done by G.F. Watts (see 2.17). It faces a title page decorated with a vignette of Pan playing his pipes to two cherubs holding a garland of flowers which stretches around the perimeter. Apart from this, the book lacks illustration and will not be considered further. It provides additional demonstration of Morris's popularity at the time and the profuse output of books with which publishers responded.

Commercial companies published the four illustrated editions which contain all of the poems in the 1858 book. Their listings in this chapter comprise 2.1, 2.4, 2.5, and 2.11. Robert Steele edited 2.4, which has a pleasing layout and, alone among the group, a lengthy introduction, notes at the end, and even an epigraph from Keats. However, its illustration is a cherry on an otherwise plain sponge cake, a frontispiece only, with no interior illustration or decoration. The Collins edition (2.5) does run to four colour plates, and decorated title page and headpieces. Collins's artist Hickling does not take full advantage of the rich opportunities which the poems offer. Besides this the publisher fails to complement the pictures with supporting layout, and the final impression is that of illustration dropped in as an afterthought to sheets already printed and awaiting binding.

The other two editions, those illustrated by King (2.1) and by Harrison (2.11), merit serious attention. Both artists produced work of a high calibre, and the publisher responded with a layout which enhances the illustration. As well as the illustrations, both artists provided all the decoration in their respective books, clearly working from galley proofs to do so. Thus a unity of conception emerges which one normally finds in a private press, where all aspects of the work stem from the vision of one or a few individuals.

In contrast to the commercial origin of the complete editions discussed above, private presses provide most of the many editions which contain one or a few of the poems in the complete *Guenevere*. This probably reflects the more limited technical and financial resources of the latter. Exceptions exist, for example the Featherweights series of Hodder and Stoughton (see 2.15 and 2.16). The booklets in this series each contain a single poem. The British Library has four Featherweights titles, including two with a poem by Morris. Of the others one is *Lilliput Land* by Matthew Browne, the other *The Grey Squirrels* by William Howitt.

I have never seen a reference to further titles in the series. One can imagine booklets like this bought as a trifle for the children of well-to-do Edwardian families. Parents would see them as a painless introduction to poetry, though the Morris poems, *Two Red Roses across the Moon* (2.15) and *Summer Dawn* (2.16), scarcely fit into the category of poems for children. In young hands, booklets like this would not last long and probably there are few copies extant. They are pleasing little productions, with no pretensions to advancing the art of the book. I have scarcely any information about the Featherweights. Company officials could find no reference to them in their records, and nor could I in the company's archives deposited at the Guildhall Library in London. The company does not provide public access to its stored archival copies.

In 1900 the Wessels Company provided another example of a commercial press turning its hand to fine printing when it published *Pre-Raphaelite Ballads* (2.12). Not only do the materials and layout conform to private press standards, but in addition Wessels published the book in a split edition with special copies having the trappings of a KP book. The various states of this book have sufficient differences to need a separate description for each, with one description for features common to all. One difference lies in the statement of limitation. In the colophon of the regular copies, Wessels gives the number of large-paper copies as 100. In the large-paper copies themselves, the stated limitation is 250, the number actually printed. Clearly, the company printed the regular copies first, and then had a change of mind regarding the number of large-paper copies it would issue.

Private presses printed the last entries which contain poems from *Guenevere*. Michael and Brenda Felmingham operated one of them, the Gazebo Press, in Leamington Spa, Leicestershire, England, between about 1966 and 1970. Felmingham wrote me that he had been stimulated to start the Press by Rigby Graham and Douglas Martin of the Leicester College of Art and the School of Printing. Felmingham is unnecessarily modest about his achievements with the Gazebo Press. He wrote that he used the Press mainly to print cards, keepsakes, and ephemera for friends and relatives. However, Walsdorf records that he printed two other books at the Press (WAL #173). In commenting on the entry described in this chapter, Roderick Cave claims, without giving a source, that Felmingham actually printed only 96 copies of *Shameful Death*, rather than the 120 specified in the colophon (see 2.20). Felmingham could not corroborate this, but did write that some copies remained unbound for lack of prospective purchasers. This may account for the discrepancy. Felmingham no longer does printing work, though he maintains an interest in books and their production, as evidenced by his authorship of *The Illustrated Gift Book, 1880-1930* (see Bibliography). He now devotes himself to painting in oils and watercolour, and has become a well-recognised artist in the United Kingdom.

Asa Peavy has operated the other private press with a poem from *Guenevere* to its credit in San Francisco since 1984. He had printed ephemeral material for about five years prior to this as "Privately

Printed" and under the imprint of "Peavy Press" before adopting the current name, the Bullnettle Press. He had become interested in printing in the course of a visit to Britain in 1978 to further his university studies in library science. Subsequent to starting the Bullnettle Press, he undertook additional training under Richard-Gabriel Rummonds in Alabama and later in Britain again. The early work of the Press was also ephemeral, the first substantial publications being two books of contemporary poetry. Since then he has published a wide range of works by contemporary poets and artists, and lesser-known writing from the last four centuries.

The final entry in this chapter originated as a favour Morris did for a colleague. After graduation from Oxford University in 1856, Morris articled in an architect's office for a few months. During this time he met Edmund Sedding, who was similarly occupied. Sedding had engaged himself in compiling a collection of old Christmas carols. In the course of doing this he obtained a twelfth-century French tune, for which he asked Morris to write an accompanying carol. Morris did so, and *Masters in This Hall* eventually appeared in Sedding's book *A Collection of Ancient Christmas Carols* published in 1860 by J. Alfred Novello, and later by other publishers.

Masters appeared in another anthology of Christmas carols as early as 1885, *A Christmas Garland: Carols and Poems from the Fifteenth Century to the Present* (London: Nimmo). It appeared again in *Ancient English Carols* in 1914 (London: Chatto and Windus). *Masters* was not among the carols illustrated in these works, and anthologies up to the present time which include it are in general not illustrated. In the early part of the twentieth century Schirmer published *Masters* as sheet music for choral use, this time with a score composed by Gustav Holst. In 1929 John S. Farr printed the first edition which stands as an independent work, a limited edition from his own press. Subsequent ones appeared in 1973 from the Hermetic Press in Minneapolis and again in 1996 from the Poole Press in Berkeley, California.

Maryline Poole Adams established the Poole Press in 1979. She specialises in printing miniature books, and does the designing and binding herself. For their illustration she uses her own drawings, engravings, linocuts, and woodcuts. This press produced the only edition of *Masters* with illustration. It forms the final entry in this chapter.

2.1
The Defence of Guenevere/ and Other Poems/
by William Morris/
Illustrated by Jessie M. King/
John Lane. The Bodley Head/ London and New York. MDCCCCIV

Binding: Bright red cloth over boards. Author and title in gilt on spine and bottom of front cover, illustration above. Top edge gilt. Formal decorations also on centre of spine and back cover.

Pagination/Size: [2] 310 / 188 x 126 mm.

Contents: Pp. 1-2 blank, p. 1 half-title, pp. 2-3 blank, p. 4 frontispiece, p. 5 full title, p. 6 blank, p. 7 dedication as in edition of 1858, p. 8 blank, pp. 9-10 contents, pp. 11-14 list of illustrations, p. 15 half-title of first poem, p. 16 blank, pp. 17-310 text.

Comment: Lane used machine-made paper unpleasantly stiff, and with smooth finish, but durable, and free of foxing in the copies examined.

Illustrator: JESSIE MARION KING. Born in Bearsden, about ten kilometres northwest of Glasgow, in 1875. She showed artistic talent at a young age, but had to overcome the opposition of her father, a Presbyterian minister, before she was allowed to enter the Glasgow School of Art in 1892. During that period the School was enjoying a flowering under the inspired direction of Francis Newbery. His leadership encouraged the emergence of gifted young artists, whose combined work evolved into a distinctive Glasgow style. King was a part of this movement. She won several awards for her work including the Silver Medal in the National Competitions two years in succession (see Appendix 2). Newbery regarded her so highly that he invited her to teach a course even before she completed her own studies in 1900. Her main strength was in decorative art, and throughout her career she was active in the design of jewellery, wallpaper, ceramics, and fabrics. Indeed, she extended the technique of batik by her innovations. However, in the first decade of the new century she worked mainly as a book illustrator, while also doing watercolour painting. She married Ernest A. Taylor, another artist, in 1908. They lived briefly in Salford, Lancashire, where Taylor was working, and their only child Merle was born at this time. They moved to Paris in 1910 and extended their artistic activities to teaching when they opened an art school. Demand for all things artistic evaporated during the war years, and they returned to Scotland, settling permanently in Kirkcudbright, on the southwest Scottish coast, in 1915. There they continued their careers in the pattern they had established in Paris. King died in Kirkcudbright in 1949. See also 2.2, 2.3, Appendix 2. (See White.)

Illustrations and decoration: Decorations abound throughout, with decorated half-title and title pages, head-pieces for all the poems, and tailpieces wherever space permits their inclusion. Most of the head-pieces

GALAHAD · RISE · AND · BE · ARM'D ·

JESSIE M. KING
"Sir Galahad, A Christmas Mystery"
The Defence of Guenevere, p. 85

mirror action in the poem, though a few do not, "The Haystack in the Floods," for example. King places a separate half-title page, with further decoration, before many of the longer poems.

Illustration is equally profuse, with full-page line drawings throughout. Counting all decorations on spine, front and back covers, preliminary pages, and head- and tailpieces, the total reaches 99. Of these, 26 are full-page illustrations, with a caption referring to the text. The picture on the front cover, from the title poem, shows the angel with the two pieces of cloth, a dramatic figure standing full-length with arms raised to form a cross, one cloth draped over each arm.

Altogether this book is an ambitious undertaking. King was an artist of unquestionable talent and creativity. However, she drew images with a dream-like quality, which, while of great charm, evoke a purely decorative effect. This is appropriate when used for title pages and head- and tailpieces. However, the decorative aspect dominates her full-page pictures, robbing them of the intensity demanded by the text. They fail to convey to the viewer the drama, the angst of the poem and have a sameness which eventually palls. Her glum, ethereal ladies match perfectly her glum, ethereal knights, some of whom "looked more like insects in the process of metamorphosis than nobles championing the cause of a beautiful lady," as King's biographer put it. Many of the poems in *The Defence of Guenevere* describe scenes of horrific violence, such as "The Haystack in the Floods," or emotion at the snapping point, as in the title poem itself. This turmoil finds no counterpart in King's drawings. Indeed, some of the more violent poems, such as "Shameful Death" or "The Haystack in the Floods," she does not illustrate at all. Her illustrations of "The Defence of Guenevere" focus on scenes which do not call for depicting strong emotion, but instead stay with a "safe" subject, for example the angel with the two pieces of cloth. They invite comparison with Meteyard's illustration of the same poem (see Appendix 2). However, in spite of her limitations as an illustrator of this book specifically, both the book and its off-prints (see 2.2 and 2.3) have charm by virtue of their decorative qualities. King's style would be more successful when applied to fairy stories, such as Hans Andersen's *Fairy Tales and Stories*, which Houfe states she illustrated the same year for an edition by Routledge. Indeed, the sameness in her style seems to extend to almost all her work from this period. She does show more vigour in the series of drawings she submitted to the National Competition in 1899 (see above).

2.2 Note: The following title appeared as No. 22 in the *Flowers of Parnassus* series. All titles in the series have a standard format, with the same size and binding. Apart from the difference in binding material, standard and deluxe versions are identical.

2.2
The Defence of Guene-/vere.
By William Morris./
With Illustrations/ by Jessie M. King/
John Lane: Publisher/ London and New York/ MDCCCCV

Binding: Olive green leather (deluxe) or olive green cloth (standard) over boards. Title with decorative surround in middle of front cover and vertically on spine with further decoration, all gilt-stamped. Top edge gilt.

Pagination/Size: 46 [2] / 141 x 109 mm.

Contents: P. 1 half-title, pp. 2-3 blank, p. 4 frontispiece, p. 5 full title, p. 6 printer's name, p. 7 list of illustrations, p. 8 blank, pp. 9-43 text, p. 44 blank, p. 45 tailpiece, p. 46 blank, pp. 1-2 list of titles in the series.

Illustrator: JESSIE M. KING. See 2.1.

Illustrations and decoration: Two stanzas occupy the first page of text, below the same decorative headpiece as in 2.1, and four stanzas each of the following pages, printed on the same kind of smooth paper as used for the main edition. All six of King's illustrations for this poem appear in this offprint of the title poem. Lane made a minor change in layout, omitting the decoration of the title and half-title pages. Besides this he exchanged the frontispiece with a picture which had appeared in the body of the text in the full work. The tailpiece in this new book had been used for the half-title page in the main work. In this book as in the previous one, Lane failed to place any full-page illustration opposite the text which it seeks to depict.

2.3
The Defence of Guenevere/
by/ William Morris./
Illustrated by Jessie M King/
The Scolar Press London

Colophon: This Scolar Press edition reproduces the text and illustrations first published 1904 in *The Defence of Guenevere and Other Poems by William Morris Illustrated by Jessie M. King* by John Lane, The Bodley Head.

Date of publication: 1979.

Limitation: [12 copies of the deluxe version (White)].

Binding: Deluxe. Extremely light beige silk over boards, with same illustration on front cover as on cover of 2.1, and title vertically on spine, all gilt-stamped. Endpapers plain and same colour as cover. Top edge gilt.
 Standard. Brown suede, title on upper front cover in decorated rectangle supported by pillars to base of page, all gilt-stamped. Plain else. Plain brown endpapers of same colour as cover.

Comment: White states that Scolar bound some copies in green cloth. I have never examined one such.

Pagination/Size: 46 [2] / 165 x 113 mm.

Contents: Pp. 1-2 blank, p. 3 half-title, p. 4 frontispiece, p. 5 full title, p. 6 colophon, p. 7 list of illustrations, p. 8 illustration, pp. 9-41 text, p. 42 blank, p. 43 decoration, p. 44 blank, p. 45 tailpiece, p. 46 and pp. 1-2 blank.

Comment: Scolar used a heavier paper for the deluxe copies and for these copies only utilised the blank first and last sheets in lieu of free endpapers. The layout of text parallels that of 2.2, with two stanzas on the first page and four on each of the rest. This edition too contains only the title poem.

Illustrator: JESSIE M. KING. *See* 2.1.

Illustrations and decoration: In standard copies the decoration on the half-title page repeats in black ink that on the front cover. This decoration appeared originally as the half-title page of 2.1. The publisher restored the decorated title page used in 2.1 and employed a fractionally larger type. Finally, Scolar placed illustrations to appose the text they depict. In materials, type and layout, this book surpasses 2.2. The deluxe copies are especially fine, with all the care and attention one hopes to see in a private press book. The silk cover stamped with gilt gives promise which is fulfilled in the hand-made paper and its untrimmed edges and the tasteful layout (the last shared with the standard copies).

2.4 Note: The original edition 2.4a forms one in the de la More series *The King's Poets.* All of the titles in their series have the same format, with identical binding, layout and size. The later editions of the book described below retain these features, but do not necessarily constitute a part of the same or any other series. Both 2.4b and c have the designation *The King's Poets* on page iii, as does 2.4a. However, on the spine the two publishers refer to their editions as in the series *The King's Classics.* Quite possibly de la More changed the series name once they began to include prose texts. The last edition (2.4d) does not carry a series designation anywhere. Indeed, the one copy I have examined of 2.4d lacks pages iii-vi, those which carry the series designation internally in the other editions.

2.4a
The Defence of/ Guenevere and/ Other Poems
by/ William Morris/
Edited by Robert/ Steele/
Alexander Moring Limited/ The De La More Press 298/ Regent Street London W 1904

2.4b
The Defence of/ Guenevere and/ Other Poems
by/ William Morris/
Edited by Robert/ Steele/
London: Chatto and Windus/ Boston: John W. Luce and/ Company: Publishers 1907

2.4c
The Defence of/ Guenevere and/ Other Poems
by/ William Morris/
Edited by Robert/ Steele/
The Caxton Society 1908/ Pittsfield, Massachusetts

2.4d
The Defence of/ Guenevere and/ Other Poems
by/ William Morris/
Edited by Robert/ Steele/
Philadelphia/ George W. Jacobs & Co./ Publishers

Date of publication of 2.4d: n.d. "1906" (LeMire).

Binding: Pale blue dust jacket with author, title, price (2/6ᵈ for 2.4a) and publisher on spine. Quarter-bound, Japan vellum and blue paper over boards. Paper label on spine 2.4a and d, lettering on spine direct 2.4b and c. Top edge gilt.

Pagination/Size: lviii, 256 / 150 x 115 mm.

Comment: The publisher's numeration includes the frontispiece, even though it is tipped in, and not part of the gathering. Lacking pages iii-vi (see note above) the numeration of 2.4d becomes inappropriate since the first numbered page xiii, that of the introduction, retains the same designation as in the other editions.

Contents: Pp. i-ii blank, p. iii series title, p. iv blank, p. v heraldic shield of series, p. vi blank, p. vii half-title, pp. viii-ix blank, p. x frontispiece, p. xi full title, p. xii epigraph from Keats' "Ode to a Nightingale," pp. xiii-li introduction, p. lii blank, p. liii dedication, p. liv blank, pp. lv-lvi contents, p. lvii half-title of first poem, p. lviii blank, pp. 1-236 text, p. 237 half-title "Notes," p. 238 blank, pp. 239-52 notes, pp. 253-55 index, p. 256 printer's name.

Comment: As already noted 2.4d lacks the two sheets with the series designation. With this exception the format of the four editions is identical and reflects their common printing origin from Richard Clay and Sons of Bungay in Suffolk. Robert Steele wrote the introduction and notes on the poems at the end of the book. The paper is of good quality and the type clear. Each of the longer poems has its own half-title page. The whole effect is unpretentious and pleasing.

Illustrator: DANTE GABRIEL ROSSETTI. Born in London in 1828. His father was a literary figure who had fled to England in 1824 to escape political persecution in his native Italy and became Professor of Italian at King's College in 1831. Rossetti's mother also sprang from a family with literary inclinations. Christened Gabriel Charles Dante Rossetti, their son showed an early interest in both art and poetry, and absorbed his father's passion for Dante to the point of changing his name to Dante Gabriel Rossetti. He had considerable gifts as a poet and indeed wrote and published a major body of poetry in the course of his life. However, he early decided to pursue a career as a painter. He enrolled in a private art school in his teens. He also studied at the RA schools briefly, but had difficulty settling to the routine required at such institutions. Beyond this point he was largely self-taught, though both Ford Madox Brown (see 18.12o) and later Holman Hunt (see 18.12o) accepted him as a pupil, perhaps influenced by his great personal charm and engaging sense of humour. At about this point these three and a group of artists around them formed the Pre-Raphaelite Brotherhood to enunciate their thinking on artistic theory and practice. Brown declined to join formally even though the ideas were predominantly his. The group sought to give expression to their tenets in a publication, *The Germ*. While the PRB was short-lived as a formal group, their ideas had a long-lasting influence on British art, most immediately on William Morris himself (see Introduction) and on Edward Burne-Jones (see 3.1).

Rossetti had a difficult personal life. About 1850 he met Elizabeth Siddall and persuaded her to act as his model. Over the ensuing decade he became infatuated with her, but she would not consummate their relationship until they finally married in 1860. However, throughout this period Rossetti engaged in numerous liaisons, including many with prostitutes. This may have been one factor in Siddall's suicide in 1862. For the remaining twenty years of his life, Rossetti's emotional state became increasingly precarious, with addiction to alcohol and later to chloral hydrate, an ever more difficult problem. Through the 1860s Fanny Cornforth, a woman of sumptuous beauty but dissolute habits, became his model and his lover. This period saw the development of the sensuous aspect in his painting, in contrast to the austerity of his earlier work. William Morris's wife Jane became Rossetti's mistress some time in the late 1860s and continued to serve as his model, a role she had played since the 1850s. The affair largely ended in 1874 on the initiative of Jane, who feared the negative influence Rossetti might have on her two young daughters. However, she did still see Rossetti at intervals until 1877. He spent his last years in a state of declining mental and physical health and drug dependency. However, he continued to paint and produced significant works up to the end of the decade. He died in Kent in 1882. See also 2.19; 18.3p; 18.12o; 18.13p. (See Ash.)

Illustration: This book deserves only a courtesy acknowledgement as illustrated. It has a frontispiece photo-reproduced from Rossetti's picture *King Arthur's Tomb*. It portrays the last meeting of Launcelot and Guenevere, clasping hands in farewell over the tomb itself. The only other decoration is the heraldic design on page v, which shows six ravens on a shield and the caption "The King's Poets" above it, on a belt with a buckle, which surrounds the shield and is itself surrounded by curled scrolls and a laurel wreath. The designer identified him or herself only as BMcM.

2.5 Note: Collins published the following entry as one in their series *The Cameo Poets*, so designated on the half-title page. The series appeared during the first quarter of the twentieth century, and was devoted mainly, though not exclusively, to nineteenth-century poets. Titles in the series have a uniform size and number of pages, though some variation in binding.

2.5
Defence of Guenevere/
William Morris/
London and Glasgow/ Collins' Clear-Type Press

Comment: The half-title reads "The Defence of Guenevere," the title page as given.

Date of publication: n.d. 1911 or earlier. See Date of publication of 2.8.

Comment: An inscription in one of my copies reads, in part, "Xmas 1911."

Binding: Deluxe 1. Embossed maroon leather with decorated title in gilt on front cover and title, author, and decoration in gilt on spine. All edges gilt. Pictorial endpapers in colour, depicting Cupid and Psyche, signed indistinctly in part "Sheeh…"
  Deluxe 2. Grey-green linen over boards. Front cover has border of stems, leaves, and oranges. Below upper border, "Guenevere" in gilt outlined in black with "Morris" in black beneath it. Below this, enclosed by two lines, outer ruled, inner dotted, a bright blue panel with cloth garland suspended from upper corners, with fruit depicted on it. More bunches of oranges in rest of panel. Similar decoration on spine, also "William Morris" vertically and outlined in black. Back cover plain. All edges gilt. Pictorial endpapers as in deluxe binding 1.

Comment: Other titles in the series have bindings uniform with both these types of binding. Possibly they represent issues put out at different times.
  Standard. Red cloth over boards. Top edge gilt. Decoration of cover and endpapers as in deluxe binding 1.

Comment: In addition to the bindings described above I have seen a single copy which differs from them, both in binding and in size. The

Cover, *Defence of Guinevere*
Deluxe binding 2

contents (see below) are identical with those of the others. This book measures 132 x 94 mm. The binding is of brown suede of the same tone as that seen in *Songs of Chivalry* (see 2.7) and with the same yapped edges. It differs in being limp, but like 2.7 has the title blind-stamped in the same position within a similar decoration on the upper inner part of the front cover. The top edge is gilt, and the endpapers carry the same picture as appears in the bindings of other copies of 2.5. The type is the same as the other copies, and the lesser height of this book reflects its smaller margins, mainly the lower one. The picture facing page 234 which illustrates "The Night Watch" is absent. This may represent a further point of difference or may be a defect limited to this one copy. The retention of the pictorial endpapers and the similarity of the binding to others used by Collins point to this binding being original with the publisher, but confirmation awaits examination of additional copies. If this book is truly distinct, rather than a trimmed and rebound copy of the standard edition, it would warrant a separate entry following 2.5.

Pagination/Size: 252 [4] / 148 x 95 mm.

Contents: P. 1 half-title with title in red, p. 2 blank, inserted frontispiece and facing title page (obverses blank), pp. 3-4 contents, pp. 5-252 text, pp. 1-4 blank.

Illustrator: PERCY BELL HICKLING. Born in Nottinghamshire in December 1876, but living in Leicestershire by 1881, and in London in 1901, where he married in 1904. He may have come from a family of painters and illustrators; three artists with the name of Hickling were living in Nottingham in 1881 (ECR) and if related to him would have provided early teaching and encouragement. This could account for the date of his first published illustration at the early age of eighteen, a cartoon for a humorous magazine called *Fun,* modelled along the lines of *Punch.* It reveals an artist in full command of his technique. He did his last work, covers for a series of children's books, about 1950. These covers seem curiously dated to the Edwardian era. He was a profuse illustrator in the intervening period, this activity seemingly constituting his main professional career. See also 2.6-10; 18.4o.

Illustrations and decoration: The title page has a decorative vignette in colour of a youth playing a lyre, the artist identified only by three indistinct initials, possibly AAD (see 2.6). Throughout the text the name of the poem appears at the top of each page in red capitals. Each poem follows a line drawing of a landscape, decorative only, since it does not depict a scene or action in the poem. These head-pieces are narrow rectangles, which occupy the whole width of the page. Each appears from one to five times in the course of the book, with ten different scenes in all. A decorative tailpiece appears at the end of a poem wherever space permits, with nine designs seen. Most have a floral motif, while others include an anchor, two heads, and two bees. The floral designs include the national flowers of England, Scotland, and Ireland. The end-piece, below the end of the last poem, depicts a pillar inscribed "Finis." The

D.G.   *Page* 168

'Our tough spears crackled up like straw.'

PERCY B. HICKLING
"The Gilliflower of Gold"
Defence of Guenevere, **p. 168**

disparate nature of the designs suggests that Collins reused them from previously published books.

The illustrations comprise the frontispiece and three in the body of the text, all in colour. They face the poem they portray, though the actual line of text in only one instance. In a pocket-book size the pictures do not have great impact. Hickling executed them competently, and seems to have sought to capture a range of moods. Two of the pictures show a single standing figure, which evokes an air of contemplation, while the third portrays a scene of violent action, "Our tough spears crackled up like straw" (see illustration) and the fourth one of emotion at the breaking point, " . . . beneath an apple tree / Our heads stretched out toward the sea." Hickling and Harrison, another artist who illustrates the poems in *The Defence of Guenevere* (see 2.11), both drew this scene. It is a dramatic climax in "The Sailing of the Sword," in which three sisters watch for the return of their respective lovers. The narrator doubts the fidelity of her man, and the artists have sought to portray her emotions in their depiction of both her facial expression and posture. Harrison is more successful in catching the mixed fear and hope of the protagonist, though Hickling does a pleasing and accurate portrayal of the scene.

The last two pictures are thoroughly in tune with the spirit of the poems; the two contemplative illustrations are not. While the reader can accept one contemplative illustration, even in poems as full of action as are these, the presence of two unbalances the overall pictorial content.

2.6
Poems by William Morris   [half-title page]
William Morris/   [full title page]
London & Glasgow/ Collins' Clear-Type Press

Date of publication: n.d. 1912-1915.

Comment: The vignette on the title page carries the earlier date. An inscription in one of my copies includes the later one. Collins reissued the book at least once. Another copy, new at the time, has an inscription dated 1924.

Binding: Limp suede, copies coloured variously emerald green, red or purple. Author's name inside decorative garland gilt-stamped (1915) or blind-stamped (1924) on front cover. Title vertically on spine in gilt. Pictorial endpapers (1915), marbled endpapers (1924). Top edge gilt.

Comment: I have examined a single copy bound in paper over boards. The front cover has a light yellow background and profuse leafy and floral decoration in light blue enclosed in brown ruled lines close to the edges. In the upper part similar lines enclose a horizontal rectangle containing "Wm. Morris." Another rectangle in the lower half, the same length as the upper one, but twice as deep, contains more decorative leafy sprays above "Poems." The spine has "William Morris" printed vertically surrounded by more blue leaves. The back cover is plain grey, and the endpapers lightly marbled as in the 1924 issue (see above). The contents are the same as those of the suede-bound copies, but the paper is matte and thicker. The thicker paper, which suggests a separate issue, the similarity of endpapers to those of a copy with an unquestionably original binding, and the worn state of the cover of this hardback copy all point to its binding being original. If so this version would constitute 2.6b. However, confirmation awaits the location and examination of further copies with the same features.

Pagination/Size: 128 / 140 x 90 mm.

Contents: P. 1 half-title, p. 2 blank, inserted frontispiece and facing title page on glossy paper (obverses blank), p. 3 contents, p. 4 blank, pp. 5-127 text (with two illustrations tipped in, facing pages 65 and 96), p. 128 tailpiece.

Comment: This edition contains eighteen of the poems from the full *Guenevere*. However, it has only half the number of pages, because Collins omitted two of the longest poems, "Sir Peter Harpdon's End" and "Rapunzel." The order in which the poems appear compared with their order in the full work seems random, but may reflect an attempt by the layout editor to place the poems in apposition to their illustrations. The single sheet carrying the two pictures is inserted at start and finish of the third signatures, such that the first picture lies between pages 64 and 65 and the second between pages 96 and 97.

Illustrator: PERCY B. HICKLING. See 2.5.

Illustrations and decoration: The front endpapers have an illustration in colour of a shepherdess and her swain, she sitting with her crook by her side and he lying on the ground beside her, resting on his elbows and playing a whistle while the sheep graze around them. On the back endpapers, the same couple are wending their way home, he carrying the crook over his shoulder, she alongside him with eyes downcast, a rosy glow on her cheeks, and the sheep meandering in front of them. Neither picture carries a signature. A vignette on the title page depicts a thoughtful-looking young woman seated on a bench and leaning forward, pen in hand and a sheaf of paper on her knee. A dove perches beside her and a bowl of fruit rests there too. Above the back of the bench grows a profusion of flowers with a tree arching over them. The air is filled with seagulls. The whole is enclosed by double lines with roses between them at regular intervals. The artist signed himself AAD '12, most likely Arthur A. Dixon, a painter and book illustrator active at this time, who did other work for Collins (see also 2.5). The head- and tailpieces are identical to those adorning the same poems in 2.5, with two exceptions. Collins used a different headpiece for "Near Avalon," the same as that used in both editions for "The Judgement of God," and a headpiece which does not appear in 2.5 for "Spell Bound."

With the exceptions noted above, the illustrations and type of *Guenevere* (2.5) and *Poems by William Morris* are identical. Collins left out the picture facing page 169 in *Guenevere*, since it illustrates "The Gilliflower of Gold," one of the poems omitted in this smaller book. Furthermore, the frontispiece in 2.5 is replaced in *Poems* by the picture which illustrates "The Sailing of the Sword." The two illustrations in the body of this book appear in apposition to the poems they depict. The end-piece, on a separate page, represents a ship reminiscent of a Viking galley under sail.

2.7
Songs of Chivalry/
William Morris/
London & Glasgow/ Collins' Clear-Type Press

Date of publication: n.d. Probably about 1912 (see 2.5).

Binding: Usually brown suede over boards, one copy seen in limp purplish suede. Title and author in gilt vertically on spine and blind-stamped on the top left of the front cover inside a floral border. Top edge gilt. Endpapers lightly marbled in pale brown.

Pagination/Size: [40] / 140 x 107 mm.

Comment: This book lacks pagination completely, even though page references appended to the captions of the illustrations direct the reader to the relevant page of text.

Contents: P. 1 half-title, p. 2 epigraph from Shakespeare's Sonnet XVII, tipped-in frontispiece and title page, pp. 3-40 text with three inserted illustrations.

Comment: The title of the poem appears at the head of each page in italics.

The absence of a contents page and the lack of numeration, coupled with the page references on the pictures, betray inconsistency in planning. The book is pleasing to a superficial inspection, but the inattention to detail has resulted in a disappointing shoddiness of execution. As in the other Collins books containing a selection, the order of the poems seems random, but may reflect an effort to have the poems as close as possible to the accompanying illustrations, which lie between pages 8/9. 16/17, and 23/24. Not the least bizarre aspect of this book is the absence of one of the poems for which Collins supplied an illustration. The picture which in other books illustrates "The Night Watch" serves double duty here for "Riding Together."

Illustrator: PERCY B. HICKLING. See 2.5.

Illustration and decoration: The title page has a decorated pedestal outlined in yellow occupying the bottom of the page. The pedestal encloses the name of the publisher printed in black. Blue vases sit one at each end of the pedestal, a brown stem rising from each to end in a profusion of green leaves stretching across the width of the page at the mid-level, and forming a base above which appear the title in red and the author in blue. Further stems originate from the leaves and some droop to the base while others rise to enclose this lettering. The latter stems carry fruit, possibly oranges, at each upper corner. Finally, a multicoloured garland of flowers hangs in a semicircle from each side of the leaves, a ribbon tied in a bow at its lowest point. The designer signed his decoration PJB, which probably stands for Percy J. Billinghurst, a little-known artist active around 1900, who was noted for such decorative work as bookplates. The frontispiece and title page are tipped in on beige matte paper of the same texture as the other pages. Each of the five poems has a decorative head-piece, and a tailpiece where space permits. These head-pieces resemble the tailpieces in the Collins editions already described, except that they are broader, occupying the whole width of the page. One occurs twice, and shows three flowers, a thistle on the left, a rose in the middle, and a shamrock on the right. One is Christmassy, with bells and holly, one has a laurel wreath, and the last shows a laurel branch superimposed on a lintel.

The illustrations in the body of the text appear on a full page of the same glossy paper, inserted into the gathering. All four of Hickling's pictures appear in this book. The frontispiece is the picture illustrating "The Gilliflower of Gold." Thus each title in the series to this point has a different frontispiece. The pictures lie close to the poems they illustrate, though only one is in true apposition to it.

2.8a & b
Gems/ from/ William Morris/
London & Glasgow/ Collins' Clear-Type Press

Date of publication: n.d. Ivan Sayers, an expert on period dress, dated the clothing of the woman portrayed in the pictorial front endpapers (see below) to 1903. This sets an earlier limit for the date of publication, but does not exclude the possibility that the artist painted the picture later and sought to create an effect of a past time. Assuming that a book which contains all of Hickling's pictures precedes those which contain only some, this also sets an earliest possible date for the publication of 2.5.

2.8a Binding: Deluxe: Limp red suede, blind-stamped rule close to all outer (yapped) edges. Title on front cover in upright rectangle with decorative edges and vertically on spine, all in gilt. Plain maroon endpapers the same as those in Collins' Illustrated Pocket Classics series (see 18.4).

2.8a Size: 134 x 94 mm.

2.8b1 Binding: Standard: Stiff, shiny, thick white paper cut to same size as pages of text, title vertically on spine in blue. Front cover with title and decoration. All edges gilt. Pictorial endpapers.

2.8b2 Binding: Standard: Limp orange suede, yapped edges, stamped rule close to all outer edges. Title vertically on spine in gilt. All edges gilt. Pictorial endpapers.

2.8b Size: 101 x 74 mm.

Comment: The designation of 2.8a as deluxe rests on its larger size, better quality of paper, extra illustration, and decoration of all pages of the gatherings. However, it lacks some of the decorative features of 2.8b1 & 2, namely all edges gilt and pictorial endpapers. In addition 2.8b1 has an illustrative and decorated front cover absent in the other two versions.

2.8a & b *Pagination:* 96.

2.8a & b Contents: P. 1 half-title, p. 2 decoration (2.8a) initials WSC [monogram of publisher] (2.8b), inserted frontispiece and title page, pp. 3-95 text with inserted illustration (in 2.8a only), p. 96 initials WSC.

? J. MALCOLM PATTERSON
Gems from William Morris, pictorial endpapers (2.8)

Comment: Collins used much thicker paper for 2.8a, such that this version is nearly twice as thick as 2.8b. In addition the frontispiece and title page are tipped in on grey matte paper in the deluxe version. Both versions contain the same fourteen of the shorter poems in *The Defence of Guenevere.*

Illustrator: PERCY B. HICKLING. See 2.5.

Illustration and decoration: Alone among the three versions, the second binding of 2.8b1 has a decorative and pictorial component. The border of the front cover has red roses at intervals and twining stems between, set 1 cm. in from the edges. This border encloses the title and a circular vignette, the latter surrounded by a similar border to that around the outer edges. A lyre below the lower edge of the picture touches both it and the outer border. The vignette depicts a Mediterranean city with a wood in the foreground and a lake and mountains behind.

The endpapers of 2.8b1, reproduced on page 36, both show an old-fashioned English garden. Those at the front portray a young woman in full-length Edwardian dress standing by a sundial with a hedge cut to form an arch in the background. Those at the back portray an old man in similar period dress, apparently in the same garden, walking in front of a house. This second picture appears on both front and back endpapers of 2.8b2. The artist identifies himself only as "Malcolm." It seems that the publisher cropped the bottom of the picture, removing the last name in the process. Conceivably the artist was the Malcolm Patterson who drew the title-page illustration for the Collins edition of *The Life and Death of Jason* (see 18.4). Certainly, the two pictures share a similar style.

The only textual illustration in 2.8b is the frontispiece, Hickling's depiction of "The Sailing of the Sword." It retains the same size as the picture in the larger editions. The publisher decreased the margins and cropped the picture itself, mainly in the vertical dimension, to fit this smaller book. In 2.8a this picture appears uncropped in the body of the text between pages 56 and 57, and the frontispiece is that which accompanies "The Gilliflower of Gold" (see 2.5).

Both versions have a decorated title page printed on the same glossy paper as the frontispiece, with a vignette, which differs between 2.8a and b. In 2.8a one sees two female figures, the first standing with her back to a pillar holding a parchment, the other crouched at her feet and reaching for a sickle. Both are dressed in full-length draperies, the first in blue and second in red. A border of leaves and flowers similar to that adorning the pages of text surrounds the vignette only, excluding the title above. The artist does not identify himself. The vignette of 2.8b occupies the centre of the page, between the title and the name of the publisher, in contrast to 2.8a where it is located on the lower half of the page and incorporates the publisher's name. This vignette consists of a bouquet of Easter lilies with two stylised hearts above them and twining rose stems around the type. Like that of 2.7, it bears the initials PJB.

The layout of the text is the same in the two versions, as are the head- and tailpieces accompanying the poems. All the poems have headpieces, some with a floral pattern and four with a landscape picture similar to those used in 2.5. Most poems have a tailpiece, some with a floral decoration, and some with a small circular landscape.

Beyond these basic features, the deluxe version shows significant additional adornment. On the obverse of the half-title page is a decorative device, which Collins replaced with their monogram in 2.8b.

However, the most significant difference between the two versions lies in a decorative border in colour around the margin of each page of 2.8a. It consists of three pendant garlands of flowers at the top of the page, one central and the others flanking it, a vertical stem on each side of the page, and a scroll at the base. The overall effect resembles that which Collins achieved in 2.10, without being identical to it. This decorative border occupies the space provided by the extra size of 2.8a.

2.9
The Defence/ of/ Guenevere/
William Morris/
London and Glasgow/ Collins' Clear-Type Press

Date of publication: n.d. Probably about 1912.

Binding: Glassine dust jacket over shiny white paper glued to cover at spine with free edges folded over the outer edges of true cover, of plain white stiff paper. Title top front of false cover, picture below it. Title vertically on spine. Endpapers lightly marbled.

Pagination/Size: 96 / 101 x 71 mm.

Contents: P. 1 half title, p. 2 statement of manufacture, inserted frontispiece and facing title page (obverses blank), pp. 3-96 text.

Comment: Besides the title poem, the selection includes "Concerning Geoffray Teste Noire" and four short poems, none duplicating those in *Gems* (2.8).

Illustrator: PERCY B. HICKLING. See 2.5.

Illustration and decoration: The picture on the cover, painted predominantly in light blue, portrays a couple in medieval dress standing side by side in a walled garden with shallow arches in the background, and a shrub rose to one side. The man holds a scroll which both are reading. This illustration has no obvious relationship to any of the poems. The only scene that comes to mind is from "The Man Born to Be King," after Cecily has substituted the letter ordering her marriage to Michael for that commanding his execution. The artist wrote his initials somewhat indistinctly; they look like A.D. The last name is clearer as ' "Macleoid" [sic].'

The title page contains the title, author and publisher, with an unsigned vignette between the last two. The vignette, a line drawing, depicts a seated female figure with a quill in her hand and a scroll on her knees, her head turned to look into a mirror held up by a naked child. Possibly the artist got inspiration from Titian's *Venus at her Toilet*, and sought to portray the goddess and her attendant Cupid. If so, the scroll and quill are puzzling; Venus's reputation does not rest on her literary pursuits. Each poem has a decorative headpiece, and a tailpiece where space permits.

Only Hickling's frontispiece illustrates the text, depicting Guenevere in the walled garden, "I went without my ladies all alone" (see 2.5).

2.10
The/ Gilliflower of Gold/
William Morris/
London and Glasgow/ Collins' Clear-Type Press [HLH]

Date of publication: n.d. About 1912 (see below).

Binding: Thick but flexible, shiny white paper, with pictorial and decorated front cover, title and author at top. Front and back fixed endpapers with opposite halves of a single picture. No free endpapers.

Comment: The cover is sewn in with the gathering. If the binder had only covers, with the complete picture on one side and lettering of the cover on the obverse, he could not have used a second such sheet, facing the first, to provide the full picture inside front and back covers.

Pagination/Size: 32 / 108 x 87 mm.

Contents: P. 1 half-title (facing front fixed endpaper), p. 2 blank, inserted frontispiece and title page, pp. 3-31 text, p. 32 publisher's monogram (facing back fixed endpaper).

Comment: The paper of the frontispiece and title page is slightly thinner and more shiny. The text consists of seven poems from *The Defence of Guenevere.*

Illustrator: PERCY B. HICKLING. See 2.5.

Illustrations and decoration: Hickling's picture illustrating the title poem appears on the cover and again as frontispiece (see reproduction under 2.5). The frontispiece constitutes the only use of textual illustration in this book. A leafy border in light blue encloses picture and lettering on the cover. The same border frames every page of the book, except the endpapers and the inserted title page and frontispiece. The two halves of the picture on the endpapers can stand alone, but at the cost of losing the conception of the artist. The left half, on the front endpaper, depicts a cottage set in trees and surrounded by a fence, while a stream and meadows appear on the back endpaper. The artist executes the scene in the same lush style employed for the endpapers of 2.8. The title page has an unsigned vignette below title and author and above the name of the publisher. It shows two women in full-length gowns before a pillar, one standing and the other kneeling before her, possibly a portrayal of Psyche before Venus. The picture and publisher's name are enclosed in a decorative border.

2.11a
Early Poems of/ William/ Morris/
Illustrated by/ Florence Harrison/
Blackie & Son Ltd London/ Glasgow and Bombay/ 1914

2.11b
Early Poems of/ William/ Morris/
Illustrated by/ Florence Harrison/
New York/ Dodge Publishing Company/ 214-220 East Twenty-Third Street/ 1914

Binding: Bluish-grey dust jacket with title across top, a horizontal panel below it. A standing knight in armour divides panel vertically and extends almost to foot of jacket. Left half of panel contains "Illustrated by" and right half "Florence Harrison." Spine has title and illustrator at top, publisher at base and floral and leafy decoration between. All lettering and decoration in dark blue. Some copies in box of bluish-grey thick, stiff paper, with pasted sheet on lid and side carrying the same colour and design as front and spine of dust jacket. Boxed copies have a glassine wrapper. Bound in very light blue cloth over boards. Lettering and decoration on cover and spine replicate that on jacket, but stamped in gilt. Top edge gilt, others left untrimmed. Pictorial endpapers dull olive-green, same picture front and back.

Comment: One rarely sees either boxed copies or those still in a dust jacket. However, when found such a copy is likely to be in pristine condition, its gilt undimmed and every page as crisp as on the day of publication, a memorable sight.

Pagination/Size: xvi, 194 [2] / 254 x 182 mm.

Contents: P. i decorative female figure, p. ii blank, p. iii half-title, p. iv advertisement for other books illustrated by Harrison, inserted frontispiece with tissue guard, p. v title page, p. vi decorative female figure, pp. vii-viii contents, pp. ix-xi list of colour plates, p. xii decorative female figure, pp. xiii-xiv list of black and white plates, p. xv decorative female figure, p. xvi blank, pp. 1-194 text with 16 inserted colour plates, p. 1 decorative female figure, p. 2 printer's name.

Comment: The publisher used a thick, matte paper throughout, included the twelve black pictures and their blank obverses in the numeration, and protected each colour plate with a tissue guard. The order of the poems is slightly rearranged.

Illustrator: EMMA FLORENCE HARRISON. Born Florence Emma Harrison, in Redditch, England, in 1863 (ECR). She was studying at the NATS by 1881, lived in London, and exhibited at the RA between 1887 and 1891. She specialised in figure drawing and book illustration and remained active in these fields to 1932. She also wrote verse; Blackie & Son published several of her books of poetry between 1905 and 1918, with her own illustrations.

Illustrations and decoration: Harrison's decorations show the influence of the Art Nouveau movement. She seems to abhor blank areas of paper and covers them wherever it is appropriate. On the endpapers she places on the recto an airborne woman in flowing dress blowing a trumpet, while on the verso three earthbound onlookers gaze up at her. The word "Romance" appears across the top of the verso. She decorates the preliminary pages even more profusely. The full title page has a border reminiscent at first glance of those seen in a KP book, but which she fills with roses and birds quite unlike Morris's motifs. The various pages for lists of contents, colour illustrations, and for black and white pictures have decoration around the headings, and a tailpiece, each different from the others. All the poems have a different headpiece and a tailpiece, the latter only where space permits. Some headpieces are

E. FLORENCE HARRISON
"Then Godmar turned again and said:
'So, Jehane, the first fitte is read!
Take note, my lady, that your way
Lies backward to the Chatelet!'"

"The Haystack in the Floods"
Early Poems of William Morris, facing p. 174

decorative, but many illustrate the poem which follows. The body of the text is generously illustrated, with both black line drawings and tipped-in colour pictures. A few of the shorter poems do not have illustration, but most of them have at least one picture. The drawings are so placed as to face the text which they illustrate and capture the scene or action which the poet has described. Facial expression and bodily movement convey the thoughts and feelings of Harrison's subjects, whether bliss, rage or desolation. This sense of bodily movement gives the pictures a life and energy, most noteworthy in the illustrations for "The Wind" among several others. King's picture for the same poem is quite lacking in these characteristics (see 2.1). Harrison makes full use of the opportunities offered by colour. In her picture illustrating the lines "No one walks there now: / Except in the white moonlight / The white ghosts walk in a row" ("The Tune of Seven Towers") she heightens the sense of the macabre with her blue tones and white highlights and her etiolated figures. In the lines "… we kissed in meeting that spring day / I scarce dare talk of the remember'd bliss" ("The Defence of Guenevere") she captures the intensity of the lovers' passion in the intense and rich colours of their dresses. In contrast to the naturalism of the colour pictures, the black line drawings look rather stylised, but no less attractive. One or two, particularly the one illustrating "Spellbound," are reminiscent of the work of Howard Pyle (see 11.3).

This book is most satisfying. The artist has done very competent work, the layout editor has integrated illustration and text, and the publisher has used material of good quality to create the finished oeuvre.

Note: The preceding entry represents the last illustrated edition published containing all the poems in *The Defence of Guenevere and Other Poems*. The remaining entries in this chapter contain only one or a selection of the poems.

2.12a, b & c
Pre-/Raph/aelite/ Ballads/
By/ William/ Morris/
With many/ illustra-/tions and deco-/rative borders/ in black and/
white . . . by/ H.M. O'Kane/
Now done into type/ from the original/ text and reprinted by/ A. Wessels
Co./ at New York City/ in the year MDCCCC

Colophon: Here endeth the Book: Pre-Raphaelite Ballads, written by
William Morris, and now newly done into type from the original text,
being embellished with many decorative borders, illustrations and
initials by H.M. O'Kane, and published by A. Wessels Company at Nine
West Eighteenth Street in New York City: August MDCCCC

2.12a Limitation: Of this edition of *Pre-Raphaelite Ballads* there have
been printed five hundred numbered copies on "Old Stratford" paper, and
one hundred numbered large-paper copies on Imperial Japanese paper,
of which numbers one to ten inclusive have been specially bound in full
English vellum and the initials drawn in and hand illuminated by H.M.
O'Kane.
    This copy is number *60* of the edition on "Old Stratford paper."

2.12b & c Limitation: Of this edition of *Pre-Raphaelite Ballads* there
have been printed five hundred numbered copies on "Old Stratford"
paper, and two hundred and fifty numbered large paper copies on
Imperial Japanese paper, of which numbers one to ten inclusive have
been specially bound in full English vellum and the initials drawn in
and hand illuminated by H.M. O'Kane.
    This copy is number *8* of the edition on Imperial Japanese paper
(2.12b).
    This copy is number *171* of the edition on Imperial Japanese paper
(2.12c)

2.12a Binding: Bluish-grey paper boards with linen spine. Front
cover carries same decorated border as title page, surrounding same
inscription as on title page in red and with different layout. Author
and title horizontally on paper label on spine. Decorative free and fixed
endpapers, front and back.

2.12a Size: 192 x 140 mm.

2.12b Binding: Limp vellum with two orange-pink ties. Title and author
vertically on spine in gilt. Endpapers plain and white.

2.12c Binding: Cream-coloured paper boards, title and author in gilt
on upper front cover and horizontally on spine. Lettering on front cover
reproduces that used on half-title page. Endpapers plain and white.

2.12b & c Size: 210 x 163 mm.

Comment: The larger size of 2.12 b & c allows for wider margins than in 2.12a. The area occupied by the text is the same in all versions.

2.12a, b & c Pagination: [xiv] [44] [6].

Comment: The book lacks pagination. Wessels bound all versions with a French fold. However, most of the inside folds contain printed text. The numeration given above includes the pages with this obscured text.

Contents: P. i half-title, pp. ii-iv blank, p. v statement of limitation, pp. vi-viii blank, p. ix second half-title, pp. x-xi blank, pp. xii-xiii double-spread title page, p. xiv statement of copyright, pp. 1-42 text, p. 43 tailpiece, p. 44 and pp. 1-2 blank, p. 3 colophon, pp. 4-6 blank.

Comment: The printer, Clarke Conwell, used Satanick type. At the bottom of each page on the inside of the French fold he placed the title of the poems printed on its obverse.

Illustrator: HELEN MARGUERITE O'KANE. The following biographical sketch has been provided by the grandson of the artist, James O'Kane Conwell, and is reproduced with his gracious permission and in his own words, with minor editorial changes.

> Marguerite O'Kane was born on April 3, 1879, possibly in a naval hospital at the Kittery Naval Yard in Maine. Her parents were Captain James O'Kane and the former Consuela Nella Corning. James O'Kane graduated from the US Naval Academy in 1860 and had a distinguished career in the navy, serving in the Civil War and after. Marguerite was the oldest of three daughters. Her father died on January 5, 1897. Almost immediately following the settlement of his estate Marguerite used her inheritance to move to France to study art. We have no information about her earlier education or interests. Family tradition has it that she studied at the Sorbonne but I cannot confirm this. However, her later work suggests that she was greatly influenced by Jacques-Emile Blanche and Aubrey Beardsley (see 18.7p). I do not know when she returned to the United States, nor where, when or how she met her future husband, Myers Clarke Conwell, whether in France or on her return to America. Family members like to believe it was the former. Neither do I know the date of their marriage, nor much of Clarke's life prior to it. Most of their energy must have gone into the Elston Press, which Clarke founded in 1901. Twenty books came from the Press in the short span of its existence. Following several disastrous fires Clarke closed the Press in 1904. He appears to have had an ample amount of money at his disposal, which would have enabled him to resume the adventurous and rakish style of living which characterised his early years. He and Marguerite separated some time after the birth of their son James O'Kane Conwell, born on August 31, 1908. She took custody of James when she and Clarke parted, and obtained her final divorce decree on March 15, 1917.

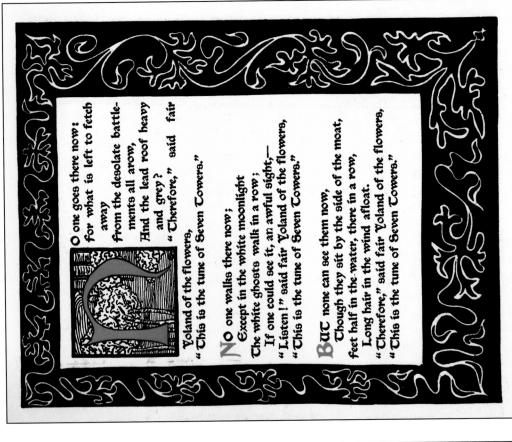

H. MARGUERITE O' KANE
"The Tune of Seven Towers," first page
contrasting hand-coloured dropped capital (2.12b)
with standard dropped capital (2.12c)

She settled in New York, where she became known as O'Kane Conwell, although among friends she preferred to be called Marguerite. In New York she began an insecure career as a costume and set designer for Broadway shows and movies; an arbiter of clothing fashions and a fashion writer; an artist whose drawings became covers for Vanity Fair, Harpers and the like; a newspaper writer and a social companion to well-known actors, actresses, directors, producers, and professional athletes; in brief, immersed in the artistic and creative swirl of the city. She and her son lived a comfortable and sometimes extravagant life when her work sold and a hard one when it did not. She died penniless in a charity ward of a New York hospital on January 1, 1927.

O'Kane worked in pencil, charcoal and watercolours. However, most of her energy went into design for the theatre, film and fashion industries. Christie Walsh recognised her expertise in the last field by selecting her as a contributing writer for their original column "Woman the Decorative." See also 2.13.

Illustrations and decoration: The layout is decorative in itself. Conwell capitalised the first word of every stanza of all the poems, with the initial letter in red. The initial letter at the top of each page he made into a larger dropped capital. The first letter of each poem is a large dropped capital in red, set in a box which contains a small illustration. Each differs from the others, but all show a rural scene. A woman appears in the corner of the picture accompanying "In Praise of My Lady." In the ten copies of 2.12b, O'Kane limited her hand-illumination to the letter at the start of each poem. She used opaque pigments, probably gouache, mainly blues and purples in my copies, which obscure the picture around the letters in the rest of the edition. She painted the capital itself in one colour and the background in two more. The actual colours vary from one poem to another and from one copy to the next. These shades provide less contrast to the otherwise black page and are therefore less pleasing than the red capitals of the regular copies.

Borders, with white outlines on a black background, surround the pages of text and illustrations, the latter on the verso and the poem it illustrates on the facing recto. The border of the first poem, "Two Red Roses across the Moon," consists, appropriately, of roses and intertwining stems. The border of the second page is a semi-abstract leafy design, somewhat reminiscent of ivy, done in a thin line; the third is a wavy frond, more like seaweed than any land plant. The editor uses these three patterns on subsequent pages in an irregular sequence. The only additional border decorates the first page of the last poem, "The Gilliflower of Gold." Naturally enough, the border is a bouquet of gilliflowers (i.e. carnations), linked by their stems. This border appears only once. In all the borders, the decoration on a verso is a mirror image of that on the facing recto. Conwell placed further decoration on the endpapers of 2.12a only and on page 57 as a tailpiece in all versions, the same figure at all these locations. The decoration consists of a stylised potted rose bush, printed in black except where it appears as the tailpiece of 2.12a. Here Conwell used red ink.

The poems "Two Red Roses" and "The Gilliflower of Gold" throb with action. Morris wrote the third, "In Praise of My Lady," as a love poem to his wife. The last, "The Tune of Seven Towers," evokes a Gothic atmosphere of impending death and dissolution. How well does the artist reflect the mood of each poem? Her success varies. In the love poem her style works quite well, portraying a languid couple in medieval dress lying in a meadow by a stream which flows out of a wooded background. The composition of this picture is very similar to that of the first one she did for *Sir Galahad* (see 2.13).

For "The Tune of Seven Towers," O'Kane has the couple standing in the foreground, Yoland gesturing toward distant towers, as she asks Oliver to fetch from them her "coif and kirtle, with pearls arow," while "the priests and I . . . / Will pray that you may not die," though "[She sayeth inwardly] / (The graves stand grey in a row . . . .)" O'Kane draws Oliver looking disconsolate instead of grateful for the chance to risk death for his psychopathic fair lady. In this picture, the artist catches, whether by chance or design, the man's natural feelings, but fails to convey the menace implicit in the towers or the callousness of Yoland's request.

In each of the "action" poems O'Kane portrays a female figure; she hints at the subject-matter most obliquely. The picture illustrating "Two Red Roses" shows the tiny head of a horse, but no rider, through the window behind the standing figure. For the other poem O'Kane chose to illustrate the lines ". . . your quiet head / Bow'd o'er the gilliflower bed," this after fourteen stanzas of mayhem. Her picture shows a woman kneeling in a meadow in front of a wall, picking carnations, a far cry from Hickling's spirited rendering, in which two armoured knights clash in clouds of dust, their shattered lances exploding in all directions (see 2.5). Harrison and King chose the same subject as O'Kane, the former only as an unobtrusive tailpiece.

In this book, the whole is greater than the sum of its parts. Although the pictures generally do not reflect the essence of the poems, they balance the text visually so that together they create a pleasing decorative effect. This edition resembles KP books, especially the ten copies bound in vellum. Conwell clearly followed Morris's example in this book and in the ones he subsequently issued from the Elston Press.

2.13
Sir Galahad, A Christmas Mystery,
by William Morris.   [Half-title]

Colophon: Here endeth this book, Sir Galahad, A Christmas Mystery, by William Morris. One hundred and eighty copies, with decorations by H.M. O'Kane, have been printed by me, Clarke Conwell, at the Elston Press in New Rochelle, New York, and are to be sold thereat. Finished this Tuesday, the second day of December, MDCCCCII.

Binding: Light blue paper boards with a beige linen spine with title and author vertically on a paper label. Endpapers of same hand-made paper with deckle edges as rest of book.

Pagination/Size: [x] [22] [8] / 320 x 243 mm.

Contents: Pp. i-vi blank, p. vii title page, p. viii statement of copyright, p. ix half-title, pp. x-1 double spread with title on verso and first line on recto, pp. 2-21 text with illustrations on pp. 7 and 19, p. 22 blank, p. 1 colophon, pp. 2-8 blank.

Illustrator: H. MARGUERITE O'KANE. See 2.12.

Illustrations and decoration: The double spread has a decorative border of leaves and flowers in black with the title in the verso. Conwell printed the initial capitals in red and 35 mm. high, the other letters 22 mm. high in black. The corresponding area on the recto holds the first line of the poem, its initial "I" in red, 61 mm. in height, the rest of the letters in black, their 22 mm. height matching that of the black letters on the verso. The initial "I" has a leafy decoration around it. The last three lines of the first quatrain appear on the second page; the first of these lines is entirely in red. Three further quatrains occupy the rest of this page. Subsequent pages bear only three stanzas. The initial letter of each quatrain is a dropped capital in red which takes the full height of all four lines. The brief prose descriptions of the arming of Galahad are in red type, interspersed with the address of each saint to him in black.

This poem explores the doubts of faith and its reaffirmation. O'Kane did two pictures; she chose her subjects well. The first illustrates the lines "I saw a damozel . . . / . . . say last farewell / To her dear knight . . . And their last kisses sunk into my mind." Had Galahad's self-denial been to no purpose? The second shows the triumphant answer from the Angel, "O Servant of the high God, Galahad / Rise and be arm'd," while a second angel and four saints bearing his accoutrements stand in waiting. The black floral borders of each picture and that of the title page all differ from one another. The type overshadows the pictures, which are not dramatic, so that some imbalance occurs between the two. However, they reflect the theme of the poem and O'Kane did them in a pleasing and workmanlike manner.

H. MARGUERITE O'KANE
["I saw a damozel . . . say last farewell to her dear knight"]
Sir Galahad, A Christmas Mystery, p. 7

2.14a & b
Sir/ Gal/ahad /A Christ/mas Mystery/
William/ Morris/
BS

Date of publication: 1904.

Colophon/Limitation: Here endeth the Poem, Sir Galahad, A Christmas
Mystery, by William Morris. This book was designed by Thomas Wood
Stevens, and lettered under his direction. The frontispiece is from a
painting by Walter H. Hinton. Of this edition there have been printed
and published by the Blue Sky Press in Chicago, five hundred copies
on paper and twenty-five copies on Japan vellum, this being number *4*
(2.14a)
... this being number *410* (2.14b)

Binding: Dark blue-green paper boards with dark blue linen spine.
Border of oak leaves parallels edges of front cover, slightly inset. Title
in gilt under border at top of page. Back cover plain. Endpapers of same
colour as covers, same front and back, with border of oak leaves and
acorns around top and outer edges of double page. Title set into the top
border on verso, "William Morris" in corresponding area on recto.

Pagination/Size: [4] [iv] [22] [2] / 206 x 125 mm.

Contents: Pp. 1-4 blank, p. i half-title, p. ii frontispiece, p. iii title page,
p. iv statement of copyright, pp. 1-21 text, p. 22 colophon, pp. 1-2 blank.

Comment: Copies are bound in a French fold, and those on handmade
paper retain their deckle edges.

Illustrator: WALTER HASKELL HINTON. Born in 1886 in Illinois,
where he appears to have lived most or even all of his life. He was a
book and magazine illustrator, with a preference for sports, action and
Wild West subjects. Fridolf Johnson (see bibliography) reproduced one of
Hinton's works, but examples are hard to find in general. He remained
active at least into the 1950s and died in Illinois in 1980.

Illustration and decoration: On the half-title page the title appears in
bold red letters, above an acorn and oak leaf panel in black, in the shape
of an upside-down L, the horizontal arm under the title. The full-title
page uses red lettering for "Sir Galahad" at the top and the monogram

"BS" at the base, and black for the subtitle "A Christmas Mystery," the name of the author, and decorative panels which repeat the oak leaves and acorns motif at top and base. The title heads each page of text in red, with "Sir Galahad" on the verso and "A Christmas Mystery" on the recto. The large initial "I" of the poem, with its oak decoration, is in red, too, but the only other use of red occurs in the "R" when Christ bids Galahad "Rise up." The frontispiece, the only illustration, is a tipped-in photographic reproduction of a detail from a painting and shows Lucy in the act of buckling on Galahad's spurs. Hinton chose his subject well; the picture illustrates a climax in the poem. Even in this small format the artist displays mastery of composition and dramatic effect.

The hand-made paper and deckle edges of the standard edition produce a more pleasing effect than that achieved by the special copies on Japan vellum. This book is most satisfying in its quality of materials, presswork and layout. Its one failing lies in the inadequate expedient of tipping in a photograph, even one of good quality and with a subject germane to the text.

2.15
Two Red Roses/ across the Moon/
Hodder & Stoughton

Date of publication: n.d. "1911" (BL)

Binding: Shiny paper with title across top and author's name at bottom, capitals in red, rest in black. Cover illustration between title and author. At front and back the cover folds over outer edge of blank outer sheet like a dust jacket, and is sewn together with rest of gathering.

Comment: The blank outer sheet over which the cover folds faces the half-title at the front and the series emblem at the back with no intervening sheets.

Pagination/Size: [ii] [10] / 150 x 81 mm.

Contents: P. i half-title, p. ii tipped-in frontispiece on shiny paper, pp. 1-9 text (on rectos only), p. 10 Featherweight emblem.

Comment: Printed in grey ink on cream-coloured paper. Sewn together by silk thread.

Illustrator: ANNE ANDERSON. Born in London in 1874. She spent her childhood in Scotland, but her father's work took him around the world, and the family lived in Argentina throughout her teenage years. It was there that she met the young woman Olive Hoskins, who later became a fellow artist, and with whom she formed a life-long friendship. Probably this friendship determined the location of Anderson's eventual residence in rural England, close to Hoskins' family home. Anderson had shown an early interest in art, and by the first years of the new century was working in London as an illustrator and studying part-time at the Slade School of Fine Art. She became a prolific and successful illustrator of books and ephemera, such as postcards. It was through this work that she met Alan Wright, another illustrator employed by the same London publisher. They married in 1912. Thirty-eight by this time, Anderson had no children, but they had a seemingly happy marriage, based on shared interests, outlook, and personality. This commonality and the similarity of their artistic style undoubtedly fostered their collaboration on many of the books for which they received commissions. While Anderson was also a painter, she was known almost entirely for the writing and illustration of children's books. Horne records that she also illustrated Dickens's *The Chimes* in 1935. After her marriage, and also for some time before, Anderson lived in Berkshire. She died in 1952. (See Cope.)

Illustration and decoration: For such a small booklet this item has generous decoration, mainly with a rose motif. We encounter this motif even on the front cover. The artist divided the available space on the cover, placing an illustration in the upper part and stylised rose stems with leaves and red flowers below it. On the monochrome half-title page she superimposed the title itself across a garland of rose leaves and two roses. The garland forms the outline of a full moon. She left the name of the publisher at the bottom of the page unadorned. Small roses printed on the paper around it also frame the frontispiece. Beyond this, the text has decoration throughout, each a single rose on a stem. One appears on the verso of each double spread, namely on pages 2, 4, 6, and 8, and also between each stanza on the rectos. All differ from one another, except that we find the same design on page 3 as the identical ones above and below the final stanza on page 9. On the obverse of page 9 the Featherweight emblem abandons the roses in favour of a dandelion. The emblem depicts a standing fairy blowing the seed head of the flower. The seeds stream into the dotted outline of a heart around her, creating an effect reminiscent of that achieved by Jessie King (see 2.1).

Both cover illustration and frontispiece are in colour. The former portrays a pensive lady in medieval dress, seen in profile. Her elbow leans on a parapet, her chin in her cupped palm. Her head is framed by a huge full moon, and two red roses hang just above her head, also enclosed in the moon's circle. A pair of red ruled lines encloses lettering and illustration, and the lettering is itself separated from decoration by a further red rule above and below. In the frontispiece we see the lady full-face, this time in an upper-storey window of a white tower against which stands a climbing rose bush, bearing flowers in pairs and reaching to the level of the window. She is watching the knight gallop past below her. The

ANNE ANDERSON
Two Red Roses across the Moon, **frontispiece**
facing first page of text

knight's shield also carries the motif of red roses. The caption reads, "There was a knight came riding by" from the second stanza. In fact both pictures portray the same scene, though with different emphases. The artist uses traditional licence to the full: on the cover she draws a full moon "at noon," and in the frontispiece we see roses in bloom "in early spring."

Anderson's style seems well suited to her main artistic activity as an illustrator of children's books. She employs bright colours, draws a sweet and cheerful-looking lady, and arranges the paired red roses, clearly enough even for the youngest child to pick up the allusion.

2.16
Summer/ Dawn/
Hodder & Stoughton

Date of publication: n.d. "1911" (BL). No later than 1919.

Comment: One of my copies has an inscription which includes the later date.

Binding: Thick, matte paper with cover illustration on shiny paper, pasted on. Title and author below picture. Otherwise resembles 2.15, with same folded cover around a blank outer sheet.

Pagination/Size: [ii] [8] [2] / 151 x 82 mm.

Contents: P. i half-title, p. ii tipped-in frontispiece, pp. 1-7 text, p. 8 decoration, p. 1 blank, p. 2 Featherweight emblem as in 2.15.

Comment: At least some of the Featherweight booklets were sold with an inserted greeting card, a sheet of blue paper the same size as the booklet, with a space at the top for a short greeting, a line drawing below, and lines at the bottom headed "To" and "From." The publisher uses the same kind of cream-coloured paper for this booklet as for 2.15, printing it with sepia ink.

Illustrator: LILLIAN AMY GOVEY. Born in 1886 and spent her childhood in Stoke Newington and North London. She spent at least part of her adult life in Sussex. She was the series editor for the Featherweight booklets, and as such probably instrumental in securing

Anne Anderson, with whom she was friendly, to produce the illustrations for the preceding entry (see 2.15). She herself was an illustrator and writer of children's books, and also did some postcard design. She died in 1974.

Illustrations and decoration: A small picture, described in more detail below, dominates the upper half of the cover. Multiple ruled lines, printed on the paper to which the picture is affixed, enclose it. On each side, outside the lines, stands a floral decoration, shaped like a furled umbrella and coloured light green and cerise. Further coloured decoration of a minor sort appears above and below the rules. As noted above, the title and author are set beneath the picture, and above three identical small doves, each enclosed by the cerise outline of a cloud. Apart from the colour noted, all the printing on the cover uses the same ink as we see throughout the booklet. The first inside page repeats the dove and cloud motif of the cover, set below the title. On this page the artist depicts only one bird and it differs from those on the cover: the cloud has a dotted and uncoloured outline and the bird several minor alterations in its form. Govey decorated the text even more profusely than we find in 2.15. The first page carries only the opening two lines, with a leaf between it and the title, and a flower below it. The decorations on the versos vary from page to page. On page 2 is a potted bush rather like the tailpiece in *Pre-Raphaelite Ballads* (2.12). Page 4 depicts a rose (also used in *Two Red Roses*, 2.15). Page 6 carries an illustration, described below. After page 1 each recto contains two sets of lines with a flower between them. The last page of text has only one set with a small picture below it. Morris wrote the poem without any division of the lines into stanzas. The divisions present in this booklet clearly result from the exigencies of layout.

The illustration on the cover portrays a red-haired woman in a red dress and a floral crown playing a lute. She is looking out of a window through which she can see a bird flying in a blue sky with white clouds. The frontispiece shows a woman wearing a diaphanous pink dress, standing full length among summer clouds, her long red hair flowing in the breeze. Govey clearly drew this woman as allegorical of a summer dawn. Whether she visualised the similar woman of the cover in the same role or as representing the one addressed in the poem is less certain.

Page 6 has a monochrome picture of a country village in front of a hill with the sun rising behind it. This picture faces another which acts as a tailpiece below the last two lines. It depicts two Viking galleys on a choppy sea with the rising sun below clouds. Both of these illustrations depict a sunrise, but seem to have no direct relevance to the text of the poem.

2.17 Note: Logically, this book would seem to belong in Appendix 1 as a paperback with an illustrative cover. However, its antiquity, stated limitation of the number of copies, and its quality of production put it outside the group of books described there. It cannot be ignored, for the reasons just given, and so appears here.

2.17
Sir Galahad/ A Christmas Mystery/
By/ William Morris/
Hillside Press/ Englewood, New Jersey/ M-CM-XV

Colophon/Limitation: here ends sir galahad a christmas mystery, a poem by william morris. set up and printed from the type by frederic m. burr at the hillside press, englewood, new jersey. press work finished in december, m-cm-xv. one hundred and fifty copies on van gelder zonen paper

Binding: Dark green heavy flexible paper. Photograph pasted centrally on front cover with title above and below it. Cover and gathering sewn with red thread.

Comment: Browning of the outer sheet has resulted from its prolonged contact with the cover.

Pagination/Size: [iv] [30] [2] / 183 x 112 mm.

Contents: P. i half-title, p. ii printed inscription, p. iii title page, p. iv blank, pp. 1-29 text, printed on rectos only, versos blank, p. 30 blank, p. 1 colophon, p. 2 blank.

Comment: The inscription reads, "Mr. and Mrs. Frederic M. Burr Send Cordial Holiday Greetings. Burarabdil, Christmas 1915." My copy carries the autograph "To Belle from Fred. Christmas 1915" on the half-title page. Probably most copies have a similar autograph.

Illustrator: GEORGE FREDERICK WATTS. Born 1817 in London into a working-class family; his father was a piano maker. He displayed artistic talent at a young age, and studied sculpture with William Behnes while still a child, going on to the Royal Academy in 1835. He became best known for his painting, though he also executed noteworthy sculptures during his long career. His rise to prominence began when he won a competition to execute murals for the newly built Houses of Parliament in 1843. However, eventually he did not contribute to the scheme in any significant way.

During his lifetime Watts's reputation rested on his portrait painting, which includes a well-known canvas of Morris, and especially on his allegorical paintings. He himself certainly attached more importance to the latter. The intellectual ferment of the mid-Victorian era affected Watts' artistic expression. Darwin's ideas influenced him, but he was equally attracted by Eastern mysticism, and he sought a synthesis of the two in his art. He had a long-lived vision of buying a house which he planned to decorate with murals depicting his vision and expressing the aspirations, emotions, and virtues of Man. Some of the works intended for this project remain as oil paintings. He donated many of them to the Tate Gallery in the 1890s, since his dream never materialised. In the meantime he and his wife had moved from London to Surrey in 1891. Here they set up a gallery devoted solely to his work, which opened only months before his death. This gallery still operates. He was elected ARA in 1867, and his achievements in art received further recognition by an offer of a knighthood. He declined it, but did accept an Order of Merit late in life.

Watts married Ellen Terry in 1864. The marriage did not last. Possibly the thirty-year disparity in their ages played a part. Terry left him after a mere twelve months, and eventually Watts formalised the de facto separation by divorce. He married Mary Fraser Tyler in 1886. His second wife was a fellow-artist, a designer and potter. Perhaps this supplied more compatibility; Watts dissolved this marriage only by his death in 1904.

Illustration and decoration: The front cover has two parallel ruled lines around a centrally placed photograph measuring 57 x 109 mm. A third line encloses them and the title, "Sir Galahad" above and "A Christmas Mystery" below the picture. Lines and lettering are all in gilt. On the title page "Sir Galahad" and a floral decoration which encloses an HP monogram appear in red, the rest in black. Burr placed a rectangular headpiece in black, filled with twining stems and leaves, above the title and first page of text. The latter starts with a dropped and decorated capital in red. Burr used a red floral design, reminiscent of two carnations, as an end-piece. The title appears in red at the top of each page of text, and the dropped capital "R" of Christ's "Rise up" is also in red, though undecorated. The only illustration, the sepia photograph on the front cover, reproduces a detail from *Sir Galahad*, a painting which Watts executed in 1862. The original hangs in the Fogg Museum of Harvard University. It depicts an armoured knight, bareheaded and standing by the bowed head of his horse. The original painting shows the lush colour and technical virtuosity characteristic of Watts' work, of which the small-scale photograph conveys the merest suggestion.

2.18
In Praise of My Lady
by – William Morris
[Spine]

Colophon/Limitation: Printed at the Aries Press, in Aries Type, in the Village of Eden, New York, by Spencer Kellogg, Jr. Composition and presswork by Emil Georg Sahlin, decoration by Elizabeth MacKinstry. Thirty-one copies have been printed on Tovil English hand-made paper and finished in the month of April 1928.

Binding: Quarter bound in black leather and bluish-green marbled paper boards. Title vertically on spine in gilt. Top edge gilt, others with deckle edges. Endpapers of same marbled pattern as covers.

Comment: In my copy and presumably in the others the free endpapers are pasted to the outermost sheet of the gathering. The binder probably adopted this expedient to provide more body to the thin marbled paper used for the endpapers. I have excluded this outer sheet from the pagination.

Pagination/Size: [6] [10] [8] / 318 x 202 mm.

Contents: Pp. 1-6 blank, pp. 1-9 text (on rectos only, versos blank), p. 10 blank, p. 1 colophon, pp. 2-8 blank.

Illustrator: ELIZABETH MACKINSTRY (married name Conkling). Born in 1879 in Scranton, Pennsylvania, and professionally active during the first half of the twentieth century. She trained as a violinist but had to abandon this career due to poor health. She subsequently studied sculpture under Rodin, but is best known as a book illustrator and as a teacher.

Illustration and decoration: The printer found it possible to dispense with such bourgeois concepts as half- and full title pages. He placed the sole illustration as a headpiece, without any title between it and the first stanza. The poem begins with a dropped capital in brown surrounded by a thin black line, the two separated by a narrow space. The first page carries three stanzas, and succeeding pages five each. The colour of the initial capital from the second stanza onwards alternates between red and blue, except that the first stanza on each succeeding page has a red capital. At the bottom of the last page of the text appears the statement, printed in red, "Here ends the ballad IN PRAISE OF MY LADY by William Morris." Kellogg added the nicety of a cream-coloured silk bookmark.

Below the colophon Kellogg placed a rectangular panel with a red background, which silhouettes the uninked parts in the white colour of the paper. Three parallel ruled lines lie at the outer margins, from the innermost of which extend stylised stems and berries in a regular pattern which widens the margin threefold beyond the breadth of the lines alone, the centre containing the words "Aries Press" in a Gothic type. The book has no decoration beyond this one panel. The illustration, a woodcut engraving printed in three colours, shows a woman in a full-length mauve dress, playing an Irish harp and seated beneath a willow overarching from the right. The trunk is brown and the foliage aquamarine. On the left a mauve rock with a fern at its base balances the composition. MacKinstry executed the picture competently but does not portray the characteristics touched on in the poem.

Comment: Sahlin, who did the printing and presswork, had worked as a printer at the Roycoft Print Shop in the early years of the century, so that he had been early exposed to the theory and practice of Morris as interpreted by the Roycrofters. However, this book owes little to their influence.

2.19
Guenevere/ Two Poems by William Morris/
The Defence of Guenevere/ and King Arthur's Tomb/
with Eight Decorations by/ Dante Gabriel Rossetti/
and a Foreword by/ Gordon Bottomley/
Printed and Published by/ the Fanfrolico Press London

Colophon/Limitation: Here ends Guenevere Two Poems by William Morris from The Defence of Guenevere 1858 with eight collographs of drawings by D.G. Rossetti and a foreword by Gordon Bottomley handset in Weiss Antiqua on Barcham Green Vellum. In the original text the first poem is divided as terza rima, & the second as quatrains; the white lines are here omitted to emphasise the dramatic nature of the speech. Jack Lindsay & W.J. Hatton made this book May 1930 the seventh printed by the Fanfrolico Press this is no *144* of 450 copies for sale. [Punctuation, or lack thereof, as given]

Binding: Brown paper boards, with black linen spine and fore-edges. "Guenevere" in gilt top of front cover and vertically on spine. Three small crosses on front cover separate title from names of author, artist, and Bottomley. Top edge gilt, others left untrimmed. Endpapers of same hand-make paper as rest of book.

Pagination/Size: [xx] [26] [2] / 233 x 172 mm.

Contents: Pp. i-ii blank, p. iii title page, p. iv acknowledgements, pp. v-xx introduction, pp. 1-26 text, p. 26 colophon, pp. 1-2 blank.

Illustrator: DANTE G. ROSSETTI. See 2.4.

Illustrations: Rossetti did not create the pictures specifically to illustrate these poems. Thus most do not correspond closely with the text. The excellence of the drawings mitigates this deficiency, but their impact does depend to a large extent on their decorative quality. The title page includes one of the pictures, between "Bottomley" and "printed." Bottomley's foreword follows the title page and contains three more sketches. The picture on the title page shows a woman in full-length dress with her arms upraised as though in exhortation standing by a seated man, his back supported by a wall, his legs outstretched, his head hanging, his demeanour weary. The first picture in the foreword repeats in larger format a detail from the first picture, the same woman alone. The only difference lies in the greater detail with which the artist has rendered her skirt. The next sketch depicts knightly accoutrements hanging on the branch of a tree. The last which appears in the foreword is more finished but more obscure, a crowded scene with women wearing crowns gazing down at something their bodies hide. This may represent the queens come to bear away the body of the dead Arthur.

The text has two pictures with each poem. In both poems the first is inset alongside the first few lines and portrays a standing female figure. That attached to the title poem resembles the figure on the title page, though with minor differences. The other presumably represents Guenevere. She is wearing a crown, inappropriately since in this poem she has entered a nunnery. The other picture accompanying the title poem shows a man in armour with drawn sword and a woman, both standing, of no obvious relevance to the text. In "King Arthur's Tomb" we find as the second illustration the same picture as Steele uses in his edition of *The Defence of Guenevere* (see 2.4). This picture does correspond well; it depicts the final meeting of Launcelot and Guenevere over Arthur's tomb. In spite of the drawbacks attached to the origin of the pictures, Lindsay achieves a wonderful unity of design between text and illustration. Altogether, this book is a most satisfying creation.

BARRY BURMAN
[Death]
Shameful Death, frontispiece

2.20
William Morris/ Shameful Death/
with Three Drawings by/ Barry Burman/
Gazebo Press

Colophon/Limitation: Hand set and printed in 12pt Baskerville (which Morris would have hated) by Brenda and Michael Felmingham 202 Rugby Road Leamington Spa. Limited to 120 copies 40 being reserved for members of the Society of Private Printers. July 1969

Binding: Limp paper bearing Morris's Sunflower pattern in red and greenish-brown. Free edges of cover folded over blank outer sheet of gathering, and pasted to it, thus incorporating outer sheet as part of cover. Patterned sheet of cover not sewn in the gathering. Pages bound in French fold except for outer sheet.

Comment: A group of students at Leicester College printed Morris's *The Message of the March Wind* in 1963 as a training project. They had used the same method of binding, which may have influenced Felmingham to adopt it too.

Pagination/Size: [vi] [6] / 218 x 158 mm.

Comment: The numeration does not include the outer sheet or the insides of the French folds (see below).

Contents: Pp. i-ii blank, p. iii half-title, p. iv frontispiece, p. v title page, p. vi blank, pp. 1-5 text (illustrations on both versos), p. 6 colophon.

Illustrator: BARRY ROGER BURMAN. Born in Bedford, England, in 1943. He studied at the RCA, after graduating with distinction from the Coventry College of Art. It was there that he met his future wife Rosy Mann, who was also training as a painter. They married in 1971. By this time he was living in Leamington Spa, where he remained for the rest of his life. He taught here part-time, at the Mid-Warwickshire College of Art, from 1974 until 1992, then gave up teaching to paint full-time. This decision stemmed from growing public recognition of his work, stimulated partly by the Group/Observer award in 1991. His early work is best characterised as photorealistic, but increasingly it began to reflect his personal obsessions with violence, death and decay. The macabre and surreal work which resulted brings to mind the art of Hieronymus Bosch, Edvard Munch's *The Scream* and Picasso's *Guernica*. Associates writing after his death variously commented on Burman's kindness, courtesy, and erudition. His long-time friend Michael Felmingham told me of Burman's light-heartedness and gaiety on social occasions. However Burman was subject to severe depression, and Felmingham went on to mention the times when Burman had confided to him, "The black dogs are after me again." Felmingham's description accords with the supposition of bipolar disorder suggested by the paintings themselves. His state was such that his wife felt impelled to extract a promise that he would not take his own life. He was unable to adhere to this, and died of an overdose of his antidepressant pills in early 2001.

Illustrations: Burman's drawings elevate this slim booklet into a minor masterpiece. Morris recounts a murder under circumstances ignominious to the victim's status as a knight and the revenge exacted for his death. Burman's choice of subjects is outstanding. The frontispiece personifies Death himself, the second picture shows the knight hanged by his enemies, and the third one of those enemies dying at the hands of the narrator. At a purely technical level, the drawings are confident, with no suggestion that the artist is extending himself or in any way daunted by his task. The execution of the frontispiece reveals Burman's mastery of his craft; no traditional skeleton here! Instead we see the upright torso and head of a corpse whose skin is stretched tightly over the bones, the other internal tissues gone. The eye sockets are empty and the tip of the nose eaten away. Here and there tiny worms wriggle out through holes in the skin. The head bears a coif, knotted at the crown, from which descends a long fold of cloth (see illustration). The second picture shows the hanged knight in an equally uncompromising fashion. His head snapped to one side, his suffused eyelids, his contorted body, his frantically kicking legs, all portray the agony of his dying. Burman rendered the last picture no less vividly. He took the lines "When . . . / . . . the smoke rolled over . . . the fen / I Slew Guy of the Dolorous Blast." The subject is conventional, a fight between two knights, but Burman set it in the fen water itself. The victor stands, water to his knees, his armour and surcoat splattered with mud, both arms above his head holding a huge broadsword ready to strike down. At what? At a right hand sinking beneath the ripples, the rest of the body no longer visible. With work of this quality, one regrets that Burman did not illustrate more of Morris's writing. He was clearly attuned to the violence of Morris's text and could produce art which complements it perfectly.

2.21
Sir Galahad: A Christmas Mystery/
by William Morris/
with a Wood Engraving by John De Pol/
Bullnettle Press/ MCMXCVI

Colophon/Limitation: Ninety copies of this poem have been printed
in celebration of Christmas and to mark the end of William Morris's
centenary year. The type is Dante, machine-set by Michael and Winifred
Bixler, printed on Hahnemule German Ingres paper using a Vandrecook
SP-15 press.
The patterned covers were made by Coriander Reisbord, who also bound
the edition.
Designed & printed by Asa Peavy.
December 25, 1996

Binding: Paper over boards, patterned in small alternating white and
grey diamond shapes, lightly embossed. Small white cross on a few of
grey diamonds. "Sir Galahad" upper front cover in rectangle devoid
of pattern. Red linen spine. Last page of gathering used as rear fixed
endpaper [not included in pagination].

Pagination/Size: [vi] [12] [4] / 191 x 127 mm.

Contents: Pp. i-ii blank, p. iii title page, p. iv blank, p. v half-title, p. vi
frontispiece, pp. 1-11 text, pp. 12 and 1-2 blank, p. 3 colophon, p. 4 blank
(facing rear pastedown).

Comment: The last free page carries the colophon, thus removing any
illusion that it is the rear free endpaper.

Illustrator: JOHN DE POL. Born in New York in 1913. In the 1930s
he studied at the Art Students League, New York, while working as
an analyst on Wall Street. He studied lithography at the College of Art
in Belfast during military service in World War II. Apart from this he
was largely self-taught. After the war he pursued a varied career as a
wood engraver, printmaker, and book illustrator, latterly as a teacher
of the first two of these art forms. In this last capacity he worked
particularly for a range of private presses, even founding his own in
1974 in collaboration with his wife Thelma. His colleagues recognised
his contributions in these fields; they inducted him into the New York
Printers' Hall of Fame and honoured him with the John Taylor Arm
Memorial Prize. He died in New Jersey in 2004.

Illustration: Peavy used red ink on the title page both for the title itself
and for the date. He employed it too for Christ's monologue, and to
highlight the names of those who address Galahad, the Angel, the four
ladies and Sir Bors. The only illustration, a wood engraving, faces the
first page of text. It shows a night scene with a stone hut, light streaming
from its open door towards a nearby lake. Perhaps De Pol intended it to

portray the chapel. While it demonstrates his technical skill, the subject of the picture is so general that it does not relate to the drama of the poem in a meaningful way. The small format in which De Pol worked, dictated in part by the size of the book, limits its impact further. Were the pictures O'Kane did for the same poem (see 2.13) shrunk to this size, we can imagine a similar reduction in their effect. Nevertheless, this book is pleasant and charming.

2.22
Masters/ in This/ Hall/ A Christmas Carol
Written/ by William Morris in 1859/
Herein Presented with His/ Decorations & the Illustra-/tions by Maryline P. Adams/
Poole Press 1995

Colophon: This book was designed, handset, printed and bound by Maryline Poole Adams. Type is Libra, with Goudy 30 and Morris' initial letters enhancements, printed on Lana Royal paper. Of an edition limited to 100 signed and numbered copies, numbers 1-30 are leather bound.
    This is number *15*
    This is number *49*
Maryline Poole Adams

Binding: Deluxe. Full, royal blue morocco, vertical rectangle on centre, front cover of same leather pasted on, surrounded by single red ruled line. Letters "W" and "M" in red with stars in gilt, one above and one below letters, all arraigned in a vertical line. Title vertically on spine in gilt. Covers plain else. Endpapers plain and bright red. Front free endpaper folded back on itself along its fore-edge and free end incorporated as a page sewn into the gatherings, separating preliminary pages from body of text. All bound in a French fold.
    Standard. Grey-blue paper over boards, surface divided into 3 mm. squares by lattice of ruled lines. Each square contains a leaf in white. "W M" on the front cover, the title vertically on spine in white. Endpapers as in deluxe copies.

Pagination/Size: [vi] [16] / 73 x 51 mm.

Contents: P. i half-title, p. ii frontispiece, p. iii title page, p. iv claim of copyright, pp. v-vi blank (the refolded end of the front free endpaper), pp. 1-10 text, p. 11 statement of end of text, pp. 12-13 musical score, p. 14 note by Adams on genesis of carol, p. 15 colophon, p. 16 blank.

Illustrator: MARYLINE POOLE ADAMS. Born in the late 1930s. Married to the actor Dana James Hutton, by whom she had a daughter and a son in 1959 and 1960 respectively. The marriage ended in divorce. She then started her career as a book illustrator, and has operated the Poole Press for several decades in Berkeley, California (see above).

Illustrations and decoration: The aesthetic appeal of this book stems from the care lavished on every aspect of its design. The French fold in which Adams bound the gatherings provides it with a bulk and proportion which it needs, given the hard cover. On the title page the initial letter of the title, in royal blue, is a large dropped capital with a red ground decorated in green and white. Adams placed the rest of the title alongside it, and a red fleuron at the end, besides three more above the name of the press at the bottom of the page. Immediately below the title she acknowledges the borders and capitals used in the book as originating from designs Morris drew for KP books. Apart from the claim of copyright the following page is covered in a Morrisian floral decoration in pale grey, which also appears on page 11 and as a border around Adams's note after the text and the colophon. Each stanza of the poem has an initial dropped and decorated capital in red, and each page has a Kelmscott border in miniature about 1 cm. wide in the more usual black ink.

In addition to the frontispiece, Adams drew two more full-page illustrations, which appear on pages 5 and 9, and a half-page illustration on page 7. All four portray significant events in the carol, and lie in apposition to the relevant points in the text. The frontispiece depicts a man standing on steps, huge roof beams of a hall above him, a closed door at his back. Presumably the figure portrays the narrator addressing the Masters of the title. The second shows the shepherds ". . . among their sheep. / No man spoke more word / Than they had been asleep." In the third illustration, their minds galvanised, we find them on the way to Bethlehem, and in the last in the manger itself. The illustrations demonstrate Adams's technical skill but suffer from their small size. They are rather dark, but more importantly lose much of the dramatic impact a larger format would impart. The impact comes instead from her exquisite workmanship in the design, hand setting, printing and binding referred to in the colophon. Adams has created a jewel akin to a Tiffany egg in this book.

Chapter 3

The Life and Death of Jason

Bell and Daldy first published *The Life and Death of Jason* for Morris in 1867. It went through several editions before Morris himself published the first illustrated edition at the KP. In the twentieth century long narrative poems fell from favour with the public. This surely explains why the last full-length illustrated edition of *The Life and Death of Jason* came out only twenty years after the first. We have to regret this neglect, since Morris's *Jason* is exciting to read, and full of psychological insight and comment on the human condition.

Morris made many minor textual alterations to the eighth trade edition which came out in 1887 and incorporated them into the Kelmscott edition. Most often the change consists of a single word; occasionally he rewrote a whole line. In Book I alone, I found at least one change on almost every page. May Morris used this revised text in Volume 2 of *The Collected Works of William Morris* which she edited in 1910, but Headley Brothers used the text of 1867 for their edition (3.2) as did Collins Clear Type Press for an illustrated anthology of Morris's poetry, which includes *Jason* (see 18.4o).

3.1
The Life and Death of Jason/ A Poem.
By William Morris. [Half-title]

Colophon: Here endeth *The Life and Death of Jason*, written by William Morris, and printed by the said William Morris at the Kelmscott Press, Upper Mall, Hammersmith, in the County of Middlesex, and finished on the 25th day of May, 1895. Sold by William Morris at the Kelmscott Press.

Limitation: [200 copies on hand-made paper and 6 on vellum].

Binding: Full limp vellum with three ties. Title and author on upper spine in gilt, edges left untrimmed. Endpapers of same paper as rest of book.

Pagination/Size: [8] [iv] 354 [10] / 289 x 210 mm.

Contents: Pp. 1-8 blank, p. i title page, p. ii Argument, p. iii blank, p. iv frontispiece (facing first page of text), pp. 1-354 text, p. 1 illustration, p. 2 blank, p. 3 colophon, pp. 4-10 blank.

Illustrator: SIR EDWARD COLEY BURNE-JONES. Burne-Jones's career as an artist could not have been predicted from his background. He was born in a slum of Birmingham in 1833 to a mother who died a few days after his birth and a father who worked hard but could not make an adequate living. He was, however, devoted to Burne-Jones's welfare, such that the boy acquired a good education. Influenced by the misery of his surroundings, Burne-Jones decided to take holy orders. He therefore went to Oxford in 1852 and shortly afterwards met William Morris. The two discovered a mutual passion for all things medieval and in the course of pursuing this enthusiasm encountered the writing of John Ruskin and the poetry and art of Dante Rossetti (see 2.4). Persuaded by these writings, they decided to follow a career in art. At this point, Burne-Jones had had no training in art, and virtually no exposure to it in any form. He left Oxford late in 1855 without taking his degree and moved to London. He existed almost penniless and half-starving, getting instruction from Rossetti and teaching himself. His situation improved when Morris moved to London and they shared lodgings. Rossetti was able to draw the attention of patrons to Burne-Jones, and he started to get commissions for his work. His position improved further in 1862 once Morris had set up his interior decorating company, since it provided work, all the more needed in that Burne-Jones had married Georgiana MacDonald in 1860. He remained a close friend and collaborator of Morris, for whose company he continued to produce work throughout his life, most particularly designs for stained-glass windows and tapestries. Morris also called on him for drawings to illustrate many of the books published at the KP from 1891 onwards. However, Burne-Jones became most recognized for his large oil paintings, mainly depicting classical myths and legends.

It was principally for this aspect of his output that he was awarded a knighthood in 1894. Perhaps surprisingly, given his origins, he did not accompany Morris into the socialist movement. He died in London in 1898. His nephew Rudyard Kipling left an account of Burne-Jones in *Something of Myself*, published by MacMillan in 1937. Kipling describes Burne-Jones's sudden death, clearly a major heart attack, and goes on to eulogise him in these terms. "His work was the least part of him. It is him that one wants – the size and the strength and the power and the jests and the God given sympathy of the man. He knew. There never was man like to him who knew all things without stirring. Last autumn, he was good enough to talk to me after work – and he talked to me like an equal – as though I were also a workman. He could work more and harder and more sustainedly than a navvy – and it was that among a million things that I reverenced him for beside all my love for him. He was never at fault in his discernings: he made all allowances, just as a God would do; and he laughed like a God." Burne-Jones was clearly a man with humanity and empathy who inspired affection, even allowing for Kipling's somewhat overblown prose. See also 4.1, 4.4-7, 6.1-2, 7.1-2, 9.1-5, 13.1-4, 17.1, 18.11p-13p. (See Fitzgerald.)

Illustrations and decoration: Morris aimed to make decorative every aspect of books he published at the KP. Someone holding a book like the Kelmscott *Jason* knows before he opens it that he has something special in his hands. He will find on turning the cover handmade paper throughout, including the endpapers, as crisp and clean (at least in a well-cared for copy) as the day it came from the press more than a century ago. Morris used the Troy type he designed for larger KP books, and it sits on the page as boldly and confidently as an eagle on a cliff-top ready for flight. The poem begins with a double-page spread, with the frontispiece on the verso and title and opening lines on the recto. Beneath the title a single sentence printed in red ink summarises the action of Book I. The poem starts with a large dropped and decorated capital. A decorative border surrounds all. A similar summary in red ink precedes each successive book of which the poem is composed. Beyond this Morris used red ink only in shoulder notes, which he placed on each page of text indicating the number of the book, I through XVII. Morris also designed a marginal twining floral and leafy border, each different from the rest, for the start of each book, and a large dropped and decorated capital for the initial letter. Similar marginal decorations and dropped capitals appear at intervals throughout the text. In quality of paper, ink, binding, decoration, and press work, the Kelmscott version of *Jason* has not been excelled.

Burne-Jones drew two pictures for this book, reproduced in the form of wood engravings, as were all the illustrations for works published by the KP. Unquestionably, they enhance the decorative effect of the book as a whole. However, as depictions of dramatic events in the text they do not work as well. The frontispiece shows Medea keeping the dragon lulled asleep while Jason steals the Golden Fleece. The second illustrates the scene where Medea seeks the counsel of Circe. Both are pivotal events in the story, so Burne-Jones chose his subjects well. However, neither of these pictures matches the vigour and intensity of Morris's writing. Just before the scene depicted in the first picture, Medea has warned Jason, " . . . if I give the word / Then know that all is lost, and draw thy sword, / And manlike die in battle with the beast." The action, then, is at a moment of high tension. The picture provides no hint of it. Medea stands as serenely as if she were in a reception line at a wedding. The appearance of the dragon justifies her sang-froid since it is small and so innocuous-looking that one could not believe it a threat even if roused and pepped up by a couple of kilograms of amphetamines. The dragon Burne-Jones drew for his *Perseus* series, reproduced in *The Doom of King Acrisius* (4.3), shows that he did not lack the ability to depict an awesome monster. Maxwell Armfield, who illustrated another edition of *Jason* (see 3.2), drew the same scene more convincingly. Admittedly, an illustration engraved on wood is a less flexible medium than a line drawing, but this drawing falls short in the conception not the medium. The second drawing has a similar passive quality, with Circe seated on a distinctive high-backed chair and Medea standing before her. It conveys no suggestion of the drama of their meeting, the horrible ambience and bleak prophecies which Circe is making about Medea's future. Comparing Burne-Jones with Armfield again, the latter's picture of Circe catches her beauty, but also her malevolence. Burne-Jones's Circe, sitting on a bishop's throne, with a halo around her head, could pass for Saint Cecilia, with Medea in front of her with hands raised in prayer.

The Life and Death/ of Jason/
W. Morris/
Illustrated by P.B. Hickling./
London & Glasgow/ Collins' Clear-Type Press

The title is misleading. The book also contains the poems in *The Defence of Guenevere*, and is described in the chapter devoted to collections and anthologies (see 18.4o).

3.2a

The Life and Death/ of/ JASON/ A Metrical Romance/
by/ William Morris/
Decorated by Maxwell Armfield/
London/ Headley Brothers/ Bishopsgate, E.C.

Date of publication: n.d. "1915" [BL].

3.2b

The Life and Death/ of/ Jason/ A Metrical Romance/
by/ William Morris/
Decorated by Maxwell Armfield/
London: The Swarthmore Press Ltd./ Ruskin House 40 Museum Street,
W.C.

Date of publication: n.d. After 3.2a, possibly 1916-17.

Comment: The attribution of the date stems from a hybrid copy with the
binding of 3.2b, including the name Swarthmore on the base of the spine,
combined with the title page of 3.2a. I interpret the anomaly as due to
the binding of left-over sheets from the earlier edition into the binding of
the later one.

3.2c

The Life and Death/ of/ Jason/ A Metrical Romance/
by/ William Morris/
Decorated by Maxwell Armfield/
New York/ Dodd, Mead and Company/ 1917

Binding: Buckram, pink in 32a, pale blue in 3.2b, purple in 3.2c.
Title, author, and publisher on spine, title only on top of front cover. On
lower four-fifths of front cover four rows of a stylised ram's head and
shoulders seen front on. Individual units about 4 cm. across, and spaced
to align horizontally, vertically, and diagonally. Lettering and decoration
stamped in white in 3.2a, dark blue in 3.2b. Lettering in gilt in 3.2c and
decoration blind-stamped. Top edge gilt 3.2c only. Pictorial and decorated
endpapers.

Pagination/Size: x, 332 / 247 x 184 mm.

Comment: Although the pages with the nineteen line drawings and their blank obverses are parts of the gatherings, they are excluded from the pagination.

Contents: P. i half-title, p. ii blank, inserted frontispiece, p. iii title page, p. iv blank, pp. v-vi note by the artist, pp. vii-viii list of illustrations, p. ix contents, p. x Argument, pp. 1-332 text (with five inserted colour plates at intervals).

Comment: Internally all the editions are identical. Indeed, in addition to publishing 3.2a Headley Brothers printed all three, using a good quality of matte paper. The Argument on page x also appears in the KP edition (see 3.1).

Illustrator: MAXWELL ARMFIELD. Born in Hampshire, England, in 1881. He studied at the Birmingham School of Art under Arthur Gaskin, at the Colarossi atelier in Paris, and also in Italy. He spent several years in the US in the second and third decades of the twentieth century. His wife, Constance Smedley, was involved with the theatre, and as a result he did some work in stage design and direction. Armfield was active in book and magazine illustration for much of his life, particularly in the first quarter of the twentieth century, and illustrated some of his own writing. He exhibited his paintings extensively in Britain, Continental Europe, and the US. In addition, he was a graphic designer and painted in watercolours but was especially known for his work in tempera, a subject on which he also wrote. He died in 1972.

Illustrations and decoration: The endpapers are a very pale purple, with a monochrome picture in darker purple of the hull and rigging of a Greek galley, enclosed in a decorated border fore and aft. The picture extends across the upper part of both front endpapers. A caption reading "THEY GAT UNTO THE OAR" appears in the top right corner. On the back endpapers Armfield placed a geometrical pattern in the same dark purple in a similar position and size instead of the picture on the front endpapers. The title page is lettered in black except for the word JASON in red. The name of the publisher also appears in red in the Headley Brothers edition. A horizontal rectangular headpiece precedes each book. It contains a geometrical pattern which suggests a ram's horns seen face on. Two parallel vertical lines which spring from the base of the horns divide the rectangle into equal halves. The number of the book appears below the horns. Each book finishes with a triangular tailpiece where space permits. It too has an internal geometrical pattern. Possibly Armfield intended to represent the tail of the sheep.

Armfield succeeds admirably in selecting good subjects for illustration from this dramatic and action-filled poem. The six colour plates serve to emphasise a character or to highlight an event of significance. The frontispiece shows Jason himself. Of the other colour plates, Medea appears in two, at points in the story where her intervention ensures

TOWARD THE BANK THEY DREW & LANDING ·D·D·D
FELT THE GRASS AND FLOWERS BLUE ·D AGAINST ·D
THEIR UNUSED FEET

MAXWELL ARMFIELD
The Life and Death of Jason, **facing p. 78**

Jason's success. Circe, looking beautiful and evil at the same time, occupies a fourth. Of the other two, one shows Chiron restraining Jason from following Diana in the chase: "Sleep again, my son / Nor wish to spoil great deeds not yet begun." Had Jason ignored Chiron's advice, there would have been nothing left to write about. The other picture, Lynceus releasing the dove, portrays another critical juncture, since the success or failure of the bird in flying between the Clashing Rocks presages the success or otherwise of Jason's quest. The colour illustrations are each protected by a sheet of tissue paper.

Armfield did most of the drawings in black ink. Like the colour pictures, they highlight points of action. Many of them have stylisation reminiscent of the work of Armfield's contemporary, Eric Gill. The quality of Armfield's pictures lies in the way they convey an emotional state with a broad gesture. They do not strain for realism in the manner adopted by Hickling (see 18.4o). The power inherent in Armfield's technique complements the text most effectively. It is the more striking in that it is not typical of much of his work; it seems he adopted this style specifically for the requirements of *Jason*.

This book is unique among those in this bibliography in having an apologia by the artist. The publishers' inclusion of this explication probably reflects the established position of Armfield as a book illustrator. He writes that in his illustrations he tries to suggest the Greek civilisation as he conceives it, "superficial and corrupt, but redeemed . . . by that wholesome life on and by the sea." He does not try to "convey an impression with line similar in kind to that conveyed by the words of the text." Rather he seeks with his decor to give "unity with the book as book, and unity also within itself." He sees the illustration as one of the physical attributes of the book, which include the binding and the layout of the page, all "purposing to present the text to the eye." As such the illustrations can serve "as a commentary on certain aspects ... not touched upon at all by the author." He feels that a simple line best serves the epic poem, since it distracts the reader less from the considerable demands made on him or her by the text.

Armfield seems to apply many of the same criteria as those outlined in the introduction to this book (see page 15). If we see the illustrated book as a work of art, of which the illustration forms one part, then the artist will draw his inspiration from the text but will provide his own interpretation derived from his experience and outlook. However, he must take the text as his starting point, or his work becomes pure decoration. In spite of his statements quoted above, which could imply a free approach to the text, Armfield does follow the text closely. In most instances he cites an actual line of text as the caption for his drawing. Where he draws a major character, he labels the picture with the name. He achieves his aim, "unity within itself," in the coherence of his illustration. He also adheres to his stated aim of a simple line. He could have lifted the accoutrements of his figures straight off a Greek vase. His conception of the Greek civilisation seems to derive from his study of the art objects it left behind, scarcely a surprise since, as an artist, one would expect him to take a visual approach to the world.

The originality of Armfield's art work, quite unlike any of the preceding illustrations of *Jason*, the layout, and the quality of the materials used for the book make this a fine addition to the corpus of illustrated editions of Morris's works.

Armfield's illustration of this book may have influenced later illustration. For example, one has to wonder if it prompted Jepson to use a scene from a Greek vase as frontispiece for his edition of *Jason* for school use (see 3.3).

3.3a & b
The/ Life and Death of Jason/ A Poem/
By/ William Morris/
Abridged and Edited for Schools by/ R.W. Jepson, B.A./ Assistant Master at Dulwich College/
Macmillan and Co., Limited/ St. Martin's Street, London/ 1923

3.3a Binding: Red buckram, plain except for triangular spray of leaves blind-stamped on centre of front cover and title and author vertically on spine in gilt.

3.3b Binding: Lime-green flexible linen on paper, title and author on spine and front cover, enclosed on latter by pillars on sides and lintel above. Series designation, *English Literature for Schools*, within lintel and between single laurel wreaths on each side, all in black. Publisher's symbol below author and editor.

3.3a Pagination/Size: xvi, 136 [2] / 169 x 107 mm.

3.3b Pagination/Size: [4] xvi, 136 [2] / 170 x 117 mm.

Contents: Pp. 1-4 blank inserts (3.3b only), p. i half-title, p. ii emblem and address of publisher, p. iii blank, p. iv frontispiece, p. v title page, p. vi statement of copyright, pp. vii-viii contents, pp. ix-xiv introduction, p. xv epigraph taken from Book XVII, p. xvi blank, pp. 1-115 text, pp. 116-128 questions on text, p. 129 glossary, pp. 130-131 geographical names, pp. 132-134 names of people, p. 135 sources of story, p. 136 further reading, pp. 1-2 inserted sheet of advertisements for other titles in series (listings different between 3.3a & b).

Comment: Some of the poem remains in its original form. However, in editing the text, Jepson wrote very condensed prose paraphrases to replace long sections of the poem, and renumbered the component books. For example, he created his last two books, 13 and 14, by dividing Book 17 of the original version.

Illustrator: Unknown.

Illustration: The book has a single illustration, its frontispiece, which reproduces an Attic vase painting of the sixth century BC. It depicts the scene in which Medea dupes King Pelias and his daughters into believing she can restore his youth by her magical powers. In the centre of the picture sits a huge cauldron from which the forepart of the ram emerges, almost upright. Medea stands to the left, one arm raised dramatically in the "Hey presto!" pose adopted by conjurers in any age. Behind her sits King Pelias, his bowed back and bent head duplicating the curve of back and head of the ram. To the right of the cauldron the daughters of Pelias stand with arms upraised in wonder. The ancient Greek artist had a sure instinct for a dramatic and pivotal situation and an equally sure hand in the execution of his work.

Chapter 4

The Earthly Paradise

The Earthly Paradise appeared, volume by volume, between 1868 and 1870. None of the British editions of this work published during Morris's lifetime is illustrated. Indeed, with the exception of a volume in *The Collected Works of William Morris*, only one edition with wood engravings by Morris has ever appeared, and that consisting of just one of the twenty-four stories (see 4.7). However, it represents the jewel of the chapter, and a pinnacle in this book overall. Two other entries have the earliest dates of publication (with the exception of an anthology containing a single poem by Morris). The first, *The Lovers of Gudrun* (4.2), appeared as early as 1870 in Boston, where the publisher was not constrained by copyright laws. This publisher, Roberts Brothers, does seem to have established a relationship with Morris, and remained his American publisher throughout his life. Ticknor and Company published the second, *Atalanta's Race and Other Stories from The Earthly Paradise* (4.3), in 1888. The publishers made these two books of inexpensive materials and marketed them for the time, not for the future. However, such publications do reveal to us the immediate and lasting recognition which Morris achieved with this poem. R.H. Russell showed more care and attention in editions of two further stories, published at the start of the twentieth century (see 4.4 and 4.5). However, it was not until 2002 that Routledge published the first edition of the whole poem to include illustrations.

In this chapter we see in significant form another phenomenon which would have dismayed Morris both as socialist and artist, that of using art work which originally came from another source to illustrate Morris's writing. As a socialist Morris would have objected to the deprivation of the artist

who would have obtained a livelihood had he received a commission to produce art for the book. Aesthetically, Morris would have been even more dismayed, seeing the book as a patchwork lacking artistic integrity. The only creative aspect in such a book comes from the designer who ferrets out the best fit he can find to match picture and text.

The first paraphrased version of Morris's writing comprises selections from *The Earthly Paradise*. Those which contain illustration are described in the second part of this chapter.

Facsimile reprints of *The Collected Works of William Morris* came to my attention too late to allow their inclusion in the text, where description of the relevant volume would have appeared after 4.6. I provide details of these reprints in *Notes Added in Press* on page 308.

4.1
The Earthly Paradise/
by/ William Morris/
Edited by Florence S. Boos/
In Two Volumes/ Volume One/
Routledge/ New York & London

The Earthly Paradise/
by/ William Morris/
Edited by Florence S. Boos/
In Two Volumes/ Volume Two/
Routledge/ New York & London

Date of publication: 2002.

Binding (same for both volumes): No dust jacket. Dark grey, almost black buckram with title, author and volume number on upper front cover and editor at bottom. Same information on upper spine and publisher at base, all stamped in silver.

Size: 227 x 151 mm.

Pagination: xlii, 688, xlvi (Volume 1), xliv, 780, lxxii (Volume 2)

Contents: Volume 1. P. i half-title, p. ii frontispiece, p. iii title page, p. iv publication information, p. v dedication, p. vi blank, p. vii contents, p. viii blank, pp. ix-x acknowledgements, pp. xi-xiii list of illustrations, pp. xiv-xli illustrations, p. xlii blank, p. 1 subsidiary title page, p. 2 blank, pp. 3-45 introduction, p. 46 title page of first section, p. 47 Morris's dedication, pp. 48-68 discussion of Morris's sources and narrative, pp. 69-687 text (with brief editorial introductions for each story), p. 688 blank, p. i statement of collations, pp. ii-xxxix collations, pp. xl-xlvi blank.

Volume 2. P. i half-title, p. ii frontispiece, p. iii title page, p. iv publication information, p. v contents, p. vi blank, pp. vii-ix list of illustrations, pp. x-xliii illustrations, p. xliv blank, p. 1 subsidiary title page, p. 2 blank, p. 3 title page for following section, pp. 4-779 text (with brief editorial introductions for each story), p. 780 blank, p. i statement of collations, pp. ii-lxv collations, pp. lxvi-lxxii blank.

Comment: Several titles included in the present book have an instructional or analytical framework supporting Morris's text (see 2.4, 3.3, and 4.3). Of the group, this edition of *The Earthly Paradise* has the most academic rigour. In the first volume a perceptive essay by Boos precedes the poem, and, as noted above, she also supplies a separate introduction for the "Apology," "Prologue," and each of the stories. In addition, she annotates the text with copious footnotes, another valuable feature of this edition. The text itself derives from that of the KP edition of 1896-97, but Boos documents earlier variants found in the original manuscript and previous editions, this in a section of collations at the end of each of her two volumes. The fidelity of Boos's text to the 1896 edition extends even to reproducing the statement "End of Vol. [I through VII]," and the accompanying statement of publication for each of the seven Kelmscott volumes in which it is present. She does not include the final colophon, of Volume VIII, perhaps because it appears on a separate page.

Illustrators: HAMMATT BILLINGS. See 4.2, where the illustration originally appeared.
    EDWARD BURNE-JONES. See 3.1.
    DANTE G. ROSSETTI. See 2.4.

Illustrations and decoration: The decoration comes almost entirely from the Kelmscott edition of *The Earthly Paradise*. The layout editor reproduced the initial title page and the title pages of individual stories of that edition among the illustrations, all of which he grouped at the start of each volume. He also used Morris's dropped and decorated capitals in the text at the same points as they appear in the KP edition. He even reproduced type from that edition for such preliminary pages as Morris's dedication of the work to his wife. Less happily, he indicated a new paragraph by capitalising all the letters of the first word of the line. Morris conveyed this information by indenting the line in his first edition of 1868 and more elegantly with a small dropped capital in the Kelmscott edition. However, overall Boos's text is clear and readable, printed on acid-free paper of good quality.

The illustrations consist entirely of photo reproductions. Several depict Morris himself, including the frontispiece of each volume. In the first we see G.F. Watts' well-known painting. It appears a second time in the body of the illustrations of this volume. The frontispiece of the second volume reproduces a drawing by Rossetti. In addition, we have two photographs of Morris alone, and one of a group which includes the Morris and Burne-Jones families. There are some pages from *A Book of Verse*, some of Morris's wall-paper designs, and some illustrations of scenes from *The Earthly Paradise* by Burne-Jones, Rossetti, and Hammatt Billings.

The only weakness of this edition lies in its graphic elements. Their failings, contrasted with the excellence of Boos's editing, endow it with a schizophrenic quality. Specifically, the first fault lies in their arrangement. In each volume, Routledge grouped them at the front, divorcing them from the story they illustrate. The reproductions of title pages of stories from the KP edition of *The Earthly Paradise* would have looked better heading the relevant story. Given the manner of production of this book, it would have been easy to place these title pages in this way. The same argument applies to the pictures which illustrate the text. Admittedly, this would have made their paucity obvious, as many stories would have no illustrations at all, while a few would have several. Secondly, many of the illustrations are irrelevant. Images of Kelmscott Manor, the multiple ones of Morris, of his family, of wallpaper patterns, of pages from another work *(A Book of Verse)* add nothing which enhances the text. Beyond this, some of the scenes drawn by artists depict events or people not present in the text, such as Rossetti's *Helen of Troy*. Admittedly, one could justify the inclusion of this on the basis of the references to her in "The Death of Paris." Finally, the quality of the images themselves fails to satisfy. Lettering and line drawings remain adequately clear and sharp. However, paintings lose definition and become fuzzy and indistinct. Some pictures, such as the four illustrations for "Pygmalion and the Image," appear in so small a format as to sacrifice power and to render important detail indiscernible.

Only a minority of illustrations do depict relevant scenes, among them Hammatt Billings's picture of Gudrun, which originally appeared as the frontispiece for *The Lovers of Gudrun* (4.2). However, Burne-Jones drew most of this group. Some have appeared before, in Russell's editions of *The Doom of King Acrisius* (4.4) and *Pygmalion and the Image* (4.5) and, as wood engravings, in the Rampant Lions Press edition of *Cupid and Psyche* (4.7). The illustrations lose some further value in that none of their captions includes a page reference to the text illustrated, nor even an explicit indication of the story to which the picture belongs. A positive feature lies in the reproduction of Burne-Jones's sketches done in the 1860s to illustrate "The Hill of Venus." Morris and Burne-Jones had planned to use them for an illustrated edition which never came to fruition (see 4.7, *Binding Contents*). The sketches for "The Hill of Venus" are of especial interest, since no one has used them before as a book illustration, as far as I know.

For further discussion of some of the illustrations re-used in this book from previous editions see 4.2, 4.4, 4.5, and 4.7.

4.2
The/ Lovers of Gudrun./ A Poem./
By William Morris./
Reprinted from "The Earthly Paradise."/
Boston:/ Roberts Brothers./ 1870.

Comment on dates of publication: Advertisements in the 1898 (see 10.1a) and 1901 (see 10.1d) reprints of *News from Nowhere* include a listing of *Gudrun* as a 16mo incorporating the frontispiece "designed by Billings." I have never seen a copy, nor any other reference to it in Pye or elsewhere. Pye does say that Longmans Green acquired unsold sheets of Roberts Brothers' editions of Morris books in 1899. Perhaps these sheets included copies of *Gudrun* which Longmans bound and sold. This fails to explain the designation "16mo," since the 1870 *Gudrun* is an 8vo.

Binding: Red, blue, or green cloth over boards, title upper cover in ornate letters, with decoration of boy sitting on globe blowing bubbles, all in gilt. Title on spine above crossed flaming torches. Back cover plain. Endpapers reddish-brown.

Comment: Copies bound in red achieve a pleasing harmony of colour with the endpapers. A copy in (emerald) green [HL] and those in blue have endpapers of the same brown colour, such that the harmony of cover and endpapers is lost.

Pagination/Size: [iv] [138] 42 / 173 x 112 mm.

Comment: To create this book Roberts bound sheets of the composite edition of which "Gudrun" is a part. The numeration of the pages, 245-382, derives from this.

Contents: Pp. i-ii blank, inserted frontispiece, p. iii title page, p. iv publisher's statement regarding pagination (see above), pp. 245-382 text, pp. 1-36 tributes to Morris from reviews and other printed sources in Britain and America, pp. 37-40 advertisements for other books published by Roberts, pp. 41-42 blank.

Illustrator: HAMMATT BILLINGS. Born Charles Howland Hammatt, in Milton, Massachusetts, in 1818. He trained as an architect and artist in Boston, where he lived most of his life. He was active in both fields, with a profuse output of book illustrations for classic American fiction, children's books, and English writers. He undertook some of the decoration of public buildings around Boston and was responsible for the design of several of its churches. He died in New York in 1874.

Illustration: The book lacks decoration except for the emblem in the front cover described in the section on binding. Buxton Forman describes the sole illustration as follows. "Facing the title-page is a frontispiece representing Gudrun, 'just come to her full height,' standing betwixt the pillars of the Hall at Bathstead." The picture matches the description in the poem exactly, and was clearly commissioned for the book. The subject matter is appropriate and competently done, though not inspired. The scene Billings portrays occurs on only the third page of the text. There are more gripping episodes later in the poem (for example see 4.8P) and one wonders if the artist stopped reading once he had found a subject.

4.3a

Atalanta's Race/ and Other Tales from the Earthly Paradise/
by William Morris/
Edited with Notes/ by Oscar Fay Adams/ with the Co-operation of/
William J. Rolfe, A.M., Litt. D./
with Illustrations/
Boston/ Ticknor and Company/ 1888

4.3b

Atalanta's Race/ and Other Tales from the Earthly Paradise/
By William Morris/
Edited with Notes/ by Oscar Fay Adams/ with the Co-operation of/
William J. Rolfe, A.M., Litt. D./
with Illustrations/
Boston and New York/ Houghton, Mifflin and Company/ The Riverside
Press, Cambridge

4.3b Date of publication: n.d. for the first issue. Houghton, Mifflin and
Company, the successor to Ticknor, presumably reprinted the title page
and bound Ticknor's sheets. Houghton reprinted the book in 1894, with
this date on the title page. [HL]

Binding: Dark green stippled cloth over boards, title and editors' names
on cover, and title only vertically on the spine. All edges trimmed and
stained light red.

Pagination/Size: [2] x, 242 [2] / 166 x 118 mm.

Comment: The Arabic numerals start at 11, following on from the
Roman numbers of the preliminary pages.

Contents: Pp. 1-2 blank, p. i half-title, pp. ii-iii blank, p. iv frontispiece,
p. v title page, p. vi statement of copyright, pp. vii-viii preface, p. ix
contents, p. x blank, pp. 11-21 introduction, p. 22 blank, p. 23 half-title
to text, p. 24 frontispiece to text, pp. 25-188 text, p. 189 half-title to the
notes, p. 190 list of abbreviations in the notes, pp. 191-240 notes, pp. 241-
242 index of words explicated in the notes, pp. 1-2 blank.

Comment: The introduction on pages 11-21 is a pastiche of extracts from
articles about different aspects of Morris's work by a range of writers on
various occasions. It concludes with Oscar Wilde's poem "The Charm of
Morris's Poetry." The text comprises "The Prologue," "Atalanta's Race,"
"The Proud King," and "The Writing on the Image" with their bridging
passages, namely the verses eulogising each month, the Preludes and the
Interludes.

Illustrators: Not identified. One landscape is signed "ehg," and a tailpiece
carries an indecipherable name, possibly starting with "Jose . . . ."

Illustrations and decoration: Decoration as distinct from illustration is fairly sparse. The frontispiece consists of a portrait of Morris above a reproduction of his signature. On the title page of 4.3a above the name of the publisher sits a heraldic shield with flowers and tassels at its edges and an open book in the centre inscribed with the letter T. In the same area in the Houghton edition a vignette in the form of an upright rectangle replaces the shield. It depicts a seated youth playing the pipes, a river in front and a tree trunk behind him. Above his head the tree's branches spread into a mass of leaves which extend the width of the picture. Superimposed on the foliage is a scroll reading "Tout bien ou rien" ("Everything perfect or nothing"). Another scroll at the base containing "The Riverside Press" presumably identifies the vignette as the emblem of the printer. Decorative tailpieces adorn the end of the introductory poem "Of Heaven and Hell I Have No Power to Sing," and the end of "The Prologue." The editors placed a further one at the end of the notes, this one a naturalistic rendering of birds, in contrast to the stylised form of the other two. Each of the three poems eulogising the months has an identical border of stems and flowers.

In contrast to the sparing use of decoration, illustration is quite profuse, with fourteen pictures at intervals throughout the book. The first appears as a tailpiece to "The Charm of Morris's Poetry." This poem by Oscar Wilde concludes the introduction. The scene depicts mature woodland with an undercover of flowers. The textual frontispiece, facing the first page of text, shows the west front of Peterborough Cathedral. Morris describes this edifice in his Prelude to "The Proud King," so the picture has an apt subject. Illustrations to "The Prologue" consist of four portraits, showing head and upper trunk, followed by four land- or seascapes. The first portrait is identified as Chaucer, named in the opening lines. The second depicts an old man with a profuse beard, presumably The Elder of the City. In the third one sees a king wearing a crown. This picture appears in the section which recounts the meeting of the Wanderers with Edward III of England. The last, a knight in armour, accompanies the long address to the king by Nicholas, and perhaps is intended to represent the latter. The seascape at the end certainly evokes the voyage of the Wanderers from Norway through the English Channel where Morris set the scene of the meeting.

Compared with the Prologue, the stories have few illustrations. The Prelude to "Atalanta's Race" has a tailpiece and the story itself a headpiece. The Interlude which follows also has a tailpiece. Two illustrations accompany the text of "The Proud King," and the Interlude which follows has a tailpiece. All of these head- and tailpieces are landscapes, and like those accompanying "The Prologue" are steel engravings. "The Writing on the Image" lacks illustration altogether.

The picture of Chaucer is a well-known one, and certainly reproduced from another source. The same is very probably true of the other portraits, which look as though they may have come from a school textbook of history. The landscapes have a similarity in style, possibly indicative of a common source as well. They have a generic quality, mainly depicting mountains or woods, such as one finds in illustrated books of travel or exploration from that period. However, LeMire points out that the scenes in the landscapes match scenes described in accompanying text. The editors clearly expended some effort in selecting appropriate pictures. All are executed with competence.

4.4
The Doom of King/ Acrisius/
by/ William Morris/
Illustrated with/ Pictures by Sir Ed-/ ward Burne-Jones/
New York R.H. Russell/ Publisher MCMII

Binding: Cream-coloured buckram. Two close-set parallel lines near margins of front cover and two cm. further in a series of four more ruled lines. Between the two sets of lines, at each corner, a poplar leaf. Title and author on upper front cover inside inner set of lines. Title alone on top of spine. On back cover publisher's monogram at base close to spine. Lettering, decorations, and top edge all in gilt. Other edges untrimmed.

Pagination/Size: [2] xviii, 82 [2] / 213 x 166 mm.

Contents: Pp. 1-2 blank, p. i half-title, p. ii blank, inserted frontispiece, p. iii title page, p. iv statement of copyright, p. v list of illustrations, p. vi blank, p. vii illustration, p. viii blank, pp. ix-xvi introductory essay by Fitzroy Carrington with illustrations, p. xvii epigraph from Morris's *The Idle Singer*, p. xviii blank, inserted second frontispiece, pp. 1-82 text (with full-page illustrations inserted at intervals), pp. 1-2 blank.

Illustrator: EDWARD BURNE-JONES. See 3.1.

Illustrations and decoration: The title page repeats the design of the front cover, with the addition of the publisher and date of publication in the base of the inner rectangle. Between this and the title is a stylised rose with the publisher's monogram in its centre. The title of the poem and the name of the publisher are in red, the rest in black. The introduction, the epigraph on page xvii, and the text all start with a large decorated dropped capital, and more appear at intervals in the text.

In his introduction, Fitzroy Carrington describes the genesis of the illustrations used in this book and its companion volume, *Pygmalion and the Image* (4.5). Burne-Jones had done some of the scenes from

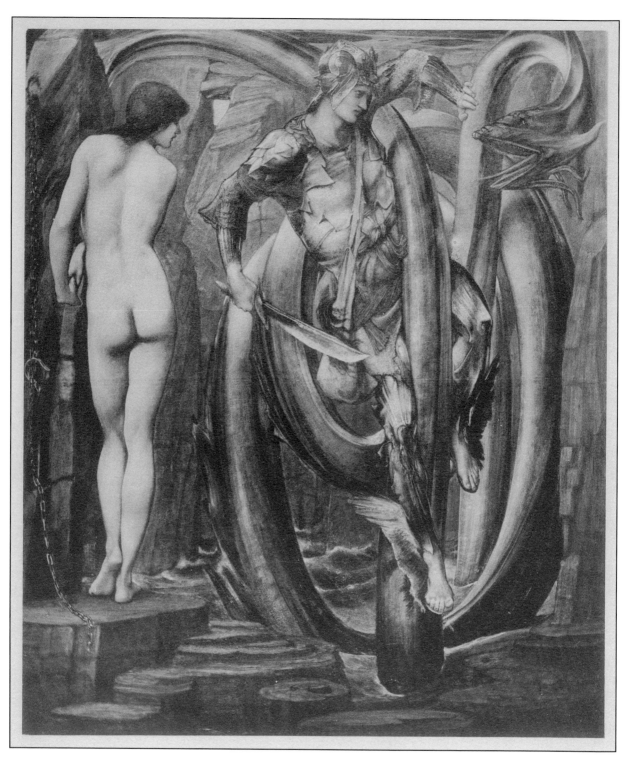

EDWARD BURNE-JONES
[Perseus Slaying the Monster]
The Doom of King Acrisius, facing p. 54

the Perseus legend as a commission for Arthur Balfour; others he had painted at various times without a particular purchaser in view. While the artist did not create them specifically to accompany Morris's text, they illustrate it admirably. The frontispiece forms an exception in depicting *The Garden of the Hesperides*, which does not figure in the story. The second picture precedes the introduction, and shows Perseus stealing the eye of the Graiae. Above the picture a text in Latin presents the Argument. Balfour spent his career in politics, but as a former Classics scholar he would have had no trouble understanding the text. This and all the other part-page illustrations are tipped in. Three more part-page pictures appear in the introduction. Fitzroy Carrington describes one of them as incomplete when the artist died, but all could stand as finished works. The first depicts Perseus hiding under the cloak of invisibility from the Gorgons seeking to avenge his slaying of Medusa, the second the slaying itself, and the third Pegasus and Chrysaor rising from Medusa's headless body.

The second frontispiece, facing the first page of the poem, represents the head of Danae in profile. In fact it depicts the artist's mistress, and was not intended for the purpose to which the editor put it in this book. Burne-Jones captures her exquisite beauty and renders the sketch with superlative skill and tenderness. The remaining ten pictures, all full-page, appear at intervals in the text. In their original form all are paintings. Frederick Hollyer, who specialised in this field, photographed them, and the reproductions in the book were made from these photographs. In spite of his expertise, they have suffered in the process. Anyone who has seen the originals can appreciate the importance of their bright colours. In the black and white reproductions in this book we lose detail which differences in colour clarify. The small format imposed by the size of the book aggravates this. Nevertheless, the skill, power and movement in the pictures remain. Between them they portray most of the dramatic episodes in the story, starting with Danae watching the building of the brazen tower through to Perseus and Andromeda looking at the reflected image of the severed head of Medusa.

4.5
Pygmalion and/ the Image/
by/ William Morris/
Illustrated with/ Pictures by Sir Ed-/ward Burne-Jones/
New York R.H. Russell/ Publisher MCMIII

Binding: Binding same as companion volume *The Doom of King Acrisius* (see 4.4).

Pagination/Size: xvi, 36 / 213 x 169 mm.

Contents: P. i half-title, p. ii blank, inserted frontispiece, p. iii title page, p. iv statement of copyright, p. v list of illustrations, p. vi blank, pp. vii-xiv introduction by Fitzroy Carrington, p. xv Argument, p. xvi blank, pp. 1-35 text, p. 36 blank.

Comment: Title page and layout generally are the same as seen in 4.4. Morris wrote the poem in seven-line stanzas. The size of the book does not permit three complete stanzas per page, so that, page after page, lines carry over. The poem ends three lines short of the bottom of the page, and Russell equalised the level by printing in upper case "The End" on what would have been the lowest line.

Illustrator: EDWARD BURNE-JONES. See 3.1.

Illustrations: The frontispiece consists of a portrait of Morris, protected by tissue paper with the caption printed on it. The introduction, Argument, and poem start with large dropped and decorated capitals, and two others appear in the body of the text. This poem is less than half the length of *The Doom of King Acrisius*, and has correspondingly fewer illustrations, four exclusive of the frontispiece portrait. However, as Carrington points out, these pictures form a unified series, counterpointing dramatic stages in the narrative. More would have been superfluous. Burne-Jones himself expressed and recognised this unity by first exhibiting them together in 1879. At this exhibition Morris supplied captions which put together form a quatrain. These captions appear on the paper guards protecting the reproductions in this book. The pictures demonstrate Burne-Jones at his best, being wonderfully executed in his characteristic style. The first picture ("The Heart Desires") shows the sculptor Pygmalion in a reverie induced by the beauty of the sculptures around him, and longing for a living woman whose beauty would match theirs. The second ("The Hand Refrains") depicts him after he has created a sculpture of a woman of such surpassing beauty that he has fallen in love with the stone image. Nevertheless the rigidity of the figure conveys its lifeless nature. Pygmalion prays to Venus to infuse the statue with life, and in the third picture ("The Godhead Fires") we see the goddess in the act of doing so. Burne-Jones catches the authority of Venus in her stance and expression and the life sparking in the statue in its new suppleness. The last picture ("The Soul Attains") portrays Pygmalion kneeling in wonder and adoration before the now fully alive woman. The pictures do not match the text in minor details, a reflection of their origin as other than illustrations for Morris's poem. However, one feels that with them the publisher has achieved a unity of all the elements of the illustrated book and created a completely satisfying work.

4.6
[The Story of Cupid and Psyche]
[In] The Collected Works/ of William Morris/
with Introductions by/ His Daughter May Morris/
Volume IV/ The Earthly Paradise/ A Poem/ II/
Longmans Green and Company/ Paternoster Row London/ New York
Bombay Calcutta/ MDCCCCX

Binding: Pale blue paper over boards. Linen spine. Paper label on top of spine with title, volume number and volume contents, plain else.

Size: 228 x 155 mm.

Contents: Pp. 4-73 text of "Cupid and Psyche."

Illustrator: EDWARD BURNE-JONES. See 3.1.

Illustrations: Illustration consists of two wood engravings originally destined for the abortive illustrated edition of *The Earthly Paradise* planned by Morris and Burne-Jones in the 1860s. Both portray Psyche in time of peril, once in Charon's boat as he ferries her over the Styx and again as she stands at the gates of Hades. For further discussion of this series of wood engravings see 4.7.

4.7 Note: The publisher put out a deluxe edition (4.7a) which consists of a two-volume set and a portfolio. Their standard edition (4.7b) contains only the two-volume set. However, they did also issue a separate portfolio (4.7c) to accompany it at the discretion of the purchaser.

4.7a & b
William Morris: The Story of Cupid/ and Psyche,/
with Illustrations Designed/ by Edward Burne-Jones, Mostly Engraved/
on the Wood by William Morris;/
the Introduction by A.R. Dufty./
Clover Hill Editions, London/ and Cambridge 1974. [Volume 1]

4.7a & b
William Morris: The Story of/ Cupid and Psyche,/
with Wood-Engravings Designed/
by Edward Burne-Jones and Mostly Engraved by/
William Morris, with an Introduction by A.R. Dufty;/
published by Clover Hill Editions, London/ and Cambridge 1974. [Volume 2]

4.7a
William Morris/ The Story of/ Cupid and/ Psyche/
The forty-four Wood-Engravings/ Designed/ by Edward Burne-Jones/
and Mostly Engraved by/ William Morris/
with the Forty-seven Drawings/
Reproduced in Collotype/
Clover Hill Editions/ London/ and Cambridge 1974 [Portfolio]

4.7c
William Morris/ The Story of/ Cupid and/ Psyche/
The forty-four wood-engravings/ designed/ by Edward Burne-Jones/
and mostly engraved/ by William Morris/
Clover Hill Editions/ London/ and Cambridge 1974/ [Portfolio]

4.7a & b [Volume 1] Colophon: The Story of Cupid and Psyche, Volume One
     The Introduction was designed and printed by Will and Sebastian Carter at the Rampant Lions Press, Cambridge, in Monotype Ehrhardt; the plates were printed by the Cotswold Collotype Company; and the paper was made by J. Barcham Green.

4.7a & b [Volume 2] Colophon: The Story of Cupid and Psyche, Volume 2.
     The text with the engravings was designed and printed by Will and Sebastian Carter at the Rampant Lions Press, Cambridge, in the Kelmscott Troy types cast at the foundry of the Oxford University Press from the original matrices in the possession of the Cambridge University Press, on paper made by J. Barcham Green. Bound by Sangorski & Sutcliffe. (4.7a)
     . . . Bound by John P. Gray, Cambridge. (4.7b)

4.7a [Portfolio] Colophon: This Portfolio was designed and printed by Will and Sebastian Carter at the Rampant Lions Press, Cambridge; the paper was made by J. Barcham Green; and the drawings were reproduced by the Cotswolds Collotype Company.

4.7c [Portfolio] Colophon: This Portfolio was designed and printed by Will and Sebastian Carter at the Rampant Lions Press, Cambridge; the paper was made by J. Barcham Green.

4.7a, b & c Limitation: This publication, the eighth of the Clover Hill Editions consists of:

130 copies, numbered I to CXXX, each with a portfolio containing a set of collotype prints of the 47 original 'Cupid and Psyche' drawings and a set of proofs of the 44 wood engravings.

270 copies numbered 1 to 270.

100 portfolios numbered i to c, each containing a set of proofs of the 44 wood-engravings.

This is copy number . . . .

4.7a Binding: Both volumes together in slipcase of paper over boards decorated with Morris's willow pattern. Leaves light blue on dark blue background. Books bound in full dark blue morocco, with title, author and volume number in gilt on orange-brown leather label on spine. Top edge gilt. Endpapers of very heavy paper, with same willow pattern as slipcase.

Portfolio in clamshell case quarter bound in dark blue morocco and paper over boards with willow pattern matching slipcase of volumes and leather label also matching those on the volumes, giving title, author, and contents "The Engravings and the Drawings." Case lined internally with plain blue paper. Unbound sheets in wrappers of same colour, folded over from all four sides.

4.7a, b & c Size: Volumes 1 and 2 and Portfolios. 338 x 237 mm.

4.7a Pagination: Volume 1: [8] xiv, 38, 26 [8]
Volume 2: [6] [viii] 92 [8]
Portfolio [8] [44] 47

4.7a Contents: Volume 1: pp. 1-8 blank, p. i half-title, pp. ii-iii double-spread title page, p. iv statement of copyright, p. v statement of limitation, p. vi blank, p. vii acknowledgements, p. viii blank, p. ix contents, pp. x-xi list of plates and engravings, p. xii blank, p. xiii foreword by A. R. Dufty, p. xiv engraving from the title page of *The Earthly Paradise*, pp. 1-30 introduction by A. R. Dufty, pp. 31-32 lists of illustrations proposed by Morris, pp. 33-35 abbreviations and references, p. 36 sources of illustrations reproduced, p. 37 title page for plates, p. 38 blank, pp. 1-26 plates, p. 1 blank, p. 2 colophon for Volume 1, pp. 3-8 blank.

Comment (4.7a & b): Pages 31-32 consist of a double-size sheet, the outer half of which folds towards page 30. The side of the sheet which faces page 30 when folded carries the page number 31, and the identification of the contents on its obverse. Its inner half, which faces page 33, is completely blank. When unfolded the double spread facing page 30 contains the lists on its inner aspect. The stub of the sewn end appears between pages 36 and 37.

4.7a Contents: Volume 2: pp. 1-6 blank, p. i half-title, pp. ii-iii double-spread title page, p. iv statement of copyright, p. v statement about the engravings, p. vi blank, p. vii Argument, p. viii blank, pp. 1-92 text, pp. 1-2 blank, p. 3 colophon for Volume 2, pp. 4-8 blank.

4.7a Contents: Portfolio: two printed sheets sewn together with white thread. P. 1 title, p. 2 blank, p. 3 title page, p. 4 statement of copyright, p. 5 statement concerning contents, pp. 6-7 contents (with engravings reproduced in miniature), p. 8 statement concerning design and materials of portfolio. Forty-four loose, unnumbered sheets, each with an engraving. Forty-seven loose numbered sheets, each with one of Burne-Jones's drawings reproduced in collotype, the last a double spread.

4.7b Binding: Both volumes together in dark blue slipcase of linen over boards. Books bound in paper boards, with same willow pattern as slipcase of 4.7a. Spine of narrow strip of dark blue paper, with title and author in gilt on same type of leather label as 4.7a. Top edge gilt. Endpapers of same paper as used for rest of book.

4.7b Pagination: Volume 1: [4] xivi, 38, 26 [4]. Volume 2: [2] [viii] 92 [4].

4.7b Contents: Volume 1: pp. 1-4 blank. Beyond the initial blank pages, pagination is identical with that of 4.7a. The final section is laid out as p. 1 blank, p. 2 colophon for Volume 1, pp. 3-4 blank.

4.7b Contents: Volume 2: pp. 1-2 blank. Beyond the initial blank sheet, pagination is identical with that of 4.7a. The final section is laid out as pp. 1-2 blank, p. 3 colophon for Volume 2, p. 4 blank.

4.7c Binding: Clamshell case of same materials as slipcase of 4.7b. Interior lined with same willow-pattern paper as above. Label on hinge of case and wrappers for sheets same as those used for portfolio of 4.7a.

Comment: The printers designed the binding of this portfolio to match that of 4.7b, though the publisher sold it separately.

4.7c Pagination: [8] [44].

4.7c Contents: Two printed and folded sheets sewn together with white thread. P. 1 title page, p. 2 statement of copyright, p. 3 colophon for portfolio (including its number in the series), p. 4 blank, p. 5 full-page note on the engravings, pp. 6-7 contents (showing the same listing as in the contents pages of 4.7a), p. 8 statement concerning design and materials of the portfolio. Forty-four loose sheets, each with an engraving.

Comment: The contents of the two sewn sheets in this portfolio differ significantly from those in the portfolio of 4.7a.

Illustrator: EDWARD BURNE-JONES. See 3.1.

Illustrations and decoration: No other edition of an illustrated text by Morris comes close to this one in conception, materials and execution. The colophon states baldly the paper, type, and form of the binding. The reality of them, the magnificence of the leather binding, the crispness of the hand-made paper carrying the distinctive and distinguished type, must be seen to be fully appreciated. Clearly the publisher took seriously Morris's precepts about the requirements for a fine book. At first glance one thinks they also followed his example. With a Kelmscott type and wood engravings made from illustrations by Burne-Jones, we can see the family resemblance. However, this book is a descendant, not a clone. For example, while, in the Kelmscott tradition, Will and Sebastian Carter designed a decorated title page, it has a distinctly modern look. They placed within a pair of ruled black lines a vertical grey rectangle which occupies most of an otherwise blank page, with the title in large black type, one word to the line inside the rectangle. They used the same design for the title page of each portfolio, employing a smaller type, with additional lettering designating the contents appropriately. By eschewing the use of decorative borders they created an open, airy feel to the text, which is thoroughly refreshing. Similarly, the designers were sparing in their use of dropped capitals. A large one opens the poem, and smaller ones appear at intervals, as well as fleurons at the beginning of each paragraph, but they do not overwhelm. In brief, the decorative effect comes from the layout, rather than decorative devices as such.

Morris and Burne-Jones had envisaged an illustrated edition of *The Earthly Paradise*, of which the engravings reproduced in this book were to have formed a part. The plan did not proceed further, and the engraved blocks were eventually deposited with the Fitzwilliam Museum in Cambridge. The Taylorian Museum acquired the drawings. The Trustees of the KP used one of the engravings as a frontispiece for the last Kelmscott publication, and one appears in *The Collected Works of William Morris* (see 4.6). Apart from this they were virtually unused (see Introduction) until the Carters got permission to print from them in the work under discussion. A major part of the first volume consists of A.R. Dufty's introductory scholarly essay on *The Earthly Paradise*, the origins of the story, and details of the circumstances summarised above in which Morris and Burne-Jones created the blocks.

Two engravings illustrate Dufty's essay and 44 the poem. In the poem the first two appear side by side as a joint headpiece and others at frequent intervals throughout the text, always at the top of the page, usually singly, but occasionally in a group of two or (once) three. They sit apposed to the relevant text and are of high technical quality. The dark colour of these wood engravings complements the dark type. Burne-Jones had a good sense for dramatic points in the narrative and chose well the scenes he illustrates. They enhance the already highly charged

And at the gate she met the beast threefold,
Who ran to meet her open/mouthed, but she
Unto his jaws the cakes cast cunningly,
But trembling much; then on the ground he lay
Lolling his heads, and let her go her way;
And so she came into the mighty hall,
And saw those wonders hanging on the wall,
That all with pomegranates was covered o'er
In memory of the meal on that sad shore,
Whereby fair Enna was bewept in vain,
And this became a kingdom and a chain.
⚘ But on a throne, the Queen of all the dead
She saw therein with gold/embracèd head,
In royal raiment, beautiful and pale;
Then with slim hands her face did Psyche veil
In worship of her, who said: "Welcome here,
O messenger of Venus! thou art dear
To me thyself indeed, for of thy grace

83

EDWARD BURNE-JONES
["And at the gate she met the beast threefold"]
Cupid and Psyche, Vol. 2, p. 83

action of the poem. Many portray Cupid or Psyche or both together, and demonstrate Burne-Jones's mastery in the depiction of form and drapery. These pictures, done in 1868, demonstrate how early Burne-Jones came to his mature style. It was largely unchanged even twenty-five years later.

The richer binding, the addition of the portfolio, and the decorated endpapers in 4.7a give an altogether more sumptuous look, scarcely surprising with a publication cost of £450 in comparison with the £120 for 4.7b (plus £60 for the separate portfolio, 4.7c).

Comment: In general, rebound copies lie outside the purview of the present book. However, two such copies of this book require comment. Both are out of series, made up from extra sheets which Colin Franklin obtained from the publisher. Franklin had the two volumes bound in limp vellum, harking back to the practice of the KP. However, while he used leather strips in the binding, they do not appear as ties to secure the book in a closed position. He radically changed the organisation, combining both volumes of 4.7a as his first volume, and creating his second volume from the portfolio of 4.7a. This does not improve the set. He does introduce a valuable feature by binding in a copy of the pre-publication prospectus at the end of his first volume. (I base this description on examination of only one of the two copies.)

Paraphrased Versions of *The Earthly Paradise*

The many editions of the works of William Morris up to the late 1920s attest to his popularity up to that time. Publishers sought to capitalise on this by bringing out versions adapted for children's reading. As Morris's best known and most popular book *The Earthly Paradise* attracted much attention from paraphrasers seeking to make the rough places plain for their young readers. The narrative poems of drama and adventure in *The Earthly Paradise* lend themselves to retelling. No fewer than four selections of the stories came out, starting in 1906. Arnold and Longmans Green published the last jointly in 1915. However, reprints of some of these books straggled out into the mid-1930s. The second half of this chapter contains descriptions of the paraphrased versions.

The first book in the group of paraphrases, published by Harrap, resembles the Collins' Clear-Type Press editions of *The Defence of Guenevere* (see 2.5-10) in that the publisher issued several editions, under different titles, with varying content. In the Collins books, assigning a date of publication creates much of the difficulty. Harrap, by contrast, evinced a punctilious regard for chronology, to the point of giving even the month of issue for each edition and its reprints. The difficulty resides in their multiplicity, outlined above. Harrap uses Madalen Edgar's text for several editions. They comprise deluxe, super deluxe, and standard versions of the first book, grouped together here as 4.8Pa, b & c, two American editions published by Crowell (4.9-10P), and a truncated edition illustrated by a different artist (4.11P). The last of the group, with its cheaper appearance and diminished content, would seem designed for a larger if more impecunious readership. Paradoxically, this title proves the least common, with online listings of copies appearing at about a tenth the frequency of 4.8P. Harrap's books and the rest of the paraphrases in this chapter have features in common with each other, and with parallel books of the period, which I shall touch on in the course of the descriptions.

4.8Pa, b & c
Stories from the/ Earthly Paradise/
Retold from William Morris/ by/ Madalen Edgar M.A./
    "In their times of idleness and ease
      They told of poets' vain imaginings,
      And memories vague of half-forgotten things,
      Not true nor false, but sweet to think upon."
                  – William Morris
London/ George G. Harrap & Company/ 15 York Street Covent Garden W.C. / 1906

Comment: After 1919 the layout of the publisher's address changes slightly.

Dates of publication: <u>November 1906</u>, <u>March 1907</u>, <u>October 1908</u> ["1909" on title page: 4.8Pa & b only], April 1910 (4.8Pb only). <u>February 1912</u>, <u>September 1916</u> (only 4.8Pa seen), August 1917, <u>July 1919</u> (4.8Pa only), February 1923, <u>July 1933</u>.

Comment: While Harrap supplied the same publishing history in both deluxe (4.8Pa) and standard (4.8Pc) versions I have no certainty that both versions actually appeared on all the dates given. I have, for example, never located a copy of 4.8Pa published in 1917.

Note on binding: The binding of 4.8Pa changes after the reprint of 1916. I give separate descriptions of the two forms. Both of these forms and those of 4.8Pb & c are uniform with contemporaneous bindings of other titles in the *Told through the Ages* series.

4.8Pa (1906-1916) Binding: Quarter-bound in rust-red leather and dark green cloth over boards. Spine and front cover have profuse and ornate floral decoration, with "Earthly Paradise" on middle of front cover and title horizontally on spine. First edition only has Edgar's name and publication date on spine. Decoration and lettering in gilt. Decoration on spines of 1906 and 1907 editions has a simpler pattern, lacking the horizontal rules of 1909 and later editions. Same lettering and decoration on front cover in 1916 in light green. Top edge gilt in 1906-1912, plain in 1916. Endpapers a mottled brown in 1906-1909, plain beige in 1916.

Comment: The only copy of the 1912 reprint examined has the same covers and spine as the other reprints in the group. In addition it features pictorial endpapers of a dull blue monochrome, with line drawings done by M. Lavars Harry. Harrap was employing this artist for other work besides this reprint at the time (see 4.11P).

4.8Pa (1919 & 1923) Binding: Dark brown paper over boards, the covers patterned with stamped thin black lines, to create the illusion of leather. Series title *Told through the Ages* across top of front cover within and above geometrical decoration, and below it the title. Ruled lines parallel to edge of cover. At each lower corner a griffin facing outwards. Spine has similar geometrical decoration, with the title in upper part and publisher at base. Lettering and decoration in gilt. Back cover plain. Endpapers light brown.

Comment: I have not examined a copy of the 1917 reprint if it exists, and can make no statement about the binding, whether it resembles that of 1916 or of 1919. The only copy of the 1933 reprint I have examined has a bright blue cover with a geometrical pattern on the front and spine. While the cover looks as though it dates from the period, it may not be the original binding.

4.8Pb Binding: Bottle-green cloth over boards, finely stippled. Leafy and floral decoration on margins of front cover, similar on spine within rules. Title on upper spine, all in gilt. Back cover plain. Top edge gilt.

Comment: Harrap advertised the deluxe version of another title in the *Told through the Ages* series in the 1909 Christmas supplement of *The Bookman*. The illustration on the cover shows similar but not identical decoration to that of 4.8Pb described above. I have seen this super deluxe binding only on reprints of 1909 and 1910, and do not know whether Harrap used it also for later reprints.

4.8Pc (all issues) Binding: Buckram, usually dark blue. One copy seen in orangey brown (1919). All lettering and decoration on cover in black ink. Title on top of front cover and Morris's name at bottom, with a picture between. Title on top of spine, the publisher's name at the base, and a decoration at mid-level.

Comment: This version originally had a dust-jacket, if uniform with companion volumes in the series, which certainly did. I have never seen one on a copy of 4.8Pc. Nor have I examined a copy of the 1933 reprint with an unquestionably original binding. The only copy I have seen has a binding of dark green leatherette, plain on the covers, but with the title and Edgar's name in gilt on the top of the spine above gilt decoration occupying the rest of it. This decoration does not resemble that seen on the spine of 4.8Pa. However, the binding has a 1930s appearance and may be original with Harrap. Original binding or not, the thickness of this book at 13 mm. confirms it as a copy of 4.8Pc.

4.8Pa, b & c Pagination/Size: xvi, 240 / 187 x 130 mm.

Comment: The reprints of 4.8a & b of 1909 and later are slightly broader at 137 mm. All issues of 4.8c have the breadth given above.

4.8Pa, b & c Contents: P. i half-title, p. ii blank (1906; reprints from 1907 on have lists of other titles in series), inserted frontispiece, p. iii title page, p. iv publication information, p. v contents, p. vi blank, pp. vii-viii list of illustrations, pp. ix-xvi introduction, pp. 1-239 text, p. 240 blank.

Comment: Copies of 4.8Pb have an additional title page preceding the regular one and facing the frontispiece. Title and publisher's monogram are in red and series title and name of publisher in black enclosed in black ruled lines. From 1909 onwards Harrap used much thicker paper for all reprints of 4.8Pa, increasing the books' thickness to 2.7 cm. exclusive of binding, compared with 1.5 cm. for the first edition of 4.8Pa and c. By contrast, 4.8Pc remains much the same thickness throughout all its reprints. The thickness of 4.8Pb is the same as that of the 1909 reprint of 4.8Pa.

In reprints of both 4.8Pa and c after 1917 Harrap reduced the number of illustrations from sixteen to eight. I have not examined a copy of the 1917 reprint, and rely on a bookseller's notation of "eight illustrations" in assigning 1917 as the date of this change. The shorter list of illustrations fits onto one page. Thus in such issues the description of contents would read: p. vii list of illustrations, p. viii blank. In the reprints of 1923 and later Harrap omitted the date of publication from the title page and instead gave a complete publication history on p. iv along with the addresses already present in the earlier issues.

Illustrators: GERTRUDE DEMAIN HAMMOND. Born in 1862. She studied at the Lambeth School of Art and the RA schools and later exhibited at the RA between 1886 and 1903. She was elected to the Royal Institute in 1906. Her work centred on book illustration, and she was especially known for her depiction of Shakespeare's works. She lived in London, dying in 1934. See also 4.9P-10P.
EVELYN M. B. PAUL. Born in London about 1883. She studied in South Kensington, I believe at the NATS, and was living in London at the time she illustrated this book. She was known as a book illustrator. See also 4.9P-10P.
SIR EDWARD JOHN POYNTER. Born in Paris in 1836, son of the artist A. J. Poynter. He spent his childhood in London. A fortuitous 1853 meeting with the artist Frederick Leighton in Rome made him decide to follow the same career. He studied briefly at the RA schools, and then in Paris between 1856 and 1859. He exhibited at the RA in 1861, and there and at many other London galleries in the following years.

His paintings show a strong PRB influence, though his career took him into the academic art camp: he became Professor at the newly opened Slade School of Art at University College in London in 1870. He held this professorship until 1875, when he assumed the post of Director for Art and Principal of the NATS. He remained active as a teacher and administrator for the rest of his career, which culminated in his election as the President of the RA in 1896, with an accompanying knighthood. (He had been elected RA in 1876.) He retained the Presidency for twenty-two years. A connection to the Pre-Raphaelites he would not have wished to sever was his wife, Agnes MacDonald, whom he married in 1866. She was the sister of Burne-Jones's wife. By this marriage, he became connected to one of the great Pre-Raphaelite painters (see 3.1) and uncle to Rudyard Kipling and Stanley Baldwin, the future Prime Minister, sons of the other two MacDonald sisters. Poynter died in London in 1919.

CHARLES PROSPER SAINTON. Born in London in 1861. He studied at the Slade School of Art and in Florence and Paris. He became known for his portrait and landscape painting and as a book illustrator. He lived in London but died in New York in 1914.

Illustrations and decoration: I have described the decoration of the various covers of 4.8Pa in the sections devoted to the binding. The picture on the cover of 4.8Pc shows a man in tunic and cross-gartered leggings, holding a sword. He stands looking through trees at a castle tower in the background. The artist did not sign his work. The picture does not seem to illustrate a scene in any of the stories, but does evoke the era in which Morris set the narrators of the stories in *The Earthly Paradise*. Similarly, a companion volume in the series *The Iliad* carries the same layout of the front cover and a picture of an oared Greek galley. In the early issues of 4.8Pc the decoration on the spine comprises the head of a helmeted man in left profile, enclosed in a circle. Harrap replaced it with a floral spray by 1912. Both 4.6Pa and c lack internal decoration. The coloured frontispiece "Away to Fairyland" by Sainton has no obvious relevance to the text. Possibly the publisher sought to set a mood as with the cover of 4.8Pc.

Each of the fourteen stories has at least one accompanying illustration. These internal pictures, all in black and white, seem to be reproductions of paintings. This is certainly true of "Atalanta's Race," which Poynter executed in 1876. It depicts a pivotal scene, in which Milanion throws one of the golden apples in front of Atalanta to beguile her from the race, and so let him gain the advantage. Other pictures seize on points of drama. In "The Man Born to Be King" we see Cecily in the moment after she first catches sight of Michael and supposes him to be her future husband. (See 4.16P for further discussion of this picture.) Yet again in "The Writing on the Image" the artist Evelyn Paul portrays the thief in the act of reaching to steal the dead queen's necklace off her body. Most of the other pictures seize on a similar dramatic moment in the story. One or two are rather passive: Hammond's picture for "Ogier the Dane" merely shows him kneeling in prayer. However, they represent the exceptions. Overall, the pictures are of high technical quality, lie apposed to their text, and serve to draw the reader to the story, emphasising its

"I have done thy Will—is it enough?"   184

EVELYN PAUL
"The Lovers of Gudrun"
Stories from The Earthly Paradise, facing p. 184

climactic point and complementing the text. Nevertheless, the lack of other decoration creates a sense of two parts, text and illustration, which have not melded into a unified whole.

In 1917 when Harrap reduced the number of illustrations depicting the text from fifteen to seven, all but one duplicated the omissions already perpetrated by Crowell in 1907 (see 4.9P). Crowell presumably published this edition under licence from Harrap, so the latter would have been familiar with the new layout. Among the smaller number of pictures which Harrap retains is "The Garden of the Hesperides," which does not appear in Crowell's edition. The omissions affect the representation of Paul's pictures disproportionately. Of her eight pictures in the early editions, only two remain after 1917. Poynter's suave picture is also lost.

4.9P
Stories/ from/ Morris/
Madalen Edgar/
New York/
T.Y. Crowell & Company/ Publishers

Date of publication: 1907.

Comment: Crowell claim copyright "1906 and 1907." I have never found a reference to an edition they published on the earlier date, nor seen any such copy.

Binding: Light brown buckram with pictorial cover. Title in red above Edgar's name in lower right. Title, adapter, and publisher on spine in gilt.

Pagination/Size: xiv, 336 [2] / 166 x 105 mm.

Contents: Inserted frontispiece with tissue guard, p. i title page, p. ii statement of copyright, p. iii contents, p. iv blank, pp. v-xiv introduction, pp. 1-336 text, pp. 1-2 blank.

Comment: Unlike 4.8, this book lacks a half-title page. The stories, even to their order in the book, and the illustrations, where present, are identical in these two publications.

Illustrators: GERTRUDE D. HAMMOND. See 4.8.
EVELYN PAUL. See 4.8.

Illustrations and decoration: On the left side of the front cover a Viking stands full-length in battle gear, with a Norse galley afloat on a choppy sea in the upper right, all coloured in red, black and light blue. The picture harks back to the premise of *The Earthly Paradise*, a group of Norsemen fleeing the plague in their native land. The title page has a line drawing of a woman in full-length dress and flowing cloak standing on a beach, gazing at three approaching sails. Behind her is a castle perched on the top of a high cliff. Possibly the artist had Aslaug in mind in drawing this vignette. However, the subject is rather general and definite identification uncertain. The picture is unsigned except by an ambiguous monogram, which could represent DD or IOI or M. Beyond this the book has no internal decoration.

Crowell used only nine of the illustrations present in 4.7, replacing the frontispiece of the British edition with the picture which illustrates "The Writing on the Image." The pictures which Crowell left out comprise one of the two accompanying "The Man Born to Be King," and those which illustrate "Atalanta's Race," "Bellerophon in Lycia," "Acontius and Cydippe," "The Golden Apples," and "The Lovers of Gudrun." Crowell's artist tinted the frontispiece in rather subdued colours but left the other illustrations in black and white. This book does not include a page listing the illustrations, but identifies the artist as part of the caption. Crowell omitted five of the eight pictures done by Paul, and Poynter's sole illustration, but retained all six of those done by the better-known Gertrude Hammond. I regret this choice since Paul's work complements the narrative more effectively than some that Crowell includes. One, and arguably a second, by Hammond show only a static figure. See also the Illustration section of 4.8P.

4.10P
Stories from/ William Morris/
Retold by/ Madalen Edgar M.A./
   "In their times of idleness and ease
   They told of poets' vain imaginings,
   And memories vague of half-forgotten things,
   Not true nor false, but sweet to think upon."
               – William Morris
New York/ Thomas Y. Crowell & Company/ Publishers

Date of publication: 1907.

Comment: See comment under 4.9P.

Binding: Tartan cloth with sett resembling dress MacDonald over boards. Paper label on top half of front cover reading "Stories from Morris, by Madalen Edgar, M.A." in black, initial letters of title, name, and degree in red. Line of five Norse galleys in black silhouette below letters. Paper label on top of spine carries title and adapter with another Norse galley below, all in black.

Pagination/Size: xiv, 336 [2] / 153 x 97 mm.

Contents: Same as 4.9P.

Illustrators: GERTRUDE D. HAMMOND. See 4.8.
    EVELYN PAUL. See 4.8.

Illustrations: Crowell used the same electroplates to print this edition as for 4.9P, except for the title page, which lacks the vignette and decoration. They achieved the smaller size of 4.10P by reducing the width of the margins. Finally they also reduced the number of illustrations, replacing the frontispiece with Paul's picture for "The Man Born to Be King," and leaving it as a black and white drawing. The body of the text contains only three further pictures, two by Hammond and one by Paul, all of which also appear in 4.9P. They comprise the illustrations for "The Fostering of Aslaug," "The Proud King," and "The Lady of the Land." For further comments about these illustrations see 4.8 and 4.9P.

4.11P
Tales from/ William/ Morris/
Retold by/ Madalen Edgar M.A./
London: George G./ Harrap & Co. Ltd./ 2 & 3 Portland St. Kingsway WC/ and at Sydney

Comment: The listing of the publisher's offices varies with each reprint.

Dates of publication: June 1911, January 1917, <u>April 1921</u>, <u>January 1926</u>, <u>June 1931</u>.

Comment: I have seen a reference to a further reprint in 1933 but cannot verify its accuracy.

Note on binding: Harrap decorated the cover in either of two ways. Possibly Binding 1 represents an early form and Binding 2 a later one. I have seen copies of the 1921 reprint in both types of binding, perhaps representing a transitional phase. I have not had the opportunity to examine enough copies to give a more definite opinion.

Binding 1 (1921): Dust jacket with brightly coloured pictorial front cover, showing a man and two women dressed in medieval clothing standing on a rough path at base of a cliff. Title and adapter's name across top. Spine has title and Edgar's name at top, publisher at bottom. At mid-level a laurel wreath encloses three pillars with a common plinth and capital and two crossed diagonal bars behind the pillars. A short ribbon hangs from base of wreath. List of other titles in series on back of jacket. Book bound in bright red buckram, lettering in black and decoration in grey. Most of front cover and spine decorated in profusion of swirling stems and leaves. "William Morris" in italic letters on upper front cover in plain oval. Black decoration surrounds the panel and is pendant down centre of cover, at its base picture of seated man playing an Irish harp. Back cover plain. Full title on top of spine, publisher at base.

Comment: This book is one in the series *All-Time Tales*. The design of the dust jacket is standard for the series, though the picture differs for each of the titles. However, the scene on the dust jacket of *Tales from William Morris* does not obviously depict any of the stories in the book. The picture is signed Stephen Reid and dated 1909, so it seems safe to assume that Harrap used it for the dust jacket of the first edition as well as later ones.

Binding 2 (1921-1931): Buckram, blue (1921 and 1926) or red (1931). Lettering essentially same as in Binding 1, and similar swirling decoration. In centre front cover a large circular area free of decoration but with depiction of Pegasus enclosed in circle, his outstretched wings extending beyond the circumference. Lettering and decoration in black. Back cover plain.

Comment: For most copies with the second binding, Harrap used blue buckram. I have seen a copy of the 1931 reprint in red. Possibly red was also used for earlier reprints.

Pagination/Size: viii, 158 [2] / 183 x 123 mm.

Comment: Harrap used Roman numerals for the eight preliminary pages, and then started Arabic numbers at nine on the first page of text. Thus inclusive of the final blank sheet the pagination totals 160.

Contents: P. i half-title, p. ii list of other titles in the series, p. iii blank, p. iv frontispiece, p. v title page, p. vi publication information, p. vii contents, p. viii blank, pp. 9-158 text, pp. 1-2 blank.

Comment: This edition contains only five of the stories present in 4.8P. In both forms of the 1921 reprint the frontispiece is on glossy paper and inserted. Probably the same applies to earlier issues. All the reprints later than 1921 have the frontispiece printed on the same paper as the rest of the book. Harrap used paper comparable in thickness to that of the later issues of 4.8Pa for the reprint of 1931. Consequently the overall thickness of the book is about fifty per cent greater than that of the 1921 reprints. The thickness of the 1926 reprint is intermediate between the two. There are differences in numeration and total number of titles in the series between the lists on the back of the dust jacket and those on page ii of the books themselves.

Illustrator: M. LAVARS HARRY. NIF. Harry illustrated a title in the *Told through the Ages* series (see 4.8) and designed pictorial endpapers for another in the same series about the time Harrap published the first edition of 4.11P. Thus he seems to have worked regularly as a book illustrator during this period. There was a Mabel Harry living in New York in 1920 who exhibited in the Society of Indianapolis Artists exhibition that year. However, it seems unlikely that Harrap would have employed an artist on the other side of the Atlantic. See also Comment on 4.8Pa (1906-1916) Binding.

Illustrations and decoration: Except for that on the cover (see above under Binding) decoration consists of a vignette on the title page different in each of the reprints examined. All appear between Edgar's name and that of the publisher. The picture in the 1921 reprint has the shape of an upright rectangle. It depicts a two-storey building with a steeply gabled roof, a shop front on the ground floor facing a deserted street corner. Indistinct lettering above the shop window may read "Old Curiosity Shop." A clock tower rears in the background. In the 1926 reprint, in a horizontally oriented rectangle, one sees the head of a man in right profile blowing a long wavy instrument otherwise like a trumpet. The vignette in 1931 has a square shape, but unlike the others lacks rules around the edges. The picture comprises a galleon under sail seen from behind. Below the stern is a scallop shell, the rim downwards. Skirting the outside of the rim is a series of Xs, possibly Roman numerals or possibly decorative.

As stated on the dust jacket, the book contains eight full-page illustrations. In the 1921 issue the frontispiece has a very light brown monochrome tint over a line drawing of the Proud King riding out through the gates of his city unrecognised and unacknowledged. Harry catches his dejection well in his bowed head and humble dress and mount. In the issues after 1921 the same frontispiece appears as a line drawing without the tint. The rest of the pictures are also black line drawings in all the issues examined. A small headpiece precedes the first story, "The Man Born to Be King," and depicts the opening scene in which the soothsayer tells the king that a low-born man will succeed him, so setting in motion the whole action. The artist continues to show a good instinct for the high points of a tale. The other picture accompanying this story shows the infant Michael in his crib cast

"HE POURED INTO HER UNHEEDING EARS THE STORY OF HIS LOVE"

M. LAVARS HARRY
"The Land East of the Sun and West of the Moon"
Tales from William Morris, **p. 157**

into the stream by the king's soldiers. Similarly, Harry chose the first meeting of Ragnar and Aslaug to illustrate "The Fostering of Aslaug," and the last departure of Ogier and Morgan le Fay after Ogier has saved France by his return there from Avalon. Harry portrayed his subjects with technical competence. However, without supporting decoration to the title page and elsewhere, and without further head- and tailpieces the book, like its predecessors by Edgar, falls short of the unity of text and illustration which is the essence of the illustrated book.

4.12P Note: Nelson published other books with a similar binding and design contemporary with the next entry, all entitled "The Gateway to . . . ." Titles include ". . . Chaucer," ". . . Shakespeare," ". . . Spenser," and ". . . Tennyson." Nelson did not dignify them with the name of an actual series.

4.12P
The Gateway to/ Romance/
Tales Retold by Emily Under-/ down
from "The Earthly/ Paradise" of William Morris/
With Sixteen Coloured Plates/ and many other Illustrations/
Thomas Nelson and Sons/ London, Edinburgh, Dublin, and New York

Date of publication: n.d. "1909" (BL).

Binding: Buckram with background colour of olive green, dark blue or grey in different copies. All copies have identical decoration on front cover and spine with twisting stems in gilt and flowers budding off them in light blue. Vertical rectangle in centre has picture in its upper three-fifths and title below it. Title on top of spine, with adapter's name at mid-level and publisher at base. Picture and lettering all in gilt. Back cover plain. Top edge gilt. The same pictorial endpapers front and back.

Pagination/Size: 304 / 228 x 176 mm.

Contents: Inserted frontispiece, p. 1 title page, p. 2 blank, p. 3 contents, p. 4 illustration, p. 5 illustrations and quotation, p. 6 illustration, p. 7 list of illustrations, p. 8 illustration and quotation, pp. 9-299 text, with fifteen inserted colour illustrations on glossy paper, pp. 300-304 advertisements for other titles.

Comment: The page of contents lists nine stories from *The Earthly Paradise*, rather than the eight mentioned in the advertisement for the book, which appears among others in the five pages at the end of the book itself. Underdown changes the title of all but one of the stories. Nelson printed the book on a heavy stock of matte paper, which conveys a sense of opulence. However, all the numerous copies I have examined show foxing of greater or lesser degree, which raises doubts about the quality of the materials used in making the book.

Illustrators: JOHN COPLEY. He was born Herbert Crawford Williamson in Manchester in 1875, but used his adopted name for many years and legalised the change in 1927. He studied at the Manchester School of Art and the RA schools from 1892 to 1897 and extended his experience by travel in Italy. Copley was known as a lithographer and painter. He married the lithographer, painter, and illustrator Ethel Gabain in 1913. He died in London in 1950.

HENRY CHARLES INNES FRIPP. Born in Bristol in 1867. He was a great-grandson of Nicholas Pocock, the marine painter, 1741-1820. The name Innes perpetuated the maiden name of Pocock's mother, Mary Innes. She must have been a much-loved and memorable lady; many descendants received Innes as a middle name extending over at least three generations. While the Fripp who married Pocock's daughter was an ordained minister, two of his sons became artists, as well as three or more grandsons. Innes Fripp lived in London. A genre painter, who also worked with stained glass, he signed his paintings using only "Innes Fripp." He exhibited at the RA in 1893. See also 4.13P.

FRANK CHEYNE PAPE. Born in America in 1878. He was a book illustrator, best known for his illustration of the works of Anatole France and James Branch Cabell. His work attained such popularity in his time that he was even mentioned in a contemporary novel, referred to in laudatory terms by one of the fictional characters. He died in England, where he spent much of his working life, in 1972. See also 4.13P.

WILLIAM GEORGE SIMMONDS. Born in Constantinople in 1876. He studied at the RA schools and became known as a sculptor, engraver, book illustrator, and painter. His works are represented in the Tate Britain and in provincial British galleries. He died after 1928.

EDWARD F. SKINNER. Active 1888-1925. He was known for his portrait and landscape painting and as a book illustrator. He lived in London.

Illustrations and decoration: The picture on the front cover shows an arched gate in a stone tower with a path leading to it. A tall turreted castle outlined by billowing clouds rears up in the background. The endpapers have a monochrome picture in sky-blue showing on the recto a castle high on a headland at the top of a huge cliff. The edge of the cliff extends into the foreground and sweeps across both pages to another headland, on which stands a flaming beacon. In the bay enclosed by the cliffs is a galleon under full sail on a storm-tossed sea. We see suicidal seamanship, but the stuff of romance indeed. This picture is signed Arnaud Hortone. On the title page, the title itself and the statement regarding illustrations appear in red, as does a small

Out of the
thicket staggered
a man with
the dart in
his body.
(See p. 79.)

INNES FRIPP
"The King's Vow"
The Gateway to Romance, facing p. 80

illustration at the bottom of the page of a woman kneeling before a knight in armour. The subtitle and publisher's name are in black. The contents page has a decorated border at top and inner edges filled with twining stems and two women, one seated in the horizontal part of the border and the other standing in its upright arm. The illustration on the next page shows a woman somewhat déshabillée tied to a tree in the forest with a mounted knight in the background presumably coming to rescue her. On the facing page a quotation from Tennyson's "The Last Tournament" sits between two small pictures, the upper one of a knight in the lists with couched lance, the lower of two knights fighting with swords. The next page has another full-size illustration of three women seated in a meadow, one with a shepherd's crook. Sheep graze in the background. The list of illustrations opposite has a decorated border, and the preliminary pages finish with a picture of a princess in full-length dress holding her knight's shield. Below is an apposite quotation from Thackeray's poem "Fairy Days." All the decoration in this section is in black, as is the decoration throughout the book. The latter consists of a headpiece for each story, a tailpiece where space permits, and numerous marginal illustrations, one on almost every double page, and often one on each of two facing pages. The head- and tailpieces generally illustrate the text, but in some cases only decorate it. The marginal pictures usually consist of a figure, sometimes a scene which appears on that page of text. The artist drew them with skill and assurance. Nelson gives no indication of his or her identity.

Fripp did eight of the colour illustrations, Simmonds three, Pape two, with Skinner and Copley contributing one each. A further one is unsigned. All these artists exhibit technical competence and a sense of suitability of subject. It is valuable to compare the same scene rendered by different artists. Harry (see 4.10P) and Fripp both portray Aslaug as she came aboard Ragnar's ship, a climactic moment which constitutes a good subject. Harry as already discussed creates a pleasing evocation, though somewhat static, with the two figures standing on the deck. By contrast Fripp has Aslaug in the act of stepping over the gunwale, her hands clasped by Ragnar as he helps her on board from the shield held by his crewmen. We are left to imagine her having stood on it while they carried it above the water, as they now stand chest deep, having hoisted it and her above their shoulders to permit her to embark. The picture throbs with the immediacy of the action and the fulfilment of all that has passed. In general the pictures have this sense of action or drama, whether it is Pape's picture of the king questioning the miller about Michael in "The Man Born to Be King," or Fripp's of Milanion supplicating Venus in "Atalanta's Race," renamed "The Apples of Venus" by Underdown. Fripp achieves the ultimate in conveying a sense of movement in the frontispiece, where he portrays Perseus aloft with the help of the slippers of Hermes. The scene appears in "The Doom of King Acrisius," renamed "The Story of a Hero" by Underdown. Nelson could not have chosen a better frontispiece for the impact which this dramatic picture possesses.

In summary this book creates a sense of opulence, with a fine melding of text and illustration. The foxing noted above, ubiquitous in copies of this title and in the companion *Gateway* volumes, detracts greatly from this initial impression.

4.13Pa & Pb Note: Nelson published 4.13Pb in their Golden River series. The name derives from the first title in the series, Ruskin's *The King of the Golden River*. The information about the inclusion of 4.13Pb in the series appears only on the dust jacket. While identical in most respects, 4.13Pa has some niceties which 4.13Pb lacks. Nelson probably saw them as deluxe and standard versions respectively. 4.13Pa has many features in common with titles in Nelson's parallel series *Told to the Children*, but I found no evidence from lists on dust jackets of titles in the series that 4.13Pa is one of them.

4.13Pa & b
The Six Gifts/ and Other Stories/
Retold from/ "The Earthly Paradise"/ of/ William Morris/
Thomas Nelson and Sons/ London, Edinburgh, Dublin, and New York/
1910

Comment: The word "Ltd" appears after the publisher's name in the 1920 reprint and in the undated 4.13Pb, which also has larger lettering for the names of the cities.

4.13Pa Dates of publication: <u>1910</u>, <u>1911</u>, 1918, <u>1920</u>.

Comment: This list may not be complete. Nelson provides the date of publication on the title page of any given copy, but no publication history overall.

4.13Pb Dates of publication: n.d.

Comment: Nelson does not supply a publication date in copies of this version but does list the cities in which they maintained offices. The changes from one printing to another provide evidence as to date of publication when compared with 4.13Pa and suggest that the two editions may have been published simultaneously.

4.13Pa Binding: Buckram, some copies bright red, more often olive green. Title in gilt on top of front cover and spine, author on latter as well. Picture of Milanion praying to Venus pasted on centre of front cover within white ruled lines. White ink replaces the gilt in the 1920 reprint. Back cover plain. Endpapers plain white in the early issues, brown in that of 1920.

4.13Pb Binding: Dust jacket with white background and lettering in black. Front cover has coloured foreground of picture of Reisler and Grima finding Aslaug in the harp. Title at top of front cover and spine of jacket, publisher at bottom of spine and back cover. On bottom of front cover, mid-level of spine, and top of back cover is identification of book as in *Golden River* series. Rest of back cover has list of other *Golden River* titles. Book bound in dark green cloth, plain except for yellow frieze, 3.5 cm. high, just below top of front cover and spine. Frieze decorated with line of dancing children in black silhouette. Title in black on spine below frieze, publisher at base. Back cover plain.

Comment: The design of the binding is uniform for the series. Nelson reproduces the picture on the dust jacket in full as one of the illustrations inside the book.

4.13Pa & b Pagination/Size: 160 / 163 x 122 mm.

4.13Pa & b Contents: Inserted frontispiece, p. 1 title page, p. 2 blank in early issues (with statement about printer in 1920 reprint), p. 3 contents (listing five of the stories present in 4.12P), p. 4 blank, p. 5 list of illustrations, pp. 6-160 text with five inserted colour illustrations additional to frontispiece.

Comment: Title and publisher appear in red on the title page of 4.13Pa and in black in 4.13Pb.

Illustrators: H.C. INNES FRIPP. See 4.12P.
　　FRANK C. PAPE. See 4.12P.

Illustrations: This book is an off-print of 4.12P, but lacks its decoration, except for the presence of many of the marginal line drawings found in the latter. The picture on the cover appears as one of the illustrations in *The Gateway to Romance* and also in the interior of this book. For further discussion of the illustrations see 4.12P.

4.14P Note: The following entry falls into the category of a collection. However, in view of its connection with the two preceding entries and the minor content of other material which it contains, I have included it in this chapter.

4.14P
Stories from/ William Morris/
Retold from/ "The Earthly Paradise"/ by/ Emily Underdown/
Thomas Nelson & Sons, Ltd./ London and Edinburgh

Comment: New York appears in the list of cities in later issues.

Dates of publication: <u>May 1925</u>, October 1926, <u>May 1929</u>, November 1931, June 1934, <u>August 1935</u>.

Binding: Red buckram plain except for capital N within an oval on front cover and title vertically on spine, both in gilt. Endpapers in light green, patterned in rows about 2 cm. high of identical old-fashioned three-storey houses with the date 1798, motif repeating horizontally and vertically over whole surface.

Pagination/Size: vi, 208 / 157 x 1037 mm.

Comment: Arabic numeration starts at page 7 and duplicates the Roman numerals of the preliminary pages.

Contents: P. i half-title (with designation as No. 11 in *Teaching of English* series), p. ii frontispiece, p. iii title page, p. iv publication history and note on source of text, p. v contents, p. vi epigraph from Shakespeare, pp. 7-197 text, p. 198 blank, pp. 199-207 epilogue consisting of exercises for students, p. 208 blank.

Comment: The epigraph on page vi comes from *Romeo and Juliet* Act I, scene III. The text contains all the stories in *The Gateway to Romance* and also sections from *The Life and Death of Jason* in the original.

Illustrator(s): Not identified. See 4.12P.

Illustrations: The frontispiece portrays Morris late in life done as a line drawing by E. Heber Thompson. A large selection of the marginal line drawings which first appear in *The Gateway to Romance* (see 4.12P) comprises the sole textual illustration. The excerpts from *Jason* do not contain any illustrations.

4.15P
Tales from/ The/ Earthly Paradise/
by/ William Morris/
Selected and Arranged in Prose by/ W.J. Glover/
with Twelve Full-Page Illustrations in Colour/ from Designs by/
Isabel Bonus/
London/ Adam and Charles Black/ 1913

Binding: Light green dust jacket, title in white on top of front cover and spine, and Glover's name at their bases. A picture, also in text facing page 208, on front of jacket. Part of picture facing page 193 on spine. On back of jacket and both flaps a list of volumes in the (unnamed) series. Book bound in grey buckram, title and author at top of front cover and spine, publisher at base of spine, all in gilt. Lettering on front cover enclosed in pendant semicircle, its diameter the top of the cover. In lower part a galleon in orange, black, and blue enclosed in circle of double lines. On each side two seated figures support the circle. Above it a design of leaves, stems and fruit in the shape of outstretched wings clasping undersurface of the semicircle in upper part of cover. On spine a knight full-length in armour. All decoration in black except as noted. Back cover plain. Top edge gilt.

Pagination/Size: viii, 280 / 208 x 143 mm.

Contents: P. i half-title, p. ii list of other titles in series and locations of publisher, inserted frontispiece with tissue guard, p. iii title page, p. iv blank, p. v preface, p. vi blank, p. vii contents, p. viii list of illustrations, pp. 1-280 text, with inserted illustrations.

Comment: Glover retained seven of Morris's titles, but changed the remaining five, "The Fairies' Gifts" in place of "Ogier the Dane," for example. He included Morris's Prologue, "The Wanderers." By so doing Glover retained the fictional framework of Morris's original poem.

Illustrator: ISABEL BONUS. NIF. This artist was living in Croydon, England, in 1919, the year she exhibited in a London gallery. The subject of her painting, Loch Ailort, a remote spot in the Western Highlands of Scotland, and her Scottish-sounding forename, suggest that she may have had a Scottish background.

THE FAIRIES' GIFTS.

" Stepping forth, he knelt before her feet and took her hand to swear homage." *Page* 113.

ISABEL BONUS
"The Fairies' Gifts"
Tales from The Earthly Paradise, facing p. 112

Illustrations and decoration: The lettering of the title page is in red, inside a rectangular black floral border. A double set of red lines encloses the border and extends nearly to the edges of the page. The title page describes the illustrations as "in colour from drawings." The effect in four of the eleven pictures, with varying depth of one colour throughout, suggests that the publisher may have tinted them from black and white originals. The rest have a full range of colours, most likely reflecting the nature of Bonus's originals.

In general Bonus picks moments of contemplation as her subjects. The captions reflect this. Thus we have "What man is this who, weak and worn and old, can smile on his coming death?" "He found Michael sitting by the stream," "He watched her pass from flower to flower in childish glee," and "The sunset burned like fire behind her." All of these four and others depict one or two figures in relaxed pose, which does not evoke the drama of the story. Bonus does select some points of tension as subjects, for example those illustrating Ogier kneeling to swear fealty to the Queen, and the terror of the thief when he encounters the bodies in the treasure-filled mausoleum in "The Writing on the Image." Gertrude Hammond (see 4.8) and Bonus drew one scene in common, the encounter of Jovinian with the angel in "The Proud King." The scene is a pivotal one in that one sees in it the redemption of the king from the sin of pride. However, it gives little scope for visual interpretation, and both artists depict the two figures without managing to hint at the epiphany which occurs. Bonus provides skilled work, and perhaps draws the attention of the reader to points he may otherwise pass over. However, her drawings are rather repetitive in their themes and apt to lose the viewer's attention as a result. Furthermore the book lacks the supporting decoration which would set the pictures and text to best advantage.

The publisher gives a page reference as part of the caption for each illustration since the picture does not appose the text it illustrates. The binder followed the common practice of placing most of the illustrations between gatherings, so that one half of a single sheet carrying two pictures appears between successive gatherings while the other half appears one or two gatherings later.

4.16Pa
Stories from/ The Earthly/ Paradise/
by William Morris/
Retold in Prose by C.S. Evans/
Illustrated/
London/ Edward Arnold/ 1915/
[all rights reserved]

4.16Pb
Stories from/ The Earthly/ Paradise/
by William Morris/
Retold in Prose by C.S. Evans/
Illustrated/
New York/ Longmans Green and Co./
London: Edward Arnold/ 1915/
[all rights reserved]

Binding: Green buckram, with title in ornate script on upper half of front cover, a stylised picture in lower half of Perseus and Andromeda encircled by the dragon, all in gilt. Border of two pairs of parallel lines around entire layout, with chequered squares at intervals between the two sets. Spine has similar pattern, with one pair of lines and chequered squares only at top and base. Title at top, below two squares, and above picture of Perseus alone. Publisher at base above two more squares. Back cover plain.

Size: 188 x 123 mm.

4.16Pa Pagination: viii, 248, 8.

4.16Pb Pagination: viii, 248.

Contents: P. i half-title, p. ii blank, inserted frontispiece, p. iii title page, p. iv publication information, p. v contents, p. vi blank, p. vii list of illustrations, p. viii blank, pp. 1-6 introduction, pp. 7-247 text (with pictures and their blank obverse included in pagination), p. 248 blank, pp. 1-8 advertisements for other titles by Arnold (4.16Pa only).

Illustrators: HILDA HECHLE. Born in 1885 or 1886 in North Derbyshire, England. She spent at least part of her childhood in Cheshire, but was living in North Wales at the turn of the century and in London by 1913. She exhibited at the RA and other London galleries from 1902 to 1938 and was elected to the RSBA in 1926. She was known for her figure, portrait, and landscape painting. She died in 1938 or early in 1939.

THOMAS HEATH ROBINSON. Robinson was born in London in 1869, the son of an engraver. He studied at the Islington School of Art. He was mainly known for his illustrations of books and magazines, contributing both line drawings and colour pictures. However, he also produced oil paintings and etchings. He married in 1902 and continued

"SMITING BLINDLY AT THE HORROR WITH HIS SWORD."

HILDA HECHLE
"The Lady of the Land"
Stories from The Earthly Paradise, p. 97

living in London until 1940, when he settled in St. Ives, Cornwall. He died there in 1953. See also Charles Robinson (1.4).

Illustrations: Robinson's frontispiece demonstrates his technical skill in figure drawing and composition, and benefits further from full colour. It depicts the same scene as Evelyn Paul drew in 4.8P from "The Man Born to Be King" in which Cecily finds Michael asleep in the garden. Paul's picture loses some appeal from being in black and white, but even so holds the viewer's attention better in the way it suggests Cecily's emotions at the first sight of the man she believes her father has chosen for her as her future husband.

Hechle executes the rest of the pictures as black ink line drawings. She displays an excellent instinct for a good subject and a sense of drama in portraying it. In her depiction of the Race she evokes better than Poynter (see 4.8P) the cool confidence of Atalanta as she swerves aside to pick up the apple, contrasting it with Milanion's frantic exertion. Where Hechle draws the thief as he steals the queen's necklace, she shows us vividly his naked cupidity in face and gesture, again excelling over the depiction of this scene by Paul, who nevertheless draws it with verve and immediacy (see 4.8P). Hechle again displays her technical competence where, in "The Man Born to Be King," she pictures Michael in his cradle thrown into the river. Harry renders this scene perhaps less skilfully but does convey in the rushing water a better sense of Michael's immediate peril (see 4.11P). The picture by Hechle reproduced here is especially noteworthy in successfully combining the ferocious appearance of a dragon with the despair it feels at its betrayal by the man striking at it.

In brief, Hechle ranks among the finest in the group which illustrates these paraphrased editions of *The Earthly Paradise.* The use of the work of the one artist for all the textual illustrations gives greater coherence to the pictorial aspect of the book, but as with the rest it lacks the unity of conception achieved by such works as Armfield's *Jason* (3.2) or Harrison's *Early Poems* (2.11).

4.17P
Stories from/ The Earthly Paradise/
By William Morris/
Retold in Prose by/ C S Evans/ Illustrated
London/ Edward Arnold/
[All rights reserved]

Date of publication: n.d. "1915" (NLS).

Binding: Dull blue buckram, plain except for title and adapter on top of front cover and spine, and publisher at base of latter, all in black. Endpapers beige in copies examined, possibly white originally.

Comment: A copy in the NLS has a different arrangement of lettering. The title and Evans' name appear at the bottom of the front cover along with the price (1/6^d) and a ruled line around the edge. The spine also has the title and name and gives the publisher at the base. It suggests the possibility of more than one printing.

Pagination/Size: viii, 216 / 177 x 113 mm.

Contents: P. i half-title, p. ii blank, p. iii title page, p. iv blank, p. v contents, p. vi blank, p. vii list of illustrations, p. viii blank, pp. 1-6 introduction, pp. 7-216 text.

Comment: The publisher omitted the last two stories present in 4.16P. Instead the last five pages of this book contain an excerpt of Morris's original verse from "The Writing on the Image." By reproducing this extract, the publisher sought to "help the reader to estimate Morris's place in literature and to perceive his method of handling a subject in verse." That Arnold needed to fill five empty pages is quite coincidental. Apart from the differences described, the two books have the same illustrations and pagination. This book has only half the thickness of 4.16P. Part of the difference comes from the smaller number of pages, but most from the use of thinner paper of poorer quality. These two books have the same relationship to one another as the hardcover and paperback versions of more recent times. However, the differences in illustration and content mandate that 4.16 and 17 be listed as separate editions.

Illustrator: HILDA HECHLE. See 4.16P.

Illustrations: This book lacks Robinson's frontispiece. Hechle's pictures all appear in this book. See 4.16P.

Chapter 5

The Story of Grettir the Strong

Morris translated *The Story of Grettir the Strong* in 1869, one of the early fruits of his collaboration with Eirikr Magnusson. No publisher has ever issued an illustrated edition of Morris's original text. However, two paraphrases exist. Allen French wrote the earlier one, published in America in 1908 during the heyday of paraphrases and illustrated books. A British publisher reissued it in 1961, presumably by agreement, since copyright had not expired. The British company may have specialised in reissues. They also put out another older paraphrase of a Morris text a few years later (see 7.4P). In both cases they used the work of new artists to illustrate their editions. The second paraphrase of *Grettir,* by Robert Newman, appeared in 1968. Newman also uses Morris's text as a basis for his rendering of the story, as he specifies in his foreword. This edition has illustrations by yet another artist.

The paraphrases of *The Earthly Paradise*, discussed in the previous chapter, and *Sigurd the Volsung* (see Chapter 7) disappoint in the extent to which the adapter bowdlerises the original. He, or more often she, may have had preconceptions about the young readers of the book. Bowdlerisation may also reflect the period; all but two first appeared before 1915. French, who also acknowledges Morris's text as the source for his own version of *Grettir*, proves much less prone to this tendency. He explains in the preface that he seeks to make the text more readable by removing archaisms and omitting some minor sub-plots. He presents Grettir as exemplifying dogged courage and tenacity in the face of fearful odds, the qualities he hopes the book will inspire in the reader. Morris's prefatory sonnet for his edition of 1869 says the same thing more concisely.

5.1P. Note: Where a feature of one reprint differs from others, requiring a separate description, I identify the reprint in question with the last two digits of its year of publication in parentheses. A previous owner rebound the one copy of the 1950 reprint available to me. The description of this copy therefore refers only to its internal features.

5.1P

The Story of/ Grettir the Strong/
by/ Allen French/
New York/ E.P. Dutton & Company/ 31 West Twenty-First Street

Dates of publication: <u>September 1908</u>, September 1916, October 1922, <u>June 1925</u>, September 1928, <u>August 1934</u> [NYPL], <u>May 1941</u>, <u>April 1950</u>, January 1952, <u>October 1957</u>, <u>January 1962</u> [UBC], <u>June 1966</u>.

Binding: Dust jacket of glossy paper with white ground and black lettering. On both front and back covers in 1925, lower two-thirds of cover carries colour picture which duplicates frontispiece, with title above. By 1957 and in later issues back cover instead has details of other books. Title on top of spine, author at mid-level and publisher at base, in all jackets examined. Back flap has list of other books published by Dutton (1925) or details thereof (1957 and later), the latter different from one edition to another. Front flap has details of another book (1925) or promotion of present book (1957 and later). Book bound in bright red buckram by 1925 and until 1941, dull red in 1908 and other reprints examined. Lettering on front cover and spine repeats that on dust jacket. On lower half of front cover a picture of two men fighting with swords. Back cover plain. Colour of lettering and decoration varies over time. Black in 1908 with light blue scroll around letters on front cover. All in gilt by 1925 and to 1934, lettering only in gilt in 1941, black with no blue scroll in 1957 and later issues.

Size: 190 x 127 mm.

Comment: The size of the various issues varies by 1-2 mm. one to another. However, the reprints of 1941 and 1950 are significantly smaller at 183 x 118 mm.

Pagination: xii, 268 [2].

Comment: The pagination given above is that of 1908. That of some later reprints deviates from this. Dutton retained the numbering of the preface (pp. iii-viii) found in the original edition for all later reprints. However, rearrangement of the preliminary pages in later issues creates an anomaly. Specifically, the list of contents, on [the unnumbered] page ix in 1908, subsequently appears before the preface, until 1966 when Dutton returned to the original sequence. In the reprints in which the contents page precedes the preface, the half-title page loses numeration, and here I supply Arabic numbers. In such reprints Roman numbering ends at x. Pages where the number is inferred, rather than present on the page itself, have the assigned number in parentheses. In view of these variations the contents for the various reprints appear separately where they differ from one to another.

Contents: 1908. P. i half-title, p. ii blank, inserted frontispiece and title page (both on glossy paper, frontispiece with tissue guard and title page including vignette in colour and publication information on obverse), pp. iii-viii preface, p. ix contents, p. x blank, p. xi list of illustrations, p. xii blank, pp. 1-268 text with inserted illustrations, pp. 1-2 blank.

1925-1950. P. [1] half-title, p. [2] blank, inserted frontispiece and title page as in 1908, p. [i] contents, p. [ii] blank, pp. iii-viii preface, p. [ix] list of illustrations, p. [x] blank, pp. 1-268 and pp. 1-2 as for 1908.

1957. P. [1] half-title, p. [2] blank, inserted frontispiece as in 1908, p. [3] title page with vignette in black, p. [4] publication history and address of printer, p. [i] contents, p. [ii] blank, pp. iii-viii preface, p. ix list of illustrations, p. [x] blank, pp. 1-268 text omitting black and white illustrations in earlier editions, pp. 1-6 blank.

1962. P. [1] half-title, p. [2] blank, inserted frontispiece in black and white, p. [3] title page as in 1957, p. [4] statement of copyright and date of publication, p. [i] contents, p. [ii] blank, pp. iii-viii preface, p. ix list of illustrations, p. [x] blank, pp. 1-268 text, omitting black and white illustrations in earlier editions and reproducing previous colour pictures in black and white, pp. 1-6 blank.

1966. P. [1] half-title, p. [2] blank, inserted frontispiece as in 1962, p. i title page, p. ii statement of copyright and publication date, pp. iii-viii preface, p. ix contents, p. x blank, p. xi list of illustrations, p. xii blank, pp. 1-268 text with inserted illustrations as in 1962, pp. 1-6 blank.

Comment: The form of the publisher's name and address differs in minor ways between the first and the later editions. The extra blank pages at the end of the reprints of 1957 and later reflect the use of an additional sheet needed when Dutton replaced the inserted title page with one which was part of the first gathering. Not having examined copies of all the reprints, I am not able to provide exact dates for some of the changes described. I do not know, for example, when Dutton first used the bright red covers and gilt for their decoration, nor when they moved the table of contents to precede the preface, both features present by 1925, but possibly earlier.

Illustrators: FRANCIS I. BENNETT. Born in Philadelphia in 1876. He studied under Robert Henri, Thomas Anschutz, Robert Vonnoh, and William Chase, and became recognised as a painter in oils, doing mainly landscapes, and figure drawings, and as an illustrator. His commitment to art was recognised by his membership of the American Artists Professional League. He lived much of his adult life in New Jersey and died in 1953.

"ACB." Not identified.

Illustrations: The vignette on the title page has the caption "Grettir the Strong" and depicts Grettir half-length in green holding a spear. The colour of this picture brings out detail which is lost in the 1957 and later reprints, in which the vignette appears in black and white.

Grettir must have had quiet periods in his life, months or even years perhaps. The reader gets little hint of them. The story soars from one adventure to another like a bee buzzing from flower to flower. The illustrations reflect this constant action. The first two depict Grettir's early escapade in which he breaks into a tomb, fights the spirit within, and emerges with the dead chief's treasure. The next two complement the point in the narrative where Grettir fights Thorbiorn and his son single-handed, and kills them both. The next shows another fight, in which Thorod attacks Grettir, who dares not kill him for fear of antagonizing Thorod's father. The artist portrays Grettir as he fends off Thorod with his shield. The picture draws the attention of the reader to the greater skill needed for such a feat compared with merely killing the antagonist.

The book has relatively few illustrations, and it suffers further in that nearly half are in black and white, drawn by ACB, and the rest in colour by Bennett. The two forms create a loss of unity in a text unsupported by decoration which might have provided some cohesion between the two and between them both and the printed page. As noted in the Contents section, by the time of the 1957 reprint Dutton had solved the problem of mismatched illustrations by omitting the black and white ones, at the cost of reducing the number from seven to four, exclusive of the vignette. In 1962 Dutton presents even Bennett's pictures in black and white, but does not restore the black and white ones by ACB from the earlier editions. Having so few pictures to cover the whole action leads to unbalanced coverage overall.

5.2P
Grettir/ the Strong/
by Allen French/
with Drawings/ by Bernard Blatch/
The Bodley Head/ London

Date of publication: 1961.

Binding: Dust jacket with pictorial cover (see below). Title and author at bottom of cover and at top and mid-level respectively of spine, publisher at base of latter, all in black. Back of jacket has advertisement for another title published by Bodley, and two forthcoming titles on back flap. Front flap describes the present book and gives price. Bound in bright red buckram, plain except for title and author in gilt on top of spine and publisher at base.

Pagination/Size: 160 / 215 x 130 mm.

Contents: Pp. 1-2 blank, p. 3 half-title, p. 4 frontispiece, p. 5 title page, p. 6 publication information (including publisher's emblem, statement of copyright and printer), p. 7 contents, p. 8 blank, pp. 9-10 preface, p. 11 second half-title, p. 12 blank, pp. 13-159 text, p. 160 blank.

Comment: In a later companion volume (see 7.4P), Bodley identifies *Grettir* as one in their series *Heroic Retellings from History and Legend*. The series had not received this designation when they published *Grettir*. In preparing this edition they abbreviated French's preface and in doing so omitted his acknowledgement of Morris as his source. However, the text remains the same as that which appears in Dutton's edition (5.1P). Each chapter begins on a recto. If the preceding chapter finishes on a recto, then its obverse stays blank.

Illustrator: BERNARD BLATCH. Active from the 1950s as a book illustrator and designer of television graphics. He has also designed ceramic ware.

Illustrations: A picture on the front and spine of the dust jacket portrays Grettir, dressed in a rough tunic and leggings, standing full-length in the act of drawing his sword. The artist suggests his huge size and strength by filling most of the vertical dimension with his body, and by diminishing the low background of snow-covered hills and scrubby trees. A large red sun hangs behind his right shoulder. His tunic is in red too, but otherwise the artist limited colour to black, white and two shades of blue. The book lacks decoration as such, and relies on the pleasing layout described under Contents and attached Comments for decorative effect. All the illustrations are line drawings which depict only the figure or figures participating in the action, without background. This device, by eliminating distraction, serves to focus the attention of the viewer, but reduces the decorative effect even further. The artist aims for realism, with the shaggy hair and walrus moustaches of his subjects, and the rough tunics and cross-gartered leggings in which he dresses them. All impart a satisfying sense of authenticity. In six of the ten pictures, nine of which depict Grettir, Blatch drew a scene relating to conflict, either preparation for it, the fight itself, or the aftermath. A lot of fighting occurs in the story, but the high proportion narrows the focus. The artist deprives the reader of visual representation of other dimensions in the narrative. The frontispiece, one of the four which does not depict a fight, shows Grettir mounted on his horse. It serves to reemphasise the huge bulk of the man by making the horse small in proportion to him and slender, a feature accentuated even more by crossing the animal's front legs, so that it tapers below almost to a point. The second non-fighting picture portrays Grettir carrying on his back the treasure he has looted from the tomb, a subject in common with Bennett (see 5.1P). Bennett's picture has more appeal, in colour, in inclusion of a background, and in the greater naturalness of the figure. Indeed a slight stiffness is evident in many of Blatch's pictures. It robs them of the vitality so necessary in scenes of action. Another of the pictures which does not depict a fight provides an exception. In it we see Thorbiorn swinging his axe to hew a flat surface out of the log on which the witch will write the curse that delivers Grettir into the hands of his enemies, a crucial point in the narrative.

5.3P
Grettir/ the Strong/
Retold by/ Robert Newman/
Illustrated by John Gretzer/
Thomas Y. Crowell Company/ New York

Date of publication: 1968.

Binding: Picture on both covers and spine of dust jacket (see below). Title and names of author and artist on upper front cover of jacket. Author horizontally on top of spine, title in two lines vertically below it, publisher at mid-level. Front flap has commentary on book, back flap an advertisement for another Crowell title. Bound in olive-green buckram, plain except for same lettering on spine in black as appears on spine of jacket.

Pagination/Size: xvi, 190 [2] / 202 x 134 mm.

Contents: P. i half-title, p. ii frontispiece, p. iii title page, p. iv statement of copyright, p. v list of other works by Newman, p. vi blank, p. vii dedication, p. viii blank, pp. ix-xi contents, p. xii blank, pp. xiii-xvi preface, pp. 1-190 text, p. 1 blank, p. 2 biographical sketches of author and illustrator.

Illustrator: JOHN STEPHEN GRETZER. Born in 1920 in Iowa, where he spent his childhood. He studied art under Thomas Benton at the Kansas City Institute of Art and before that at the University of Omaha, where he met his future wife Agneta Jenson. They married late in 1941 a few months before he enlisted in the navy. He saw action in the invasions of North Africa and Sicily. After the war he worked for a short

JOHN GRETZER
[Grettir Encounters Lopt]
The Story of Grettir the Strong, p. 98

time as art director for a publishing company in Philadelphia. However, his main artistic activity for the next quarter century comprised book illustration and commercial art. By 1970 he and his family had moved to Perkasie, Bucks County, in south-eastern Pennsylvania. The artist's son Steven Gretzer wrote that at this time a colony of painters and other artists had established itself in Bucks County and become known as the New Hope Impressionists. The group was centred some thirty miles from Perkasie and remained active to the end of the century. By the middle 1970s Gretzer had turned to landscape painting, perhaps influenced by the New Hope Impressionists. He worked during this latter phase in oils, watercolours and pastels. He died in Pennsylvania in 2004.

Illustrations: The dust jacket has a powerful picture which extends over front, back, and spine and shows on the front two men in combat with sword and battle axe, and on the back a group of fighting men. The artist uses a limited palette, olive-green and light blue on a background of black and white, with dramatic effect. Gretzer provides fifteen full-page illustrations and many more part-page ones, including a double spread, such that the reader finds pictures at least every three or four pages, and sometimes more often. All are in black ink wash, with Grettir's hair highlighted in ochre in a few. Gretzer's pictures have a refreshing energy and vigour in accord with the story itself. At the same time the dark colouration sits well with the dark events in the narrative. Unfortunately, an integral element of the artist's technique in this book, the absence of delineation around the figures, sometimes blurs the details in the picture. Unquestionably, however, Gretzer's work greatly enhances the text of this edition.

Like Blatch (5.2P) Gretzer uses the frontispiece to portray Grettir. Where Blatch conveys only brutish strength and power, Gretzer endows Grettir with an aura of the heroic, from his clean-cut features, blonde hair, and lithe body to his alert expression. He exemplifies in detail Cummings' ideal of "a yearning nation's blue-eyed pride," if one ignores the irony Cummings intended by the line. Reading between the lines, Blatch's interpretation may come closer to historical reality, but when illustrating this text it counts for little. Blatch and Gretzer draw several subjects in common. Comparison highlights the static nature of the work of the former. In the episode with the bear, Blatch shows Grettir standing still and drawing his sword, the bear some way behind him. Gretzer shows the stage in the fight in which they fall off the cliff, the bear below, Grettir above. In the fight with the berserkers, both have a heap of corpses on the ground, but only Gretzer has them looking as though they have truly died a violent death. While Gretzer portrays many scenes of combat, overall he chooses a much wider range of subjects than Blatch, including the unusual one of Grettir's meeting with Hallmund. The integration of text and illustration by the use of half-page pictures and double spreads makes this book among the most satisfying described in these pages.

Chapter 6

The Rossetti Period:
A Book of Verse
Love Is Enough

Morris met Rossetti in 1856, and their acquaintance lasted until the latter's death in 1882. The title of this chapter does not refer to this whole quarter-century span, but to the five years from 1869 to 1874 when Rossetti embarked on an affair with Jane, Morris's wife of ten years at that point. During these years Morris produced an astonishing variety and number of poems, prose translations, and a play. His personal situation may well have influenced the content of two of these works, which form the subject-matter of this chapter.

Morris wrote *A Book of Verse* for the birthday of Georgiana Burne-Jones in August 1870. It was a time of crisis not only for Morris, but for Georgiana as well. Her husband, Edward Burne-Jones, had begun a long-lasting affair with Maria Zambaco. Morris and Georgie, already good friends, must have been drawn together by a shared desolation and sympathy. There was in fact a close bond of affection between them life-long. On Morris's side this found expression in gifts of his work, of which this calligraphic manuscript was one. The original manuscript is now in the Victoria and Albert Museum in London. The Scolar Press obtained permission to reproduce it in the forms described in the following pages.

The play *Love Is Enough* has not had a wide appeal, as reflected in the sparse publication record. Morris wrote it as a morality play, a form unfamiliar to most modern playgoers and unlikely to attract a large audience. Probably for this reason it has been largely ignored by both the commercial and the private presses, except for the KP, which published the only illustrated edition. F.S. Ellis published the

first edition in 1873. The next British edition came out only in 1896 as part of a series *The Poetical Works of William Morris*.

Not the least claim to attention of *Love Is Enough* is the delineation of Pharamond in the opening scene of the play within a play. Master Oliver, who describes his behaviour, mentions symptoms easily recognisable as those of depression. It raises the question whether Morris drew on his own feelings and the resulting physical changes of that time in his portrayal of Pharamond.

6.1a & b
A Book of Verse/
By/ William Morris/
Written in London/ 1870

Colophon (in part): This facsimile of *A Book of Verse* by William Morris is reproduced by arrangement with the Victoria and Albert Museum, London . . . Printed and bound in Great Britain by The Scolar Press, Ilkley, Yorkshire and published in 1980 by Scolar Press, 90/91 Great Russell Street, London WC1B 3PY in an edition of three hundred and twenty five copies. Three hundred numbered copies are for sale of which 1-62 are bound in vellum.
This is copy number *58* (6.1a).
This is copy number *265* (6.1b).

6.1a Binding: In bottle green clamshell case, plain except for title in gilt, on red leather label on front edge. Compartment at back of clamshell holds supplementary folder (see below). Bound in full stiff vellum. Laurel wreath in centre of front and back covers surrounds the initials "G.B.J." Covers otherwise decorated with small repeating pattern of two types of flower, possibly lily and peony, all in gilt. "Verses by William Morris" vertically on mid-spine. All edges gilt.

6.1b Binding: In clamshell case same colour as for 6.1a, label in black, with title and author in gilt. Same folder as in 6.1a. Book quarter-bound in dark green leather and very pale green linen boards, plain except for oval, dark green leather patch in middle of front cover with same inscription and border in gilt as on vellum copies. Gilt line separates spine from covers. "A Book of Verse by William Morris" vertically on top of spine. Edges plain.

6.1a & b Pagination/Size: [2] [vi] 52 [4] / 273 x 205 mm.

6.1a & b Contents: Pp. 1-2 blank, p. i title page, p. ii blank, pp. iii-iv contents, p. v half-title, p. vi blank, pp. 1-51 text, p. 52 blank, p. 1 facsimile of Morris's handwriting, p. 2 blank, p. 3 colophon, p. 4 blank.

Comment: These two forms of the edition are printed on handmade paper, in contrast to the machine-made paper of the rest.

6.1a & b Contents of folder: Title and author on unattached paper cover folded over blank outer sheet. P. 1 title page, p. 2 statement of copyright, p. 3 biographical sketch of Morris by Roy Strong, p. 4 captions to plates, pp. i-iii photographs (Morris, Georgiana Burne-Jones, and combined Morris and Burne-Jones families), p. iv facsimile of Morris's handwriting (pp. i-iv on glossy paper), pp. 5-7 introduction by Joyce Whalley commenting on the manuscript, p. 8 bibliography.

Comment: Among other information Whalley mentions that George Wardle drew the first ten pages of the decorations while Morris did the rest.

6.1c

A Book of Verse/ A Facsimile of the Manuscript/ Written in 1870 by/ William Morris/
London/ Scolar Press/ 1981

6.1d

A Book of Verse/ A Facsimile of the Manuscript/ Written in 1870 by/ William Morris/
Clarkson N. Potter, Inc./ Publishers/ Distributed by Crown Publishers, Inc./ New York

Comment: The slash between "Inc." and "Publisher" appears on the title page itself; it does not represent an editorial insertion.

Date of publication: n.d. (6.1d). The Library of Congress code in the book includes a date of 1982. It appeared that year or in 1981.

6.1e

A Book of Verse/ A Facsimile of the Manuscript/ Written in 1870 by/ William Morris/
London/ Scolar Press

Date of publication: 1982.

6.1c & d Binding: Dust jacket with cream-coloured background, title and author in green on top of front cover with names of writers of introduction in black below. On lower two-thirds, decoration which appears also on page 20 of text. Title, author, and publisher vertically on spine in black. On back of jacket of 6.1d, ISBN and laudatory comment about book and about Morris. Front and back flaps of both editions have brief notes on Morris and on the book, note differing between the editions. Bound in beige buckram, plain except for title vertically on spine and publisher at base, both in gilt.

6.1e Binding: Paperback with thick, matte cover, same layout on front as on dust jacket of 6.1c. Back cover has notes similar to those on flaps of dust jacket. No endpapers, cover glued on, but gatherings sewn.

6.1c, d, & e Pagination/Size: [2] [xvi] [vi] 52 [4] / 236 x 158 mm.

Contents: Pp. 1-2 blank, p. i half-title, p. ii blank, p. iii title page, p. iv publication information, p. v contents, pp. vi-x biographical sketch of Morris, pp. xi-xiv discussion of text, pp. xv-xvi blank, p. i title page to poems, p. ii blank, pp. iii-iv contents, p. v half-title, p. vi blank, pp. 1-51 text, p. 52 blank, p. 1 facsimile of letter from Morris, pp. 2-4 blank.

Comment: Pages vi-xiv contain the material present in the folder of 6.1a & b, with minor rearrangement of pages vi-vii.

Illustrators: EDWARD BURNE-JONES. See 3.1.

CHARLES FAIRFAX MURRAY. Born in 1849, in Bow, a village northeast of London. His mother died when he was four years of age, and by twelve Murray had left home and was living in London. He showed artistic talent as a boy, which received encouragement, and was further encouraged in the early 1860s by his employer, Sir Samuel Peto. He brought himself to the attention of John Ruskin at the beginning of 1866 by sending him a portfolio of his drawings. Ruskin too recognised his talent, and arranged lodgings, art instruction, and copying work for him. Burne-Jones took him as his studio assistant that summer. By 1869 he was working for Rossetti in the same capacity and also did designs for Morris's company. He went to Italy in December of 1871 for several months to study the work of the old masters. In so doing, he continued to acquire the extraordinary expertise which later made him so effective as an art dealer. He returned to Italy two years later to copy old masters for John Ruskin. During this visit he met and married Angelica Colivicchi in 1875. He spent most of the next ten years in Italy. By 1878, his main activity centred on negotiating the purchase of art works for institutional and private clients. His effectiveness in this activity derived from the vast knowledge of art styles he had acquired, his impeccable artistic judgement, and his contacts in the art world. However, he also continued to draw and paint, influenced not surprisingly by the Renaissance painters and by Burne-Jones; he exhibited regularly at the Grosvenor Gallery during these years. He returned to London in 1886, accompanied by his wife. She went back to her native Tuscany permanently in 1887, but he visited Italy only occasionally after this time. He entered into a long-term relationship with Blanche Richmond in 1888. Four of their children survived to adulthood, in addition to the six who survived borne by Angelica. In London, Murray continued to work as a dealer in art and became extremely rich. His wealth enabled him to amass a large collection of paintings, drawings, and old and rare books. He was a major benefactor to British art institutions, donating large parts of his collection to the National Gallery and the Fitzwilliam Museum in Cambridge, especially in the first fifteen years of the twentieth century. His plans to settle back in Italy with Angelica, whom he had continued to support and see, were frustrated by the outbreak of World War I. During the war years he had a succession of strokes, and died in London early in 1919. See also Appendix 3. (See Elliott.)

Illustrations and decoration: Morris aimed in this book to create a hand-written, hand-illuminated manuscript to rival those of the Middle Ages. While the pictures of Burne-Jones and Fairfax Murray illustrate the text, they function mainly to enhance an already rich decoration. A pattern of green willow leaves fills the manuscript title page, with a medallion portrait of Morris in colour in the middle, and the title and author in gilt above, embedded in the leaves. Below the portrait a line of female figures, all playing a musical instrument, stand in front of a fence. Flowers, possibly poppies, lean over the fence, and a line of poplars grows behind it. Beyond the title page Morris used gilt for the Table of Contents title and page numbers, the titles of the poems at the top of each page, the first letter of the lines of some poems, occasional decorated capitals, and here and there to highlight a word in a poem. The capitalised letters in the page of contents are in various colours of ink, and this is true also of most of the decorated capitals in the text. The publisher used gilt only in 6.1a & b. It is absent in copies of 6.1c, d & e, where they substituted yellow ink.

Morris missed little opportunity to apply decoration. Most poems have short enough lines that he decorated the space at their ends with a mixture of twining stems, leaves and flowers the whole length of the page. Where a poem is sufficiently short he interposed decoration between the stanzas. If space remains at the bottom of a page he left it blank at one or two points, but usually filled the space with more decoration or illustration. In small areas space does not permit an integrated pattern, and here we find individual flowers and leaves. Comparison of the first ten pages of decoration done by George Wardle with the later pages done by Morris reveals that the latter's decoration is the more varied and free. Where Wardle has only individual flowerets, Morris has whole stems twining between the lines and a greater range of species of flowers. Finally, Morris's neat calligraphic script, enclosed throughout in a fine ruled line, provides the last component to make this a true manuscript book as the medieval period understood it.

The one illustration done by Burne-Jones is a headpiece for the first poem, "The Two Sides of the River." He has caught in their posture and outstretched hands nearly but not quite touching the mutual longing of youth and maiden separated by a symbolic stream. Burne-Jones used a rich palette of green, blue and yellow. In the other nine miniatures, by Fairfax Murray, one sees a similar richness of colour. Also like Burne-Jones, he tends to a symbolic representation of the poem. For "The Lapse of the Year" he provided four panels each with a female figure emblematic of Winter, Spring, Summer and Autumn. To accompany "Hope Dieth, Love Liveth" he drew an angel standing above a coffin. In others he could be seen as more literal, as in "A Garden by the Sea." In some instances he is rather obscure. He renders all his pictures with exquisite detail and skill, with some hint that Burne-Jones exerted influence on his style at this point. His pictures appear mainly as tailpieces, some in multiple panels, some in round or square format, all surrounded by the decoration of the rest of the page.

6.2
Love Is Enough, Or the Freeing of/ Pharamond: A Morality.
Written/ by William Morris   [Half-title]

Colophon: Here ends Love is Enough, or The Freeing of Pharamond,
written by William Morris, with two pictures designed by Sir Edward
Burne-Jones, & engraved on wood by W.H. Hooper. The picture on the
opposite page was not designed for this edition of *Love Is Enough*, but
for an edition projected about twenty-five years ago, which was never
carried out. Printed at the Kelmscott Press, Upper Mall, Hammersmith,
& finished on the 11th day of December, 1897.
Sold by the Trustees of the late William Morris at the Kelmscott Press.

Limitation: [300 copies on hand-made paper and 8 on vellum].

Binding: Full limp vellum with three ties, title in gilt lengthwise on
spine.

Pagination/Size: [8] [iv] 92 [4] / 290 x 211 mm.

Contents: Pp. 1-8 blank, p. i half-title, p. ii dramatis personae, p. iii
blank, p. iv frontispiece, pp. 1-90 text (with colophon at the end), p. 91
illustration, p. 92 and pp. 1-4 blank.

Illustrator: EDWARD BURNE-JONES. See 3.1.

Illustrations and decoration: In the early stages of the KP Morris
adopted a design to which he adhered throughout and which his trustees
used after his death. However, in Morris's absence they were obliged
to re-use borders which he had created for previous works. We see this
practice in *Love Is Enough,* which they published late in 1897. A floral
border surrounds the frontispiece and first page of text facing it, the
latter starting with a large dropped capital. Similar but smaller capitals
are present at the start of each new scene, which is further embellished
with a marginal decoration. The designer used Troy type for the text
and Troy and Chaucer types at different places for the directions.
The stage directions and the name of the speakers appear in red. The
directions call for music at intervals throughout the play; Morris wrote
these sections as declamations in stanza form. Each stanza starts with
a dropped capital in blue. These pages and some others have marginal
decorations the full length of the page.

Burne-Jones drew two illustrations. The frontispiece portrays a climactic
scene in which Azalais comes upon the sleeping Pharamond. It captures
his weariness and wretched state, and her pity for him. The other, at the
end, shows Pharamond and Azalais in Love's temple, standing before
the altar, with Love bending from it in the act of placing a victor's crown
of laurel leaves on Pharamond's head. This earlier picture hints at a
change in the artist's approach, in that its allegorical style contrasts
sharply with the literalness of the later frontispiece. Burne-Jones chose

the subjects well, starting with Pharamond at his nadir and leaving him in triumph. The latter picture suffers from the narrow border chosen as its surround. The empty space outside does not sit well with the fuller decoration elsewhere.

Chapter 7

Translations in the Mid-1870s:
The Aeneids of Virgil
The Story of Sigurd the Volsung

As noted in the Introduction to Chapter 5, Morris began to write translations of stories from the Icelandic and continued translations from various languages for the next twenty years. In 1875 he published his verse translation of Virgil's *Aeneid*. No illustrated edition of his translation has appeared. However, during this same period Morris had busied himself with writing calligraphic manuscripts (see Appendix 3). The most magnificent is *The Aeneids of Virgil* in the original Latin, illustrated by Burne-Jones and profusely decorated. It last sold in 1987 when Christie's auctioned the Doheny collection. Their catalogue provides excellent reproductions of parts of both text and illustrations. In editing her father's writings for their eventual publication in *The Collected Works of William Morris*, May Morris obtained reproductions of two of Burne-Jones's preparatory drawings for the manuscript, and she used them to illustrate the volume which contains Morris's translation of *The Aeneid*. Thus the first entry in this chapter describes Volume XI of her edition. While she included illustrative material in every volume, most of it does not relate to the text, consisting mainly of portraits of Morris, family members, specimens of his calligraphy and other material illustrative of his activities, his houses, and so on. One can only see the drawings depicting scenes from *The Aeneid* as inadvertent illustration. Equally in Volume III, which contains wood engravings to accompany "Cupid and Psyche," the selection seems based partly on Morris having cut those particular blocks (see 4.6).

The public has unjustly neglected *Sigurd*, which is a poem of great vitality and technical skill. The neglect must derive in part from the neglect of long narrative poems in general. In part, it surely comes

from the poem's portrayal of a society with values admirable in many ways, but fundamentally different from our own. Finally, the public may be less tolerant of the supernatural in an artistic work now than a hundred years ago. *Sigurd the Volsung* was therefore out of print for many years, though the Thoemmes edition has recently remedied this.

Like *Love Is Enough, Sigurd the Volsung* appeared in only one illustrated edition, and this too came from the KP. However, MacMillan published a paraphrased version of *Sigurd* in 1932. Holt reissued it in 1947, and The Bodley Head republished it in 1965, with illustrations by a different artist.

As already noted in the introduction to Chapter 4, facsimile reprints of *The Collected Works of William Morris* came to my attention too late to allow their inclusion in the text, where description of the relevant volume would have appeared after 7.1. I provide details of these reprints in *Notes Added in Press* on page 308.

7.1
[In] The Collected Works/ of William Morris/
With Introductions by/ His Daughter May Morris/
Volume XI/ The Aeneids of Virgil/
Longmans Green and Company/ Paternoster Row London/ New York
Bombay Calcutta/ MDCCCCXI

Limitation: This edition is in 24 volumes and is limited to 1,050 copies, of which 1,000 only are for sale. This is No. *959.*

Binding: Pale blue paper over boards. Linen spine, paper label on top with title, volume number and volume contents. Plain else.

Pagination/Size: [4] xxxii, 286 [6] / 228 x 151 mm.

Contents: Pp. 1-4 blank, pp. i-iii blank, p. iv statement of limitation, pp. v-vi blank, inserted frontispiece with tissue guard, p. vii title page, p. viii blank, pp. ix-x contents, pp. xi-xxix introduction with inserted illustrations, p. xxx blank, p. xxxi bibliographical note, p. xxxii blank, pp. 1-286 text, p. 1 blank, p. 2 address of printer, pp. 3-6 blank.

Illustrator: EDWARD BURNE-JONES. See 3.1.

Illustrations: Illustration comprises preparatory drawings which Burne-Jones did for Morris's manuscript of *The Aeneid*. One portrays a relatively unimportant sub-plot from Book III when Aeneas and his men are attacked by harpies. Burne-Jones takes full advantage of the artistic opportunities offered by the harpies' breasts and talons. The other picture, from Book IX, shows an important point in the epic in which Juno's emissary Iris appears before Turnus the enemy of the Trojans, to exhort him to attack them while they are at a disadvantage. The pictures would have served better had Longmans apposed them with their text. For consistency with the layout in the other volumes they did not do so.

7.2
The Story of Sigurd the Volsung and the Fall of the Niblungs
By William Morris   [Half-title]

Colophon: Here ends The Story of Sigurd the Volsung and the Fall of the Niblungs, written by William Morris. With two pictures designed by Edward Burne-Jones and engraved by W.H. Hooper. It was printed at the Kelmscott Press, Upper Mall, Hammersmith, and finished on the 19th day of January, 1898.
Sold by the Trustees of the late William Morris at the Kelmscott Press.

Limitation: [160 copies on hand-made paper and 6 on vellum].

Binding: Full limp vellum with three ties. "Sigurd" vertically on spine in gilt.

Pagination/Size: [4] [viii] 210 [6] / 326 x 233 mm.

Contents: Pp. 1-4 blank, p. i first signature, p. ii blank, p. iii half-title, p. iv blank, pp. v-vi contents, p. vii blank, p. viii decorated frontispiece, pp. 1-209 text, p. 210 colophon, pp. 1-6 blank.

Illustrator: EDWARD BURNE-JONES. See 3.1.

Illustrations and decoration: The trustees of Morris's estate published this book at the KP the year after Morris died. However, they adhered in every detail to the design Morris had established for KP books. To discuss components of these books separately obscures the unity of their conception, from vellum binding to handmade paper, to quality of ink and presswork, all of which give pleasure to the viewer. The decoration as such has the lavish appearance which is the hallmark of the Press. A border surrounds the frontispiece wood engraving and facing page with the opening lines of the poem, which starts with a large dropped and decorated capital. The Troy type appears at the start of each of the four books making up the poem. Elsewhere we find Chaucer type. Each successive book begins with a large dropped capital of the same decorative quality as that at the start. However, smaller dropped and decorated capitals abound at the start of each section and throughout. The book's designer uses red ink for section headings and for the shoulder note on each page designating the book number. Marginal decorations accompany the start of each section and a larger one the start of each book. They display the usual motifs favoured by Morris: leaves, flowers or twining stems.

The pictures are well placed in that they portray the scene on the facing page. The first depicts the hall of the Volsungs with the Branstock in the middle and the hawks flying or perched in its branches. Decorated pillars support an arched roof, and fine dishes on long tables await the diners. The end painting shows Gudrun, a torch in her hand, amid the flames which are consuming Atli's hall. Both these pictures reveal Burne-Jones

EDWARD BURNE-JONES
[The Hall of the Volsungs]
***The Story of Sigurd the Volsung and the Fall of the Niblungs**, frontispiece*

at his best, with vigorous execution, good handling, and an excellent choice of subject. The hall of the Volsungs is the setting for the opening scenes from which the whole story unfolds, and the destruction of Atli's hall completes the tragedy. Thus, as in *Love Is Enough*, the pictures span the extremes of the story. In this one, however, we see the opposite progression, from triumph to disaster. The effect and quality of these pictures are all the more gratifying in that Burne-Jones did not like the subject-matter and undertook the work with reluctance.

Paraphrased Versions of Sigurd the Volsung

Illustrated editions of full-length works by Morris had become a thing of the past by the end of World War I. The history of paraphrased editions with specially commissioned art work extends much later. In contrast to the early appearance of paraphrases of *The Earthly Paradise* (see Chapter 4) and *Grettir the Strong* (see Chapter 5), MacMillan published the first adaptation of *Sigurd* only in 1932, close on the heels of Scribner's paraphrase of *Child Christopher* (see Chapter 15). Dorothy Hosford's rendering of *Sigurd* has a long publishing history, which eventually extended over a third of a century. Only French's edition of *Grettir* (see 5.1) exceeds it at more than fifty years. With these exceptions, beyond the second decade of the twentieth century illustration of texts by Morris became the preserve of private presses.

The various paraphrases of *Sigurd* all use Hosford's text. The last, illustrated by a different artist (7.4), differs markedly from the earlier two. The earlier editions (7.3Pa & b) share the same artist and general scheme of layout, but do differ in details. Firstly, the MacMillan edition has wider margins, which account for the greater breadth of the book. Secondly, MacMillan used a much heavier paper, which makes the 1943 reprint nearly twice as thick as the Holt edition. These features give the MacMillan edition an altogether more pleasing aspect. The text de-emphasises some features of the story, such as the incestuous parentage of Sinfiotli, and ends on the high note at the end of Book 2 of Morris's text, with Sigurd and Brynhild rapturous in each other's company, rather than taking the reader through the treachery and betrayal of Books 3 and 4.

7.3Pa
Sons/ of the/ Volsungs/
Adapted by Dorothy G. Hosford/ from Sigurd the Volsung/
by William Morris/
Illustrated by Frank Dobias/
The Macmillan Company/ New York 1932

Dates of publication: <u>October 1932</u>, May 1940, <u>July 1943</u>.

7.3Pb
Sons/ of the/ Volsungs/
Adapted by Dorothy G. Hosford/ from Sigurd the Volsung/
by William Morris/
Illustrated by Frank Dobias/
Henry Holt and Company/ New York 1949

Binding: Dust jacket with picture in lower three quarters. Upper
quarter has background of sky-blue (1932) or navy (later issues) over
front, back and spine. Background of lower part is cream (1932) or gold
(later issues). Title and adapter on upper front and spine of jacket in
yellow matching background of lower part of jacket. In 7.3Pa adapter's
name in red. Publisher at base of spine. Front flap has information about
book, same in both editions. Back flap has advertisements for other titles.

Bound in bright lemon-yellow buckram, a deeper shade than jacket,
with title across top of cover and on top of spine. Adapter's name at base
of front cover and publisher at base of spine. On middle of front cover a
stylised Norse design like a helmet seen from above with outstretched
wings extending from its top. All lettering and decoration in dark blue.
Bright blue front and back endpapers with picture of three Norse galleys
each with swelling sail on swelling sea under a vast open sky (7.3Pa
1932). Plain white endpapers (7.3Pa 1943). Plain dull blue endpapers
(7.3Pb).

7.3Pa Size: 215 x 158 mm.

7.3Pb Size: 212 x 135 mm.

7.3Pa & b Pagination: xiv, 170 [4].

Contents: P. i half-title, p. ii address of publisher (7.3Pa) blank (7.3Pb),
p. iii blank, p. iv frontispiece, p. v title page, p. vi statement of copyright,
p. vii dedication, p. viii blank, pp. ix-x contents, p. xi list of illustrations,
p. xii blank, p. xiii decorated chapter heading, p. xiv blank, pp. 1-169
text, p. 170 blank, p. 1 brief decorated epilogue, pp. 2-4 blank.

Comment: The Roman numeration of chapters in the contents pages does
not appear in the text. Instead the designer marks a chapter by starting

it on a recto with a decorated heading, the page otherwise blank as is its obverse. The text follows on the facing recto, below an illustrative headpiece.

Illustrator: FRANK DOBIAS. Born in Austria in 1902. After studying at the Kunst Gewerke Schule and the Kunst Akademie, Vienna, he moved to the USA in 1924. Book illustration seems to have been a major artistic activity for him. He was listed as an illustrator for a wide range of titles between 1928 and 1955.

Illustrations and decoration: The picture on the dust jacket has a deep yellow background with a Viking galley under sail, dragon's head at the prow, and a row of shields along the gunwale. Dobias highlighted the striped sail, prow, bulwark, and helmsman's oar in red, the rest in the same shade of blue as the background of the upper quarter of the dust jacket. The ship breasts a choppy sea, and headlands lie in the background off the port bow. The picture extends over both covers of the jacket and is signed "Franz Dobias." The decoration comprises three Norse designs, including the one on the cover (see Binding above), which appears also on the title page. The designer uses another as a headpiece for the pages both of contents and of the list of illustrations. The third appears at intervals as decoration for chapter headings, interspersed with the other two. The second Norse design takes the form of a twining horizontal band with a vertical flame-like projection at each end, and the third resembles a broad bracelet with complex carving seen edge on.

Dobias provides only four full-page illustrations, including the frontispiece. However, he has chosen as his subjects crises or turning points in the story. The first depicts the desperate defence of the Volsungs against the treacherous Goths, the second Sigmund's last battle, in which, apparently on the verge of victory, Odin is about to shatter his sword, the third (the frontispiece) Sigurd mounted on Greyfell setting out on his quest, and the last Sigurd and Brynhild united. Besides these, a headpiece which occupies a third of the page at the start of each chapter illustrates a crucial event in the chapter. The first shows Sigmund in triumph having pulled the sword out of the Branstock. The second portrays the Volsung ships as they sail to visit the Goths. For this the designer uses the same picture as adorns the endpapers of 7.3Pa (1932). Similarly, heading the appropriate chapters, we see the forging of Sigurd's sword, Sigurd killing Fafnir, and Sigurd coming upon Brynhild after braving the ring of fire. All the illustrations are black line drawings.

The designer got every aspect of this book right. The dust jacket when present carries immediate promise, which the pictorial endpapers sustain into the text, where the sense of space created by a separate sheet at the start of each chapter confirms the initial impression that we have an artistic unity in our hands. This unity comes partly from the layout but also from the quality of Dobias's illustrations, which leave nothing undone. This book deserves to be recognised as one of the inspired achievements stemming (admittedly indirectly) from Morris's

Far away beneath lay the silver ocean's hem.

FRANK DOBIAS
Sons of the Volsungs, **facing p. 168**

text. Its failing has nothing to do with its physical aspects, but comes from its betrayal of Morris's artistic intent, since it covers only the first half of the poem. Were the decoration of this book wedded to the original text, Morris enthusiasts would not rest without a copy. See also 7.4P.

7.4P
Sons/ of the/ Volsungs/
Adapted by/ Dorothy G. Hosford/ from/ Sigurd the Volsung/
by William Morris/
Drawings by/ John Holder/
The Bodley Head/ London

Date of publication: 1965.

Binding: Dust jacket with picture on front cover. Title and adapter's name spread across top and vertically on spine. Back of jacket has list of other titles in series *Heroic Retellings from History and Legend.* Front flap has commentary on contents, back flap advertisement for another book in series. Bound in plain blue buckram, with title and name of adapter vertically on spine and publisher at base.

Pagination/Size: 126 [2] / 214 x 128 mm.

Contents: P. 1 half-title, p. 2 list (in different order from that on jacket) of other titles in series, p. 3 decorated title page, p. 4 dedication and publication details, pp. 5-6 contents, pp. 7-126 text, pp. 1-2 blank.

Comment: The publisher re-used Hosford's text of 1932 (see 7.3P) supplying a Roman number at the head of each chapter and retaining the chapter headings, but no decoration.

Illustrator: JOHN HOLDER. NIF.

Illustrations and decoration: The illustration on the lower half of the dust jacket appears on a white ground and depicts the fight between Sinfiotli and Gudrod. The upper half has a blue ground, the two background colours creating the impression of a beach and sea. The sea bears a stylised Norse galley broadside on with hoisted sail striped in alternating blue and white. In front of the galley, just above the margin between white and blue background, stand a row of warriors.

On the title page is a small rendering of two fighting men, which appears as a full-page picture in the body of the book, illustrating the last battle of Sigmund. The only other decoration appears on the obverse of the title page, a tree with a stag standing beneath it. This seems to be an emblem for the series since it appears also in other titles, such as *Grettir the Strong* (see 5.2P). Holder executed all the pictures as line drawings, seven full-page, several of half-page size and one tailpiece. He chose his subjects fairly well: Sigmund just after pulling the sword out of the Branstock, the spearmen of the Goths as they prepare to assault the Volsungs, Sigmund and Sinfiotli waiting in the cellars of King Siggeir's hall to begin their attack, the last fight of Sigmund, Sigurd after acquiring Greyfell, Sigurd obtaining his sword from his mother, Sigurd after he has slain Fafnir and Regin, and Sigurd with Brynhild.

Holder strives for historical realism. His rendering of the interior of King Volsung's hall during the feast has dogs among the diners. Sigurd on Greyfell looks like an ordinary youth on an ordinary pony. In most circumstances one applauds historical realism, but not in a narrative which aims at evoking mythic dimensions. Morris's text describes the hall of the Volsungs as a place where "Dukes were the door-wards there, and the roofs were thatched with gold: / Earls were the wrights that wrought it, and silver nailed its doors; / Earls' wives were the weaving women, queens' daughters strewed its floors . . . ." Holder depicts it as a single-storey log building. These pictures carry no hint of the heroic. The final one, of Sigurd and Brynhild, exemplifies this best of all, especially when compared with the same subject done by Dobias (see illustration accompanying 7.3P) in which the two seem ready to bestride the world. Holder's realistic approach works better in his depictions of fighting men. Here the action itself carries a sense of the heroic, and Holder shows considerable skill in depicting accoutrements and movement. However, even here Dobias excels over Holder. Both artists illustrated the last fight of Sigmund, against the army of King Lyngi. Holder's rendering has two men in single combat. Dobias conveys the sense of a battle with combatants all around and Sigmund at that moment dominant over all. Similarly, when Dobias portrays the embattled Volsungs on the crest of the hill awaiting the onslaught of Siggeir's Goths, he has a forest of spears surrounding them, not the three of Holder, who fails to depict the Volsungs at all.

Chapter 8

Political Writing and Socialist Pamphlets and Poetry:
The Pilgrims of Hope

Morris must have possessed a keen sense of social justice from a young age. For example, when his wife entered into an affair with Rossetti in late 1869, Morris acted on his conviction of the autonomy of the individual. He did not interfere or try to dissuade Janey from the course of action she had chosen, in spite of the pain it must have caused him (see Introduction to Chapter 6). He wrote many letters to the newspapers throughout his life, many on social issues. In 1880 he wrote an address intended to bolster Liberal opposition to the war-mongering policy of Disraeli, the Prime Minister at the time. Disraeli was offering British support for the Turks against Russian advances into Turkish territory. The major European powers had already interceded in the dispute between Russia and Turkey, and tension had eased by the time Morris dated his completed text. In these circumstances Morris did not proceed further with the subject. The full address remains in manuscript form in the British Library. May Morris included part of it in a two-volume set *William Morris: Artist, Writer, Socialist*, which she edited and Blackwell published in 1936. The William Morris Society published the full text in 2008 with an introductory essay by Florence Boos. This edition has relevant illustrations of Morris's text, and forms the first entry in this chapter.

Morris lectured frequently as part of his work for the socialist cause. He later published most of his lectures in order to reach a wider audience. Some appeared as pamphlets at the outset, while some he put in *Commonweal* initially. The vast majority had at most a decorative headpiece, but one or two carry illustration in addition. These latter pamphlets and a single illustrated edition of a socialist poem form the subject of this chapter.

The earliest illustrated pamphlet, *Art and Socialism*, is unusual in two respects. Firstly, it was published in two forms, one a regular and the other a large paper edition. Secondly, it did not appear under a socialist imprint, but as one in a series of pamphlets covering a range of social and literary topics.

London workers staged large-scale demonstrations demanding their rights in November 1887. The rallies centred on Trafalgar Square. The size of the gathering alarmed the authorities, who ordered the police to disperse the crowds. The police force did so using mounted men, who rode down and killed a young man. Morris wrote a pamphlet to raise money for the support of the victim's family and to express his outrage at the police action. This pamphlet constitutes the third item in this chapter, *A Death Song for Alfred Linnell*. Morris reprinted the poem in 1891 in the collection he called *Poems by the Way* (see Chapter 12).

The last pamphlet, *Monopoly*, first appeared in parts in three successive issues of *Commonweal* (Volume V, numbers 204-206) late in 1889. The Socialist League issued it as a separate pamphlet the following year, No. 7 in their series *The Socialist Platform*. It thus represents one of the last items Morris wrote before his break with the League. Morris reprinted the pamphlet in 1893 under the aegis of the organisation he founded, the Hammersmith Socialist Society. However, this later imprint does not have the cartoon, present in the 1890 version, which justifies the inclusion of the latter in this book. A further reprint appeared about 1900, put out by yet another socialist group. This one includes the cartoon, despite Buxton Forman's unflattering remarks on the subject (see below).

Morris used all of his vast talents, not least his poetical gifts, to promote Socialism. His poem, *The Pilgrims of Hope,* is one example, a *cri de coeur* against the social injustice he perceived around him. It appeared first in *Commonweal* in serialised form in 1885 and 1886. Buxton Forman re-issued it as a booklet dated 1886, but most likely printed about ten years later. The polemical nature of the subject-matter has ensured comparative obscurity for the poem, at least with the general public. Mosher published an edition in 1901, and Longmans Green put out others, both in their Pocket Library Editions and in *The Collected Works*. However, the only illustrated edition comprises just a short section of the total poem *The Message of the March Wind*, which appeared in 1938. Morris included this one section in *Poems by the Way*. The Leicester College of Art and Printing also published an elegant version of this same section as a student project in 1963, but that is not illustrated.

8.1
William Morris/ Our Country Right or Wrong/ A Critical Essay/
Edited by/ Florence S Boos/
William Morris Society/ 2008

Binding: Paperback with cream-coloured cover. Author at top of front cover, main title in red below, sub-title below it. Line of horizontal S's in red separates title from name of editor. Shorter line of S's in red at base. Author, title, and "WMS" vertically on spine in red. At top of back cover author in black above title in red, and editor below that. Notes about book in lower two-thirds. Inner aspect of covers has reproduction of last page of autograph manuscript.

Pagination/Size: 96 / 215 x 128 mm.

Contents: P. 1 half-title, p. 2 frontispiece, p. 3 full title page, p. 4 publication information, p. 5 contents, p. 6 list of illustrations, p. 7 acknowledgements, p. 8 blank, pp. 9-48 introductory essay, pp. 49-51 introduction, p. 52 blank, pp. 53-89 text, pp. 90-94 notes, p. 95 note about William Morris Society, p. 96 blank.

Illustrators: DIMITER GUDZHENOV. Identified in the caption as "Professor." NIF.
    Other illustrators not identified.

Illustrations: This book makes little or no pretension to printing as art (to filch a phrase from a recent book of that title). However, it is a pleasing and workmanlike production which presents the material clearly and well. Not the least of the strengths of the book lies in its illustrations. None of them is original to the book, but the individual who selected them did so with a good sense of their appropriateness to the subject matter of the essay. (The person responsible may be Peter Wright, whom Professor Boos recognises in her acknowledgements.) All of the pictures portray events or individuals from the time Morris was writing his essay. Indeed, most of the pictures themselves date from that period. Most depict events connected with wars in which Britain was involved, either directly or indirectly, in the 1870s and early 1880s. Some show scenes from the battlefields themselves. In general they have an appearance typical of illustrations in the magazines of the period, such as *The Illustrated London News*. Others date from the twentieth century, namely the ones concerned with the Zulu wars. These pictures are reproductions of old photographs and appeared before in books on the subject dating from 1963 and 1974. The frontispiece is a cartoon from *Punch* which lampoons Disraeli's jingoistic foreign policy. Two of the illustrations depict events preceding and during the Russo-Turkish war of 1877. One, and possibly both, come from a book published in 1966. They are reproductions of paintings, one by Dimiter Gudzhenov, portraying the arrival of Russian troops in Bulgaria and the crushing of a Bulgarian revolt by the Turks in the period before the war. All the pictures show a high level of competence and relevance to the subject-matter of the essays.

8.2a & b
Art and Socialism: a/ Lecture delivered [January/ 23rd, 1884]
before the Sec-/ ular Society of Leicester,/
by William Morris,/ author of "The Earthly/ Paradise,"/ etc./ And
Watchman: What of the Night?/
Cum Privilegio Auctoris./
Imprinted for/ E.E.M. and W.L.S./ Anno 1884./
Sold by W. Reeves, 185,/ Fleet St., London, E.C.;/ and by Heywoods,/
London and Manchester.

Comment: The lettering below "Cum Privilegio Auctoris" is in two columns separated by a stylised sun surrounded by short tapering lines and with eyes, nose and mouth on its face. The text to its left finishes with "1884," the rest appearing on the right side.

8.2a Binding: Thick but flexible yellow paper with red lettering. Front cover repeats wording of title page with addition of horizontal band of decoration above and below it. Above upper band the name of the series, Leek Bijou Reprints, below lower band the statement "Large Paper" and price, 1s. [shilling]. On inside of front cover two quotations relevant to socialist thinking. Back cover has advertisement for *Justice*, the magazine of the Socialist Democratic Federation, on outside, and one for *Today*, another socialist magazine, on inside.

8.2a Size: 145 x 135 mm.

Comment: In the copy examined the breadth of the uncut pages varies from 130 to 140 mm.

8.2b Binding: Outermost two sheets blank. Outer one of relatively thick, beige paper, inner white. Immediately within, salmon-pink printed cover. Lettering duplicates that of 8.2a except for absence of "Large Paper" and lower price, 3d [pence]. Inside of front cover has publisher's announcement about the large paper copies.

Comment: The publisher issued a second edition of 8.2b, indicated by the imprint "2nd Edition" at the bottom left of the front cover. The title page is unchanged from the first edition, and has the same date, 1884.

However, the printer reset the cover as "Art and/ Socialism:/ by William Morris,/ Author of "The Earthly/ Paradise," etc./" From "Cum Privilegio Auctoris" onwards the lettering is the same as in the first edition. The one copy of the second edition examined lacks the two blank outer sheets of the original edition. I do not know whether later editions of the large paper copy appeared.

8.2b Size: 127 x 97 mm.

8.2a & b Pagination: 72 [16].

8.2a & b Contents: P. 1 illustrated half-title, p. 2 quotation from John Ruskin's *The Stones of Venice*, p. 3 title page, p. 4 William Wordsworth's Sonnet xxxiii, pp. 5-58 text, p. 59 half-title to second section, pp. 60-72 quotations from various authors relevant to socialist thought, p. 1 half-title to section of advertisements, pp. 2-16 advertisements for the other Bijou Reprints and other socialist pamphlets.

Comment: The quotations in the second section all offer comment on social or political issues from a standpoint in accord with socialist thinking. The reprints advertised in the final section under the heading "The Bijou Advertiser" seem to have the same format as *Art and Socialism*, which is No. 7 in the series. They deal with a variety of topics, some political, some religious, and some poetical.

Illustrator: Not identified. Walter Crane (see 8.3) could have drawn at least the frontispiece pictures, judging by the style. However, no evidence to support this exists in either Masse's bibliography of Crane's illustrated first editions or the supplementary bibliography which Spencer appends to her biography of Crane, or her account of Crane's comments to Morris about the pamphlet.

Illustrations and decoration: The publisher took some pains to enhance the appearance of this pamphlet with decoration. A floral headpiece in the form of a horizontal band precedes the text, which starts with a dropped and decorated capital. The page numbers sit above the text within brackets which, while not really decorative, do catch the viewer's eye. The text finishes with a tailpiece, another horizontal bar filled with a floral motif. The half-title for the next section, on the page facing the tailpiece, has a similar device below the title. Another appears on page 72 at the end of this section. Even the title page which precedes the advertisements has decoration, a richly ornamented vase on a pedestal with surrounding flowers. On the obverse of this page the advertisements for the previous reprints start with a pictorial presentation of them. It portrays a pastoral scene, with trees in the foreground and middle ground, a bright sun above, and decorative clouds around. The names of the authors of the reprints being advertised are written in relation to one or another tree, or, in Morris's case, in the middle of the sun itself. In the lower left corner a scroll reads "Leek Bijou Reprints," and a similar scroll in the lower right corner "Trees of Liberty." This picture is drawn rather crudely.

The only true illustration, and allegorical at that, occupies the top part of the half-title page to the main text. It shows two knights jousting, one sprawling on the ground. The caption reads "Superstition Unhorsed by the Reprints." The picture is well executed, and suffers only from its small size.

8.3
Sold for the Benefit of Linnell's Orphans./
Alfred Linnell/ Killed in Trafalgar Square,/ November 20, 1887./
A Death Song,/
by Mr. W. Morris./
Memorial Design by Mr. Walter Crane./
Price One Penny.

Binding: No cover. The pamphlet consists of two sheets of newsprint paper folded once and stapled.

Pagination/Size: 8 / 253 x 177 mm.

Contents: P. 1 title page, pp. 2-4 account of the circumstances of Linnell's death, pp. 5-7 musical score, p. 8 text of song.

Comment: Buxton Forman reproduces the title page in his bibliography. The picture occupies much of the page. Like Morris's poem, the music printed in the pamphlet was composed for the occasion.

Illustrator: WALTER CRANE. Crane was born in Liverpool in 1845, but the family moved to Torquay the same year, and he spent his childhood there. He showed early talent and received encouragement and training in art from his father, who was also an artist. The Crane family moved to London in 1859. His father advanced Walter's art education by apprenticing him to a firm of wood engravers, with whom he spent the next three years. His firm also perceived his ability and brought him to the attention of a publisher, who commissioned him to illustrate a book in 1862. Book illustration, especially for children, remained a major activity throughout his career, and his main one in the 1860s. He had skill as a poet and illustrated some of his own writing. The creativity he showed in illustration induced businesses which required decorative work to approach him, and through the 1870s and beyond he designed patterns for an increasing range of materials, including wallpapers, friezes, stained glass, pottery, tiles, and plaster work. He found time in all this to marry Mary Frances Andrews in 1871. They had a large family and a happy relationship, though Crane's art suffered in one respect: his wife would not tolerate him painting from nude female models. As a result, his paintings which include the female nude tend to lack conviction. Nevertheless, he achieved some success in this field too.

Crane was a humanist, and this found greater focus in the early 1880s, when he joined the socialist movement. He first met Morris in 1870, and the latter was certainly influential in Crane's commitment to the cause. Thereafter he contributed his artistic talent to promoting socialism, as in the work here described. Publishers of socialist books and magazines continued to use his drawings for many years (see 10.3 and 10.5). By the late 1880s, he had achieved international recognition. Exhibitions of his work were held in America and major European cities, and he often travelled with them. In the final twenty years of his life, he became increasingly active as a teacher of art. He gave numerous lectures on its various aspects, and at different times was a director at the Manchester School of Art and Principal of the RCA. He gathered his lectures and thinking on art into a series of books, the best known of which is *The Decorative Illustration of Books* published in 1897. He died in 1915. See also 10.1, 10.3-4, 11.2-3, 11.5. (See Spencer.)

Illustration: Crane's design shows a mounted policeman with cape aflutter and truncheon raised, on a horse rearing above the prostrate body of Linnell. Justice and Liberty, personified as Greek goddesses, stand protectively on the right. As Buxton Forman puts it, "Mr. Crane triumphed over the obvious difficulty of making a mounted policeman decorative." The picture is done with the assurance one expects of Crane and provides an eye-catching element which must have greatly increased the sale of the pamphlet.

8.4a

Monopoly;/ or,/ How Labour Is Robbed./
By/ William Morris/ Author of "The Earthly Paradise."/
Price One Penny./
London:/ Office of "The Commonweal."/ 24 Great Queen Street, Lincoln's
Inn Fields, W.C./ 1890.

8.4b

Monopoly;/ or,/ How Labour Is Robbed./
By/ William Morris./
Price One Penny./
London:/ Socialist League Printery,/ 273 Hackney Road, N.E./ 1891.

Comment: The difference between these two editions lies in the title
page and publisher. The description which follows applies to both.

Binding: No cover. The pamphlet and the next entry consist of a single
sheet of newsprint paper folded twice and stapled.

Pagination/Size: 16 / 184 x 124 mm.

Contents: P. 1 title page, p. 2 illustration, pp. 3-15 text, p. 16
advertisements for socialist literature, including *Commonweal* and
Morris's *The Tables Turned.*

Comment: The paper is now becoming brittle and a bit discoloured in
copies I have examined. When Morris reprinted the pamphlet in 1893 he
did not include the cartoon.

Illustrator: Not identified. The artist identifies himself by a monogram
with indeterminate letters which could include A, H, I, and R. On the
basis of AH, I considered the possibility that it might represent the
initials of Arthur Hughes. However, Leonard Roberts, who catalogued
Hughes's works, feels that the monogram is not typical of the form used
by the artist. The letters most likely present comprise R and I, with the
others only possibilities.

Illustration and decoration: The top part of the title page has the
spirited design which Walter Crane (see 8.3) created for the pamphlets
published by the Socialist League of which this is No. 7. It is a horizontal
rectangle with a standing angel, wings outstretched, in the centre, a
panel at the mid-level proclaiming the publisher, and two brawny men
kneeling at each end, both holding a banner, one reading "Agitate" and
the other "Organize."

In his bibliography of Morris's works, Buxton Forman describes the
picture as "a hideous cartoon" (see BF page 145). He probably wrote
facetiously, for he surely recognised that a cartoon carries a message,
and the outré helps in the delivery of that message. Whoever the artist,

he knew his craft. In the foreground stands a roughly dressed, muscular man identified as "Labour." Before him lies a winding path, at the end of which grows a tree with rays emanating from it and emblazoned with the words "Fruits of Labour." An armed figure guards every turn of the path, labelled respectively "Capitalist," "Landlord," "Police," and "Soldier." The cartoon achieves its aim well. It predicts the possibility of armed struggle, promises the reward if successful, identifies the opposing forces, and indicates exactly on whom the outcome depends. Far from hideous, this cartoon is a very effective piece of propaganda, complementing Morris's text admirably.

8.5
Monopoly;/ or,/ How Labour Is Robbed./
By/ William Morris./
Price One Penny./
Office of "Freedom,"/ 127, Ossulston St., London, N.W./
London: W. Reeves,/ 83 Charing Cross Road, W.C.

Comment: Below the price the lettering is in two columns separated by a ruled line. The left column ends with "London, N.W."

Date of publication: n.d. Often given as "about 1900" by dealers.

Pagination/Size: 16 / 183 x 124 mm.

Contents: No cover. P. 1 title page, p. 2 illustration, pp. 3-15 text, p. 16 advertisements for other titles published by Reeves.

Comment: This pamphlet resembles 8.4 in paper and stapling. The text seems to have been printed from the same plates as the 1890 (though not the 1893) edition.

Illustrator: See 8.4.

Illustration and decoration: In addition to the cartoon on page 2 (see 8.4) the front cover carries a decoration which depicts a standing heroic female figure with arms raised and holding a banner reading "Vive la commune!" A worker kneels on each side. The one on the left holds aloft a flaming beacon in one hand and the pole of the banner in the other. The figure on the right holds a scythe in one hand and waves a cap with the other. At the base is an inconspicuous artist's palette and brushes, presumably to symbolise the solidarity of the artist with the workers. This decoration occupies a large part of the centre of the cover, and is flanked by two open vertical lines on each side within which is printed vertically "The 'Freedom' Library." The artist does not identify himself, nor is he credited elsewhere in the pamphlet. However, the style is very much that of Walter Crane (see 8.3). Doubt arises from the French lettering; the date of the Paris Commune, 1871, which appears in the picture close to the palette; and the French style of the cap waved by the second worker. All suggest the possibility of a French artist having drawn the picture.

The Pilgrims of Hope

8.6
The Message of the March Wind
by William Morris

Colophon/Limitation: Set in Uncial Type by Arthur Rushmore. With a drawing by Elizabeth Shippen Green. 200 Copies printed by hand at the Golden Hind Press in Madison, New Jersey. A.D. MCMXXXVIII.

Comment: Rushmore signed and numbered each copy.

Pagination/Size: [1] / 381 x 458 mm.

Contents: A single broadsheet, blank on the obverse.

Illustrator: ELIZABETH SHIPPEN GREEN. Born in Philadelphia in 1871. Her father had worked as an illustrator during the Civil War, and his interest in art influenced her early to pursue art as a career. She studied at the Philadelphia School of Fine Art and had her first work published in a magazine when only eighteen. By the time she went to study under Howard Pyle (see 11.3) at the Drexel Institute in the mid-1890s, she was employed full-time by two magazines. While at the Drexel Institute she met Jessie Wilcox and Violet Oakley, with whom she became associated professionally. The three shared a succession of studios in the Philadelphia area on a long-term basis, and all achieved widespread recognition and success. Green was best known for her magazine illustrations, and after 1902 worked exclusively for *Harper's Magazine* for many years. However, she was also a book illustrator,

the message of the march wind by william morris ❧ ❧ ❧

Fair now is the springtide, now earth lies beholding
with the eyes of a lover, the face of the sun;
long lasteth the daylight, and hope is enfolding
the green-growing acres with increase begun.

Now sweet, sweet it is through the land to be straying
'mid the birds and the blossoms and the beasts of the field;
love mingles with love, and no evil is weighing
on thy heart or mine, where all sorrow is healed.

From township to township, o'er down and by tillage
fair, far have we wandered and long was the day;
but now cometh eve at the end of the village,
where over the grey wall the church riseth grey.

There is wind in the twilight; in the white road before us
the straw from the ox-yard is blowing about;
the moon's rim is rising, a star glitters o'er us,
and the vane on the spire-top is swinging in doubt.

Down there dips the highway, toward the bridge crossing over
the brook that runs on to the Thames and the sea.
Draw closer, my sweet, we are lover and lover;
this eve art thou given to gladness and me.

Shall we be glad always? Come closer and hearken:
three fields further on, as they told me down there,
when the young moon has set, if the march sky should darken,
we might see from the hill-top the great city's glare.

Hark, the wind in the elm-boughs! from London it bloweth,
and telleth of gold, and of hope and unrest;
of power that helps not; of wisdom that knoweth,
but teacheth not aught of the worst and the best.

Of the rich men it telleth, and strange is the story
how they have, and they hanker, and grip far and wide;
and they live and they die, and the earth and its glory
has been but a burden they scarce might abide.

ELIZABETH S. GREEN
[The Village]
The Message of the March Wind, headpiece

painter in an Art Nouveau style, engraver, teacher, and block printer. She married Huger Elliott, an architect and administrator, in 1911, and moved to New York. Their commonality of interests provided a basis for a long and happy marriage. Green returned to Philadelphia only in 1951, after the death of her husband. She died there in 1954. (See Golden.)

Illustration: The sheet lacks decoration as such, but derives a decorative quality from the layout and the uncial type, seen also in the other illustrated text by Morris published by the Golden Hind Press (see 9.6). Rushmore oriented the sheet horizontally, and printed the poem in two columns. He placed Green's picture as a headpiece above the left-hand column, with the title and author immediately below it in red. The opening eight quatrains occupy the left side, and the rest the right. The colophon, also in red, sits at the end, above the signatures of artist and publisher.

Green's picture, from a black line drawing, shows, with skill and exactitude, the scene Morris describes in the fourth and fifth quatrains. We see the low stone bridge with the lovers leaning over the parapet in the left foreground, the inn with its lighted windows behind, the stream occupying much of the foreground, a clump of trees in the left mid-ground, and the crescent moon and evening star in a stormy-looking sky.

Chapter 9

A Dream of John Ball
A King's Lesson

This work originally appeared in *Commonweal* as a serial, Morris having written it to advance the socialist cause. He drew his inspiration from the Peasants' Revolt of 1381 when members of the lower orders sought social justice from the inequitable medieval society in which they lived, protesting specifically against the rapacity of state and church. John Ball is a historical figure, a priest in Kent who helped to foment the revolt. The serialised version of *John Ball* was not illustrated. When Morris published it as a book, Burne-Jones supplied a frontispiece inspired by the couplet "When Adam delved and Eve span / Who was then the gentleman?" Historians claim that these lines predate the revolt, but the peasants adopted them, and Morris uses them in his text. While the couplet asserts the equality of all men, Burne-Jones uses a literal rather than an allegorical interpretation of the subject and depicts Adam and Eve in person, rather than an episode in the story.

The only illustration which appears in any English-language edition of *John Ball* is Burne-Jones's frontispiece. The Longmans, Green Pocket Edition is the only Morris title in that series to carry illustration even though the series includes a major part of his writing.

Reeves and Turner published the first edition of *John Ball* together with *A King's Lesson*. The latter is a charming story, which seeks to deliver the socialist message as cordial rather than tonic water. At about twelve pages of text, a press with limited means could still publish it without undue difficulty. In the first edition it received no illustration. Indeed while *A King's Lesson* has been republished often, both in combination with *John Ball* and separately,

only one publisher, the Golden Hind Press, ever put out an illustrated edition. This does exclude the edition published about 1912 by James Leatham at the Cottingham Press. Leatham's edition starts with a dropped capital surrounded by a small picture of a rural scene. However, it is too general to be a true illustration of the text. The Golden Hind edition appears as the last entry in this chapter.

As with several other works by Morris (see Chapters 1, 10, 11, and 14), there exists a German edition of *John Ball* with illustration. It appeared in 1953, published in Berlin by Neues Leben. It has a binding of paper over boards with a linen spine and a pictorial front cover depicting an armed peasant. Both the stories have a woodcut engraving as frontispiece. That for *John Ball* depicts another version of the Adam and Eve couplet, while that for *A King's Lesson* shows the peasants working in the vineyard before the arrival of the king and his courtiers. The caption reads "So mühten sich alle um die Frucht, / Die sie niemals essen, und den Wien, / Den sie niemals trinken sollten." [Thus they produced the fruit they might never eat, and the wine they might never drink.] In addition, each chapter carries a decorative headpiece. The Gothic German type completes the sense of unity achieved in this book.

9.1a & b
A Dream of John Ball/ and/ A King's Lesson./
Reprinted from 'The Commonweal/ by/ William Morris,/ Author of/
"The Earthly Paradise" etc./
With an Illustration by Edward Burne-Jones./
London,/ Reeves & Turner 196 Strand./
MDCCCLXXXVIII.

9.1a Binding: Quarter-bound, with a vellum spine and marbled boards, predominantly maroon. Paper label on spine has title and author.

Comment: LeMire states that Reeves and Turner printed fifty of these large paper copies. The publisher seems to have favoured marbled boards, using them also for Morris's *Odyssey*. Morris does not appear to have shared their enthusiasm for this binding as he had his own large paper copy of *John Ball* rebound. It has the same vellum spine, but grey cloth boards decorated with tiny gold leaves.

9.1a Size: 199 x 164 mm.

9.1b Binding: Maroon cloth, plain except for a printed label on spine with title, author and price.

Comment: I have seen a copy with a variant binding. It has identical maroon cloth but the title in gilt on the upper front cover and top of spine. The author's name appears in gilt at the base of the front cover and on the spine below the title. The top edge is gilt. This binding looks original with Reeves and Turner and may represent a later impression. Alternatively, this copy may have been rebound since I do not know of any other copy with a gilt top edge.

9.1b Size: 162 x 125 mm.

9.1a & b Pagination: viii, 144.

9.1a & b Contents: Pp. i-ii blank, p. iii half-title, p. iv blank, p. v title page, p. vi blank, pp. vii-viii contents, inserted frontispiece, pp. 1-143 text, p. 144 blank, inserted sheet with advertisements on first page and obverse blank.

Comment: The two versions are identical in layout and type. However, the large paper copies have a superior binding, larger margins around the text, and are printed on handmade paper retaining its deckle edges.

Illustrator: EDWARD BURNE-JONES. See 3.1.

Illustration: This illustration needs little comment. Along with the frontispiece to *The Wood beyond the World*, it is one of Burne-Jones's best-known book illustrations. The caption comes from the text. As it suggests, it portrays Eve spinning, with Cain and Abel at her feet and

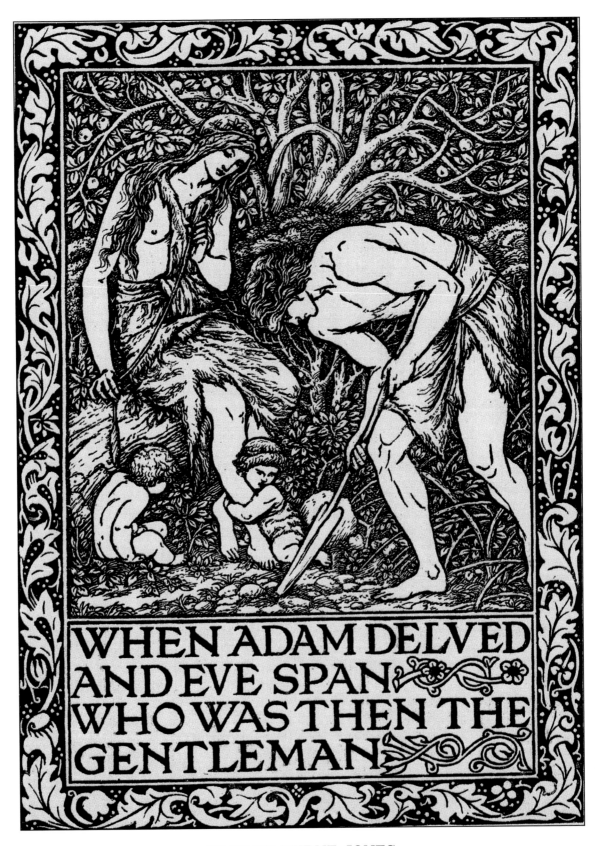

WHEN ADAM DELVED
AND EVE SPAN
WHO WAS THEN THE
GENTLEMAN

EDWARD BURNE-JONES
A Dream of John Ball, **frontispiece**

Adam digging the ground in front of them. Adam and Eve's labour and their clothed state place them outside the Garden. However, the apple tree remains symbolically in the background. The picture is a masterly composition, with a message surprising from Burne-Jones, who was not in sympathy with Morris's socialist views.

9.2
A Dream of John Ball and/ A King's Lesson.
By William/ Morris.   [Half title]

Colophon: This book, a Dream of John Ball and a King's Lesson, was written by William Morris, and printed by him at the Kelmscott Press, Upper Mall, Hammersmith, in the County of Middlesex; and finished on the 13th day of May, 1892. Sold by Reeves and Turner, 196, Strand, London.

Limitation: [300 copies on hand-made paper and 6 on vellum].

Binding/Contents: Full limp vellum with two ties, the title in gilt horizontally on spine.

Pagination/Size: [8] [iv] 124 [4] / 200 x 143 mm.

Contents: Pp. 1-8 blank, p. i half-title, pp. ii-iii blank, p. iv frontispiece, pp. 1-111 text of *John Ball*, p. 112 blank, pp. 113-123 text of *A King's Lesson* with colophon on last page, p. 124 and pp. 1-4 blank.

Illustrator: EDWARD BURNE-JONES. See 3.1.

Illustration and decoration: The frontispiece of 9.1 reappears in this edition as a wood engraving with the lettering rearranged and included within the border of the picture, which looks better in this state than in its original one. The frontispiece occupies a much larger area of the page than does the first page of text facing it. As a result Morris's floral and leafy border around both pages is much narrower where it surrounds the picture. This lack of symmetry creates an unbalanced look to the double spread. *A King's Lesson* also has a decorative border around the first page of text, but a blank page facing it. Here again it leaves a sense of imbalance. Each chapter starts with a large decorated and dropped capital. Smaller but similar capitals appear at the start of many of the paragraphs. The whole word which follows is capitalised, as are other words at intervals to supply extra emphasis. The chapter numbers and headings are in red. Each page of text has a shoulder note, also in red, giving the chapter heading. Beyond this Morris employed red for the couplet where it appears in the text, though not when it appears as the caption for the frontispiece. Finally, his use of the Golden type for the text adds a further decorative dimension in itself.

9.3a & b
A Dream of John Ball/ and A King's Lesson/
by William Morris/
Longmans, Green, and Co./ 39 Paternoster Row, London/ New York & Bombay/ 1903

Comment: From the 1907 issue onwards the cities listed on the title page in which the publisher maintained an office include Calcutta.

9.3a Dates of publication: January 1903, June 1907, January 1910, and January 1912.

9.3a Binding: Plain maroon buckram, with paper label on top of spine lettered with title, author, and publisher. Top edge gilt.

9.3b Date of publication: March 1903.

9.3b Limitation (in part): 250 copies reprinted on hand-made paper, March 1903.

9.3b Binding: Blue paper boards with linen spine. Title and author in black on paper label on upper spine. Edges untrimmed.

9.3a Pagination/Size: viii, 170 [2] / 149 x 117 mm.

9.3b Pagination/Size: [4] viii, 170 [6] / 161 x 117 mm.

9.3a & b Contents: Pp. 1-4 (9.3b only) blank, p. i half-title, pp. ii-iii blank, p. iv frontispiece with tissue guard, p. v title page, p. vi publication history, pp. vii-viii contents, pp. 1-153 text of *John Ball*, p. 154 blank, p. 155 half-title of *A King's Lesson*, p. 156 blank, pp. 157-169 text of *A King's Lesson*, p. 170 address of printer, pp. 1-2 (9.3a) and pp. 1-6 (9.3b) blank.

Illustrator: EDWARD BURNE-JONES. See 3.1.

Illustration: Like the KP edition (see 9.2) this book uses a wood engraving of Burne-Jones's picture, recut to fit the smaller size of this edition. This entails some loss of clarity and detail, and the illustration suffers further from the much lighter ink. This version does not include the caption in the engraving. It appears below as printed lettering, thus reverting to the layout of the first edition in this respect. The floral border is also absent.

9.4
A Dream of John Ball/ and A King's Lesson/
by William Morris/
Pocket Edition/
Longmans, Green and Co./ 39 Paternoster Row, London/ New York, Bombay, and Calcutta/ 1913

Comment: The publisher's address and the list of cities in which they had an office vary in later reprints.

Dates of publication: <u>September 1913</u>, July 1918, <u>April 1920</u>, <u>April 1924</u>, and <u>January 1928</u>.

Binding: Deluxe. Olive-green leather, covers plain, title and author at top of spine, publisher at base. Rest of spine decorated with galleon seen from the front and leafy stems below, all in gilt. Top edge gilt, silk bookmark of same colour as cover.

Comment: This description applies to a single copy of the 1928 reprint. A leather-bound copy dated 1914 of a different title in the series has a decoration on the upper left of the front cover, stamped in gilt. It consists of a galleon under full sail with a low sun behind it casting long rays across the background, all enclosed in a circle from which hangs a swirling pattern suggestive of fabric. Probably earlier impressions of *John Ball* have this same design.

Binding: Standard. Bottle-green cloth over boards, covers plain except for decoration described above blind-stamped on front cover. Same lettering and decoration in gilt on spine as in deluxe version. Top edge gilt and green silk bookmark in 1913 impression only.

Comment: I have not seen a copy complete with its dust-jacket. The jackets of *The Story of the Glittering Plain* also published in 1913 and *The Water of the Wondrous Isles* published in 1914 in the Pocket Library series are of grey matte paper with Gere's picture (see 10.2) of Kelmscott Manor on the front, below the title, with the author at the base. The back cover carries a list of other titles in the series. In view of the irrelevance of this picture to these two stories it seems likely that Longmans used this one cover for all the titles in the series, including *John Ball.*

Pagination/Size: viii, 184 / 156 x 101 mm.

Contents: Pp. i-ii advertisements, p. iii blank, p. iv frontispiece with tissue guard, p. v title page, p. vi publication history, p. vii contents, p. viii blank, pp. 1-184 text.

Comment: The 1913 version differs most strikingly from the later ones in its greater thickness, 12 mm. against 9 mm. It reflects the heavier matte paper of the former. The advertisements for other works by Morris differ in minor respects from one reprint to another. On the title page the words "New Impression" appear below "Pocket Edition," with the later dates of publication given at the bottom of the page.

Illustrator: EDWARD BURNE-JONES. See 3.1.

Illustration: Longmans use the version of the engraving originally seen in 9.3.

9.5a & b
A Dream of John Ball/ and A King's Lesson/
by William Morris/
with Frontispiece/
Longmans, Green and Co./ London. New York. Toronto

Dates of publication: <u>March 1933</u> [HL], <u>January 1936</u>, and April 1938.

9.5a Binding: Yellow dust jacket with ruled black lines close to and paralleling the edges of front cover. Swan emblem at top, with "The Swan Library" below it, and title at mid-level, author at bottom. On spine, title and author at top, swan at mid-level, and publisher at base, all in black lettering. Back cover plain except for country of origin at base in tiny letters. Front flap blank, back flap has list of other titles in series.

Bound in black buckram, swan blind-stamped on lower right corner of front cover. Same emblem at base of spine above name of publisher, with title and author at top, all in gilt. Plain else.

Comment: This book is No. 13 in the Swan Library series, all the volumes of which have a standard format.

9.5b Binding: Limp grey matte paper, title at top of front cover, author at base, same picture as frontispiece between them, all enclosed by thick ruled line. Title and author vertically on spine, price at lower left corner of back cover. Plain else. Printing in dark brown throughout.

Pagination/Size: viii, 184 / 172 x 113 mm.

Contents: P. i blank, p. ii list of advertisements, p. iii decorated half-title, p. iv publisher's address, inserted frontispiece with tissue guard, p. v title page, p. vi publication history, p. vii contents, p. viii blank, pp. 1-184 text.

Illustrator: EDWARD BURNE-JONES. See 3.1.

Illustration and decoration: The publisher placed the swan emblem at the top of the half-title page. It also appears twice on the facing page at the top of the list of advertisements. The version of the frontispiece is that which Longmans previously used in 9.3.

9.6
A King's Lesson,
by William Morris/
Printed to Commemorate the Centenary/ of the Birth of William Morris, 1834-1934/
with a Woodcut by Charles W. Smith

Colophon/Limitation: A King's Lesson by William Morris was set in Hammer Uncial type and one hundred and forty-five copies printed by hand on Arak paper by Arthur W. Rushmore at the Golden Hind Press in Madison, New Jersey.
Finished on December the first MCMXXXIV. Copy number *65*

Binding: Dark blue paper over boards with uncoloured linen spine. Author and title separated by a fleuron vertically on spine on paper label.

Pagination/Size: [viii] 18 [6] / 209 x 159 mm.

Contents: Pp. i-v blank, p. vi frontispiece, p. vii title page, p. viii blank, pp. 1-18 text, p. 1 colophon, pp. 2-6 blank.

Illustrator: CHARLES WILLIAM SMITH. Born in Virginia in 1893. He studied at the Corcoran School of Art in Washington, and in Paris. He was known primarily as a painter and teacher. However, he also authored a book on block printing published in 1925, and wrote and illustrated several works delineating features of his native Virginia. He died in Virginia in 1987.

Illustration and decoration: The lettering of the title page occupies four lines of closely set type, all in red, with fleurons after the name of the author and at the end. Rushmore placed it at the top, leaving the rest of the page blank, with pleasing effect. He used red ink also for the colophon. He placed a monochrome brown picture of a ship under full sail at the mid-level of this page, with his signature between the two. The text is in black throughout, decorated with an initial dropped capital, and a fleuron separates each paragraph from the next.

The illustration comprises a woodblock frontispiece, but it does contain two panels. One depicts the elegance of palace life, with the king sitting in council surrounded by his courtiers in a tiled hall with arched windows. The lower half finds him learning a more profound lesson in the vineyard. Hoe in hand, he talks to the headman while one courtier lies exhausted full length on the ground beside them and another sits slumped further back. The picture, printed in yellow and black, summarises the whole story. It has the limitations imposed by the medium, but it is competently done and pleasing, with the humour inherent in the situation well caught by the artist.

Chapter 10

News from Nowhere

Like *A Dream of John Ball*, *News from Nowhere* first appeared in *Commonweal* in serialised form to promote the socialist cause. However, *News from Nowhere* retained greater popularity than *John Ball*. This may reflect its appeal to a disparate readership, those with an interest in Utopias, fantasy enthusiasts to some extent, and socialists in particular, since it seeks to show one form a society could take under a socialist system. Publishers have responded with frequent new editions, though few such editions contain illustrations. *News* was first published in book form by Roberts Brothers of Boston. They brought it out in October 1890, the same month that Morris published the last episode of the serialised version in *Commonweal*. Roberts must have had had the type set up as each episode appeared, so that they had little further type-setting to do when they received the last instalment. In spite of their claim, Morris had not authorised this edition, and it lacks the revisions he made for his own edition, which Reeves and Turner published the following year. This latter book was, however, quite without illustration. Morris's next edition came from the KP, and he did illustrate it, with the picture of Kelmscott Manor which is now so well known and which has become associated as well with *Gossip about an Old House* (see Chapter 16). Appendix 1 lists paperback editions which use this and other pictures as cover illustration.

The first German language translation of *News from Nowhere* appeared in 1892-93, in serialised form, in *Die neue Zeit*, under the title *Kunde von Nirgendwo*. *Die neue Zeit* [The New Time] was a socialist magazine published during the 1890s at a time when the socialist movement was very strong in Germany. The publisher obtained illustrations for

their translation from Hans Gabriel Jentzsch. J.H.W. Dietz of Stuttgart put out the novel in book form in 1900, reprinting it in 1914, but with only a selection of the pictures. In New York another socialist magazine began publication in 1901 under the name of *The Comrade*. While its aims were the same as its German counterpart, it was superior in the quality of paper and the range and amount of its design and illustration. In the first two volumes, the editors printed their own serialised version of *News from Nowhere* and obtained Jentzsch's pictures to illustrate it. They did not acknowledge their source. However, they had probably obtained the artist's acquiescence. One picture contains words in English, "caviar" and "alcohol," rather than "Kaviar" and "Alkohol," suggesting that Jentzsch modified this illustration for the English text. The appearance of these pictures in *The Comrade* represents the only time they have been reproduced in an English language edition. Beyond this the only other edition with illustration re-used the picture of Kelmscott Manor which first appeared in the KP edition.

Like *Commonweal, The Comrade* sought to promote the socialist cause on an ongoing basis. In its original form *The Comrade* appeared as a monthly magazine printed on a fairly good quality of machine-made paper. Some covers have colour printing, and for these the publisher used shiny paper. In this form the magazine would not be durable, and the publisher clearly put out some copies as bound volumes incorporating twelve issues complete with half-title page giving the time spanned by the volume, a list of contributors, and an index subdivided by categories (stories, poems, articles, cartoons, illustrations, and portraits). The magazines not only feature art and graphic work of high quality but are well laid out generally and would have attracted a readership by their literary content. They numbered such notables of the time as Sarah Bernhardt among their contributors.

10.1a

News from Nowhere;/ or,/ An Epoch of Rest./ Being Some Chapters from a Utopian/ Romance./
By/ William Morris,/ Author of The Earthly Paradise," "The Life and Death of Jason,"
"The Defence of Guenevere and Other Poems," "Love Is/ Enough,"
"The Story of Sigurd the Volsung," "The/ House of the Wolfings,"
"Hopes and Fears for/ Art," "The Aeneids of Virgil Done/ into English Verse"/
Boston:/ Roberts Brothers./ 1890.

Comment: The quotation marks which should precede "The Earthly Paradise" are absent on the original title page, as given above.

Dates of publication (according to Pye): October 1890, July 1891, November 1892, January 1894, and November 1897, the last with the date 1898 on the title page.

Comment: These dates, obtained partly from Pye, may include the editions of other publishers who obtained sheets of *News from Nowhere* from Roberts Brothers and bound them under their own imprint. See 10.1b, c, & d below.

Binding (1890): Dark red cloth over boards, title on upper front cover and top of spine, author at mid-level of spine and at base of cover, with publisher's monogram at base of spine. On middle of front cover, all in gilt, embellished globe reproduced from frontispiece. Endpapers have a light net-like pattern in beige.

Binding (1898): Dark red cloth over boards, plain except for a paper label on top of spine with title, author and publisher "Longmans." Top edge gilt. Endpapers plain.

Comment: In 1899 Longmans acquired the electroplates previously used by Roberts Brothers to produce their editions of works by Morris. Longmans probably got unbound sheets as well. The title page of the 1898 reprint retains the listing of Roberts as publisher. However, Longmans' name on the label on the spine, the cover (a standard Longmans binding at that time), and the advertisements for other titles by Longmans all indicate Longmans bound the book, probably using leftover sheets rather than ones new printed. Thus the book may have appeared a little later than the stated date.

10.1b Note: LeMire states that the Twentieth Century Publishing Company of New York bought unbound sheets of *News from Nowhere* from Roberts Brothers and issued an edition with their own imprint in April 1891 (LeMire A-50.03). I have never seen a copy or any other reference to this edition.

10.1c

News from Nowhere;/ or,/ An Epoch of Rest./ Being Some Chapters from a Utopian/ Romance./
By/ William Morris,/ Author of "The Earthly Paradise," "The Life and Death of Jason,"/ "The Defence of Guenevere and Other Poems," "Love Is/ Enough," "The Story of Sigurd the Volsung," "The/ House of the Wolfings," "Hopes and Fears for/ Art," "The Aeneids of Virgil Done/ into English Verse."/
New York:/ The Humboldt Publishing Co./ 19 Astor Place. [HL]

Comment: Humboldt later issued their own edition, with different binding, title page, and pagination. This later edition does not contain illustration.

Date of publication: n.d. "1892" [HL].

Binding: Rust-red cloth over boards. Front and back covers blind-stamped with three ruled parallel lines close to edges. Corners of inner line cut diagonally. In each corner a stylised rose. Title in gilt on upper spine. Endpapers a similar colour to those of 10.1a but with pattern of tiny, close-set leaves and flowers.

10.1d

News from Nowhere/ or/ An Epoch of Rest/ Being Some Chapters from/ a Utopian Romance/
by/ William Morris/ Author of The Earthly Paradise"/
New Impression/ Longmans, Green and Co./ 91 and 93 Fifth Avenue, New York/ London and Bombay/ 1901 [HL]

Comment: The address of the publisher varies in some of the reprints.

Dates of publication: <u>1901</u>, 1903, 1907, <u>1910</u> [HL] <u>1913</u> [HL] <u>1917</u>, and 1920.

Comment: Longmans, Green used Roberts Brothers electroplates to produce these reprints of *News from Nowhere*.

Binding: Dark red buckram, plain except for a paper label on the spine lettered with title, author and publisher. Top edge gilt in issues up to 1913.

10.1a, c & d Size: 177 x 115 mm.

Comment: The 1917 issue is slightly larger at 185 x 122 mm.

10.1a Pagination (1890): [2] vi, 278 [2], 8 [2].
   Pagination (1898): [2] vi, 278 [6] [2].

10.1c Pagination: vi, 278 [8].

10.1d Pagination: vi, 278 [4].

Comment: The Arabic numerals of the text follow on from the Roman numerals of the preliminary pages.

10.1a, c & d Contents: Pp. 1-2 blank (10.1a only), p. i half-title, p. ii frontispiece with tissue guard, p. iii title page, p. iv printer's address and claim of author's acquiescence, pp. v-vi contents, pp. 7-278 text.

Comment: Following the end of the text on page 278 the content of the final pages differs between 10.1a, c & d as given below.
10.1a (1890): Pp. 1-2 advertisements, pp. 1-8 review reprinted from *The Athenaeum* of *The House of the Wolfings*, pp. 1-2 blank.
(1898): Pp. 1-6 advertisements, pp. 1-2 blank.
10.1c: P. 1 blank, pp. 2-8 advertisements.
10.1d: Pp. 1-2 advertisements, pp. 3-4 blank.

Comment: As one might expect when printing from the same electroplates, every detail of typography stays the same from one printing to another. This extends even to such minor errors as the missing quotation marks before the "The" of *The Earthly Paradise* in the list of Morris's other works on the title page. John Wilson and the University Press, Cambridge, Massachusetts, printed all editions. For their edition Humboldt obtained a heavier matte paper than that used by Roberts and their edition is correspondingly thicker. A later issue of 10.1c does not include the frontispiece.

The later issues of 10.1d have minor differences in the title page, the most noticeable being the publisher's change of address in 1910 and 1913. It reads "Fourth Avenue & 30th Street, New York/ London, Bombay and Calcutta." In 1917 the New York address remains the same, but below it Longmans add their London address "39 Paternoster Row, London/ Bombay, Calcutta, and Madras/ 1917." All issues lack the vignette on the title page of the Roberts Brothers edition, and the tissue guard over the frontispiece.

Illustrator: WALTER CRANE. See 8.3.

Illustration and decoration: A vignette appears on the title page above the name of the publisher. A circle encloses a picture of a child sitting on the globe, a large book on his knee and the inscription in the lower part "Qui legit, regit." ["He who reads rules."] Roberts had used almost the same device in the second state of their edition of *Love Is Enough* of 1873. There the vignette faces the title page and depicts a cherub with a halo, wings and staff. Presumably Roberts sought a more secular image for the more secular *News from Nowhere*. The cherub looks altogether more suited to announce that love is not enough in the secular heaven proclaimed by the text which follows.

As with *John Ball*, the illustration, limited to a frontispiece, does not portray the text directly, but only in an allegorical sense. The globe encircled by a banner reading "Solidarity of Labour" on the front cover of the 1890 edition appears again, this time surrounded by five workers with hands joined, each emblematic of one of the five continents, identified by a scroll. Below them are tools used in a wide range of trades. Above, a winged and helmeted female figure with arms outstretched symbolises "Fraternity," "Freedom," and "Equality," also on scrolls. Crane did the picture with his usual bravura. While it has vibrant inspirational value, it does not in any way suggest to the reader the idyllic future Morris seeks to present in his text.

10.2
News from Nowhere: or,/ An Epoch of Rest, Being Some/ Chapters from a Utopian Ro-/mance,
by William Morris   [Half-title]

Colophon: This book, News From Nowhere or an Epoch of Rest, was written by William Morris, and printed by him at the Kelmscott Press, Upper Mall, Hammersmith, in the County of Middlesex, and finished on the 22nd day of November, 1892. Sold by Reeves & Turner, 196 Strand, London.

Limitation: [300 copies on hand-made paper and 10 on vellum].

Binding: Full limp vellum with two ties, title and author in gilt on top of spine.

Pagination/Size: [6] [vi] 306 [10] / 205 x 140 mm.

Contents: Pp. 1-6 blank, p. i half-title, p. ii blank, pp. iii-iv contents, p. v blank, p. vi frontispiece, pp. 1-305 text, p. 306 colophon, pp. 1-10 blank.

Illustrator: CHARLES MARCH GERE. Born in Gloucester in 1869. He studied and later taught at the Birmingham School of Art and also studied in Italy. His artistic activity spanned work as a watercolourist, portrait painter, and book illustrator. He exhibited at the RA and was elected to it in 1939. He died in Gloucestershire in 1957. See also 16.1-5; 18.7o; Appendix 2.

Illustration and decoration: As with all KP publications, one can see every aspect of this book as decorative, from cover to print on the page. The first decoration as such appears on the title page, where frontispiece and initial page of text have one of Morris's floral borders. Strictly speaking they have two, since the border around the frontispiece has a different form from that around the facing text. The feeling of imbalance discussed in connection with the comparable double spread of *John Ball* (see 9.2) does not intrude here, partly because the borders are closer in size, and partly because of their very difference in pattern. There is no sense that two identical halves failed to get matched. Each chapter starts with a large decorated and dropped capital, and many smaller but otherwise similar capitals appear at the start of paragraphs. Morris marked the start of other paragraphs with a device resembling a backward facing letter D. He used red ink only for the heading of the chapter, the rest in black, but did use red too for the shoulder notes on each page, which provide a headline for the main event on the page. The text is in the Golden type. This least ornate of all the KP types seems entirely appropriate for a book with the subject matter it has.

Morris limited illustration to the frontispiece wood engraving of Kelmscott Manor. The caption is incorporated within the border and reads, "This is the picture of the old house by the Thames to which the people of this story went. Hereafter follows the book itself which is called News from Nowhere or An Epoch of Rest & is written by William Morris." The picture is a skilfully executed rendition of the north face of the Manor. The subject is particularly fitting, in that the story ends with the Guest approaching the house, approaching indeed a state of perfection, which the house symbolised to Morris in his own life and thoughts. In his picture Gere catches something of the atmosphere that must have endeared the house to Morris. He has birds flying overhead and fruit trees growing alongside the path which leads to the door, while the crowns of other trees poke above the rooftop. In all these ways Gere evokes the oneness of the man-made structure with the natural world around it, surely the basis for Morris's attachment to the Manor.

10.3
News from Nowhere/ or: An Epoch of Rest/ Being Some Chapters From a Utopian Romance./
By William Morris.
[Serialised in] The Comrade/ An Illustrated/ Socialist/ Monthly
[Vols. 1 and 2, New York, October 1901-September 1903].

Binding: Finely stippled bottle-green cloth over boards. Pictorial design on front cover, back cover plain. Title, volume number, and publisher gilt-stamped on spine.

Size: 303 x 227 mm.

Pagination: Vol. 1: pp. 26-30, 61-62, 86-88, 109-111, 137-139, 160-162, 182-184, 206-208, 232-235, 255-258, 277-281.
    Vol. 2: pp. 12-16, 38-42, 64-67, 87-90, 110-114, 130-133, 158-162, 181-185.

Contents: See above under pagination.

Illustrators: WALTER CRANE. See 8.3.
    HANS GABRIEL JENTZSCH. Born in Dresden, Germany, in 1862. He studied at the Dresden Academy between 1881 and 1887 and moved to Munich in 1889 then to Pasing, outside Munich, in 1903. He was known as a painter, graphic artist, book illustrator, and caricaturist. He demonstrated his skill in all of the last three fields in the work under discussion. Another of his books is *Ein neuer Totentanz in achtzehn Bildern* [A New Dance of Death in Eighteen Pictures] published in 1904. He died in 1930 in Munich a month short of attaining 68 years.

Illustrations and decoration: The front cover of the bound volumes has a picture of a heroic female figure in flowing draperies with arms raised to shoulder height stamped in red on the front cover. The right hand holds a pointed staff, from which a large banner streaming in the wind contains the name of the magazine. From the left hand falls a shower, in the midst of which is the word "Socialism." "Socialism" also appears in the half-risen sun in the background, between the staff and the figure's hip. In the lower left corner is the proclamation "Life Labor Literature Art." Walter Crane drew the picture and it is signed by him. The whole design is enclosed by a thick black line which runs close to the edges of the cover.

In these magazines *News* shares in the overall decorative scheme seen throughout. The designers used decoration more freely in the second volume, where they placed head- or tailpieces in relation to a few episodes. These depict landscapes of a general nature, not specifically relating to the text. They also used two of Crane's designs, one as a headpiece for the section which starts on page 64 of the second volume. Crane created it as a trade union banner. Each of its two halves shows a standing majestic female figure with workmen clustered around

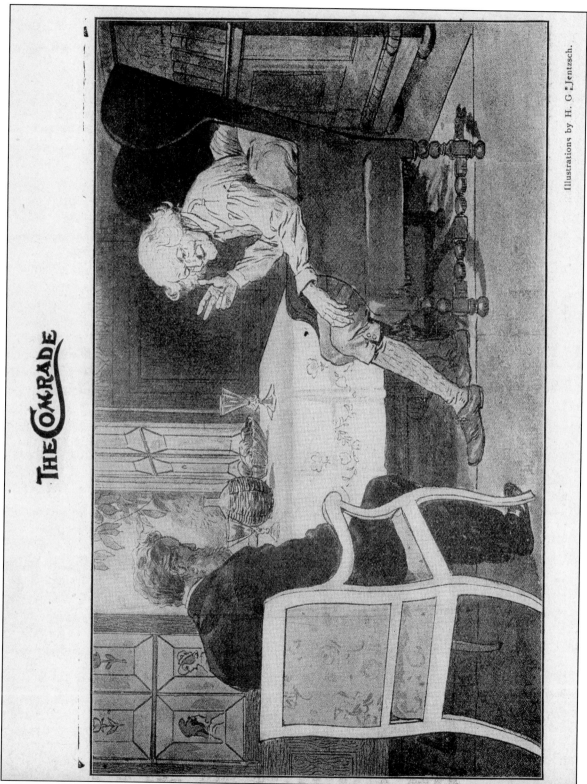

Illustrations by H. G. Jentzsch.

HANS GABRIEL JENTZSCH
[The Guest Talks with Old Hammond]
News from Nowhere (The Comrade, Vol. 1, p. 207)

acclaiming her and scrolls identifying the aspirations of the organisation. Crane's other design forms a tailpiece for the final section, another female figure and banner. Dropped and decorated capitals at the start of the chapters are also unique to the second volume. In both volumes, the first more than the second, some pictures have an appropriate border, fish for men in a rowing boat, a shelf of books for Guest in the opening scene where he discusses politics with his friends, and so on.

Jentzsch's pictures provide the most profusely illustrated editions of *News from Nowhere* ever published. Each of the nineteen episodes in *The Comrade* contains at least one illustration depicting a scene from the adjacent text. In addition to two illustrations, the first section also has an illustrative headpiece by Jentzsch.

Jentzsch had considerable technical skill and depicted a wide range of indoor and outdoor scenes with excellent composition of figures, Morris clearly recognisable in many of them. His pictures come from the mainstream artistic trends of the time, with none of the innovation of Armfield's work twenty years later (see 3.3). Thus these illustrations have a dated quality, though possessing great charm. His portrayal of the female figure is particularly good. Many of his pictures bring to mind advertisements of the period, and he may have done some commercial work. Their deficiency lies more in Jentzsch's failure to reinforce Morris's text. Morris's vision is one of a simple life close to the natural order. Jentzsch aims "to the top of every tree raise everybody." Most of his pictures show people in a style of life accessible to the tiny minority in the upper classes. The women wear rich full-length dresses; the men look elegant in tights reminiscent of the medieval era. Indoor scenes depict walls of dressed stone, extensive vistas, graceful colonnades, and fine fabrics, furniture, and wall hangings. Where Jentzsch portrayed work in progress, a group of young women raking grass for hay, there is no suggestion of the effort necessarily involved in the task. In one picture he gave rein to his talent for caricature, lampooning capitalists suppressing workers. This illustration is most effective, and has the lasting appeal of that form.

10.4a & b
**News from Nowhere/ An Epoch of Rest/ Being Some Chapters
From a Utopian/ Romance/**
by William Morris/
New York/ Vanguard Press/ MCMXXVI

10.4a Binding: Dust jacket not examined. Lime-green cloth over
boards, printing in dark blue. Front cover plain but for central diamond-
shaped emblem. On spine author at top, between sets of ruled lines, all
horizontal, one with dentelles. Title at mid-level between plain ruled
lines, and publisher at base. Back cover plain. Pictorial endpapers.

10.4b Binding: Light brown dust jacket with dark brown type. Two ruled
lines on front cover close to edges enclosing title and author at top, a
promotional text below them, and publisher at bottom. Title and author
at top of spine, price at mid-level and publisher's emblem at base, a
striding man in silhouette holding a staff in one hand and a book in the
other. On back cover a design by Walter Crane which also decorates the
endpapers. Flaps have promotional material about books from the Press.
Bound in finely stippled yellow cloth over boards, with title and author
at top of front cover and spine, emblem of striding man on cover at mid-
level, and publisher's monogram at base, all stamped in navy blue.

10.4a & b Size: 177 x 105 mm.

10.4a Pagination: 258.

Comment: The publisher mis-numbered the pages, which actually total
256.

10.4a Contents: Pp. 1-2 absent (see above), p. 3 title page, p. 4 publisher's
notes on Morris and on *News*, p. 5 contents, p. 6 frontispiece, pp. 7-258
text.

Comment: 10.4a and b have similar preliminary pages, but arranged
differently.

10.4b Pagination: vi, 258.

10.4b Contents: Inserted frontispiece, p. i title page, p. ii statement about
printer, p. iii notes as on p. 4 of 10.4a, p. iv blank, pp. v-vi contents, pp.
7-258 text.

Comment: The editor adopts American spelling, *neighbor* for *neighbour*
and the like.

Illustrator: CHARLES M. GERE. See 10.2.

Illustration: The emblem on the front cover of 10.4a comprises a man
front on, arms by his sides holding what may be a short-handled spade.

Flames rise behind his head. "V" and "P" stand on either side of the figure. The endpapers carry two of Crane's designs in red monochrome. On the fixed endpapers, both front and back, Vanguard re-used the design which had previously decorated the cover of the bound copies of *The Comrade* (10.3). The publisher modified the picture by changing the banner to read "Vanguard Press," and the bubble at the base to "The Vanguard of Thought for the Vanguard of Humanity." On the free endpapers is another female figure, also by Crane, arms raised above her head, her right hand holding a flaming torch.

The publisher used the frontispiece originally done for the Kelmscott edition (10.2), retaining Morris's border and the caption it also encloses. It is thus identical in every respect except for the smaller size required by this book. The reproduction is rather dark and loses some of the detail seen in the Kelmscott version.

10.5
News from Nowhere/ or/ An Epoch of Rest,/ Being Some Chapters/ from a Utopian/ Romance/
William Morris/
edited by Stephen Arata/
Broadview Literary Texts

Statement of publication (in part): Copyright 2003 . . . Published in Peterborough, Ontario.

Binding: Paperback with thick flexible cover carrying picture. Title and author in plain white rectangle superimposed at mid-level, right side. Spine in black with author, editor, title, and publisher in white. Back cover has information about editor and book itself. Inside of covers blank.

Pagination/Size: 356 [4] / 217 x 137 mm.

Contents: Inside of cover faces page 1 directly. P. 1 half-title, p. 2 blank, p. 3 full title page, p. 4 publication information, p. 5 editor's dedication, p. 6 blank, pp. 7-9 contents, p. 10 blank, pp. 11-44 introduction, pp. 45-48 chronology of Morris's life, p. 49 note on text, p. 50 frontispiece, p. 51 title page to text, p. 52 blank, pp. 53-249 text, p. 250 photograph of Kelmscott Manor, pp. 251-352 appendices, pp. 353-356 bibliography, pp. 1-4 blank.

Comment: This edition contains extensive editorial coverage, with an overview of Morris's writings on art, social questions, and politics, comment on other Utopias, an account of the riots in Trafalgar Square in 1887, and contemporary comments on them from various sources.

Illustrator: Charles M. Gere. See 10.2.

Illustrations: The picture on the front cover shows the face of Big Ben seen from behind at an oblique angle. Gere's frontispiece reproduces the engraving which originally appeared in the KP edition, complete with the border. The photograph which follows the text depicts an identical view of the Manor. In addition, a further picture follows Appendix E, in which various writers comment on the riots in Trafalgar Square on November 13, 1887. The illustration, from the *Illustrated London News*, shows the riot at its height, workers confronting mounted policemen.

Chapter 11

The Story of the Glittering Plain

One could argue that Morris was writing works of fantasy divorced from any historical period with his very first pieces in *The Oxford and Cambridge Magazine*. However, they pale beside the spate of full-length novels in this genre which flowed from his pen in the late 1880s and 1890s, beginning with *The Roots of the Mountains* and *The Story of the Glittering Plain*. The latter has the additional distinction of being the first book Morris published at his Kelmscott Press in 1891. It was not illustrated, but Morris remedied this deficiency by republishing it as an illustrated edition three years later. Since then illustrators have largely ignored it, though it reappeared before the public with the Dover Publications facsimile of 1987 (see 15.4) and more recently in other paperback editions, such as that from the Wildside Press (see Appendix 1).

The Story of the Glittering Plain first appeared as a serial in *The English Illustrated Magazine*. This periodical began in the later part of the Victorian era and went on well into the twentieth century. Articles covering a wide range of topics, travel, descriptions of British and foreign localities and institutions, history, and art among others, appeared in its pages. Fiction and poetry were also regular features. It had many illustrations in the body of its texts, and used headpieces for nearly every article and tailpieces less often. In the bound volume which contains *The Glittering Plain*, most of the headpieces are decorative. A significant minority depict a scene, but most have no obvious relation to the text. However, an article on Cowes Castle follows a headpiece containing ships, which could be intended to evoke the Cowes Regatta; a headpiece with a caption from a Christmas carol precedes a poem called Yule Tide; an article on Saint Michael's Mount is headed by

a pastoral scene perhaps intended to bring the neighbouring Cornwall countryside to mind. It remains uncertain whether MacMillan used these pictures for their specific illustrative content or whether they appear where they do by happenstance. The weight of probability lies with coincidence, but the possibility remains that it is otherwise. This version of *The Glittering Plain* is therefore included in this chapter on the basis of that possibility.

I mentioned a German translation of some of Morris's works previously (see introduction to Chapter 1). The other illustrated book in this group, *The Glittering Plain*, was published in 1985, with the title *Das schimmernde Land* (HL). The cover carries a detail from Frank Cadogan Cowper's painting *La Belle Dame sans Merci*. More importantly, Johann Peterka supplied a series of line drawings to illustrate the text. Each of Peterka's pictures has a Kelmscott-like border, the same for each drawing, which includes a raven and flowers. His style is reminiscent of Crane's pictures for this work (see 11.2). However, Peterka got more vigour into his illustrations. While they suffer from their small size (they occupy barely a quarter of the page of a book measuring only 179 x 115 mm.), they are the redeeming feature of an otherwise undistinguished publication.

As with *Over Sea* (see Introduction to Chapter 14) the sequence of this chapter follows the order of titles established by Buxton Forman, who lists *The Glittering Plain* after *News from Nowhere*, even though the former work appeared the year before.

11.1
The Glittering Plain; or, The Land of Living/ Men./
By William Morris, Author of "The Earthly Paradise."
[Serialised in] The English/ Illustrated Magazine/ 1889-1890/
London/ Macmillan and Co./ and New York/ 1890

Binding: Lime-green boards, with title on upper spine, year at mid-level, and publisher at base, all in gilt. All else in black. Floral border around edges of front and back covers, with semi-circles at mid-point of each side enclosing a fan-like pattern. Title on upper front cover inside the border. Decorated medallion below title and on middle of back cover includes letter M.

Comment: MacMillan put out bound copies covering a year's issues, as did the publishers of *The Comrade* later (see 10.3). The description applies to the bound volume.

Pagination/Size: Pp. 687-698, 754-768, 824-838, 884-900 / 247 x 162 mm.

Contents: See above under pagination.

Illustrators: WALTER CRANE. See 8.3.
    HENRY RYLAND. Born in Bigglesward, England, in 1856. He studied under Benjamin Constant, Boulanger, and Lefebvre, and exhibited at the London galleries from 1890 on. He died in London in 1924.
    "FLS" or possibly "AS." Not identified.

Illustrations: In common with the rest of the pieces in the bound volume, each section starts with a dropped and decorated capital. The illustrations consist of a headpiece for each of the four episodes and a tailpiece for the first. To a large extent they are decorative, or at the most symbolic. The first, by "FLS," shows two seated female figures identified as "Good and Evil Report," both blowing a trumpet. From the mouth of the trumpet of the attractive-looking figure emerges a shower of garden petals and blooms. Weeds spew from the trumpet of the ugly figure. Chapter 2, entitled "Evil Tidings Come to Hand," describes how Hallblithe hears the news of the abduction of the Hostage. One can therefore see the picture as an allegorical representation of this event, though the relevance of the "good" report is obscure. Walter Crane's tailpiece depicts a flock of twelve ravens arranged in a triangular pattern vaguely prefiguring M.C. Escher's designs. The raven is Hallblithe's emblem and that of his clan, the House of the Raven. Thus Crane's picture has direct relevance to the story. However, he did not draw it specifically for this printing. It first appeared on page 61 of the 1882 Macmillan edition of *Household Stories of the Brothers Grimm,* translated by Lucy Crane, the artist's sister. There it forms the tailpiece for the story "The Twelve Brothers."

HENRY RYLAND
The Story of the Glittering Plain, headpiece, second instalment
The English Illustrated Magazine 1889-1890, p. 754

The head-piece for Part 2, by Ryland, depicts a couple in a meadow, she lying on the ground, cradling a fiddle, and he beside her, resting on one elbow and holding twin pipes in his other hand. The chapter which follows does feature fiddles and dancing, but at an indoor feast. The connection seems tenuous at best. The unsigned headpiece to the last section fits the text of the second section better. It depicts a group of young women, whom one could identify as those who meet Sea Wolf and Hallblithe when the two arrive at the Glittering Plain. The illustration for Part 3, signed "R. Hy.," presumably Ryland, Henry, is purely decorative. It shows two sea serpents facing each other with other fanciful sea creatures mingled with them. This headpiece lacks the compositional and executional skill of the others. Even with the competence of most of the work, the pictures do not provide a sense of coherence with the text or unity of conception.

11.2
The Story of the Glittering/ Plain Which Has Been Also Called/ The Land of Living Men or the/ Acre of the Undying.
Written by/ William Morris.   [Half-title]

Colophon: Here ends the tale of the Glittering Plain, written by William Morris, & ornamented with 23 pictures by Walter Crane. Printed at the Kelmscott Press, Upper Mall, Hammersmith, in the County of Middlesex, & finished on the 13th day of January, 1894.
Kelmscott Sold by William Morris, at the Kelmscott Press.

Limitation: [250 copies on hand-made paper and 7 on vellum].

Binding: Full limp vellum with three ties, title vertically on spine in gilt.

Pagination/Size: [8] [iv] 180 [8] / 289 x 208 mm.

Contents: Pp. 1-8 blank, p. i half-title, p. ii contents, p. iii blank, p. iv decorated title page, pp. 1-179 text (with colophon on last page), p. 180 and pp. 1-8 blank.

Comment: The list of chapter headings with their page numbers on page ii also indicates the placement of Crane's pictures since one sits at the head of each chapter. The book has twenty-two chapters, and Morris placed an extra picture at the end of the first.

Illustrator: WALTER CRANE. See 8.3.

Illustrations and decoration: As noted elsewhere, books published at the KP have a unity of materials, conception, and execution which provides a decorative effect in itself. This applies with equal validity to *The Glittering Plain.* Decoration as such begins with the double spread of title page and first page of text. Its richness has an overwhelming effect especially when viewed for the first time. One sees an opulent border, with showy flowers and handsome curling leaves and stems in a typical repeating pattern. Within this border on the verso the title fills the rest of the page in large black type, including decorated capitals for the initial letters of all the words from "Glittering" onwards except the conjunctions and article. Further decoration fills the space between the letters. Crane's first picture occupies the upper half of the recto, and like all the others has its own floral border. The title appears again in small unadorned letters above the chapter heading in red, followed by the first few lines of the text. Morris used red for subsequent chapter headings also. He did not put shoulder notes in this book, but supplied further decoration with a large dropped and decorated capital at the start of each chapter, a smaller one at the beginning of each paragraph, and fleurons at the end of many sentences.

Marginal decorations abound, more in the first half of the book. Morris placed one to the left of each picture at the head of its chapter, all of them extending the full length of the page, and most along the adjacent half of upper and lower margins. Many more mark the start of new paragraphs. They have a wide range of leaves, stems, and flowers differing from one to the next, which delights with its variety and at the same time hints at the amount of care and work involved in the creation of the book. Morris complemented the decoration with the Troy type, which looks in proportion, printed as it is on a quarto page.

Each illustration depicts a scene or incident in the chapter which follows it. In general Crane selected good subjects, if displaying some over-fondness for ships, which appear in more than a quarter of his pictures. Other than this he illustrated a range of scenes. He captured physical or emotional dynamics very well in some pictures, for example the fight in the Hall of the Ravagers. Its vigour so attracted the publishers of a later edition that they reproduced it on their cover (see 11.4). Similarly, when Hallblithe and the Hostage are reunited and running to embrace, their hands already clasping, we see Hallblithe's forward impetus in one leg still outstretched behind him. Crane portrayed emotion at the opposite extreme equally well, in the distress of both Hallblithe and the King's daughter (see illustration) and in the misery of the old man at the mountain pass (Chapter XVII). Nevertheless, there is a certain stiffness to these pictures, which does not normally appear in Crane's art, and which may reflect the limitation of wood engravings as a medium for his work.

11.3

**The Story of the Glittering/ Plain Which Has Been Also/
Called the Land of Living Men/ or the Acre of the Undying/**
Written by/ William Morris/
NPC/ Newcastle/ Publishing/ Company,/ Inc./ Hollywood,/ California/
1973

Colophon: A Newcastle Book first printing: September 1973 printed in
the United States of America

Binding: Thick flexible paper cover with no endpapers, glued. Bright
blue Morris-like floral border front and back covers. Within the border
title and author in black on top half of front cover and series designation
at base, below picture in blue of Viking galley with raven emblem on its
sail. Title and author vertically on spine and publisher at base, all in
black. Back cover contains a few biographical details about Morris and
his influence on later writers of fantasy. Inside of covers blank.

Pagination/Size: xviii, 174 / 210 x 132 mm.

Comment: The picture on the cover is so similar to Crane's illustration
for Chapter III of the Kelmscott Press edition of this work (see 11.2) that
the artist must have used Crane's work as a starting point, adding an
anachronistic crow's nest and a rising sun behind the ship on the right of
the picture as well as a reversed crescent moon on its left.

Contents: P. i half-title, p. ii frontispiece, p. iii decorated title page, p. iv
publication information, pp. v-xvi introduction, p. xvii contents, p. xviii
blank, pp. 1-172 text, pp. 173-174 glossary.

Comment: The text seems to be a slightly enlarged photographic
reproduction of the first English trade edition of 1891, omitting, however,
the signatures, and the name of the printer on the last page.

Illustrator: HOWARD PYLE. Born in 1853 in Delaware into a cultured
Quaker farming family. He received early intellectual stimulation from
his mother and enrolled in a Philadelphia school of art from sixteen to
eighteen years of age. However, he largely taught himself. He moved
to New York in 1876 and achieved rapid recognition there. In 1879 he
returned to his home town of Wilmington, where he lived virtually the
rest of his life. He married Anne Poole in 1881 and had a large family.
He was also gifted as a writer and illustrated his own works, at first

historical and later mainly fiction. He was especially popular as a writer for children. His first such work, *The Merry Adventures of Robin Hood,* was published simultaneously in America and England, where his illustrations excited the admiration of William Morris. His reputation was such that the Drexel Institute in Philadelphia invited him to teach there in 1894. He proved an inspiring teacher: many of his students went on to achieve recognition in their turn (see 8.5). He left Drexel in 1900 and set up his own school at Chadds Ford. In 1910 he went to Italy to study the old masters and European painting at first hand and died there in 1911. (See Pitz.)

Illustration and decoration: A horizontal panel 2.5 cm. deep extends across the top of the title page, divided into three equal sections, with a left-facing black swan in each of the outer sections and laurel bush between them. Title and author occupy the rest of the upper third of the page. Below them the page is divided vertically into three equal sections. The middle one is subdivided, with a galleon under sail in the upper part and the publisher's name and address and emblem in the lower. The flanking panels have an identical pattern of rose stems, leaves, and flowers.

Pyle's frontispiece originally illustrated *Swanhild* by Brian Hooker, published in the January 1910 issue of *Harper's Monthly.* The caption then read, "I grow old with but one son Randver." The picture pleases one with the technical skill of its composition, but loses much in this black and white reproduction compared with its original bright colours. More cogently, its subject matter, a king seated on the throne in his palace, with people standing before him, bears no relation to the scene it purports to illustrate, the meeting of three men on a desolate mountain pass described in the text. Walter Crane draws an apposite depiction of this scene for the headpiece to Chapter XVII of the KP edition (see 11.2).

11.4
The Story of/ the Glittering Plain/ or the Land of/ Living Men/
The 1894 Kelmscott Edition/
by William Morris/
With 23 Woodcuts by Walter Crane/
Dover Publications, Inc./ New York

Colophon: This Dover edition, first published in 1987, is an unabridged republication of the work as published by the Kelmscott Press,

Hammersmith, England, 1894 (an earlier edition had been published by Kelmscott in 1891). For the Dover edition the dimensions of the original have been slightly reduced and the chapter headings, originally in red, have been reproduced in gray. Otherwise the work has not been altered in any way.

Binding: Thick flexible paper cover, beige ground colour on front and spine, white on back, glued on to sewn gatherings. Title, author, and illustrator on front cover, the last below picture. Author, title and publisher vertically on spine. All lettering in black. Informational note on back cover, advertisements on inside of both covers. A blank sheet front and back in imitation of endpapers, not included in pagination.

Pagination/Size: [2] [iv] 180 [2] / 277 x 202 mm.

Contents: P. 1 Dover title page, p. 2 publisher's statement, pp. i-iv facsimile reprint of half-title page, index and decorated title page of KP edition (pages i-iv of 11.2), pp. 1-179 facsimile reprint of text of 11.2, p. 180 and pp. 1-2 blank.

Comment: The note on the back cover provides a description of the Kelmscott original and discusses the significance of the Press generally in its influence on later printers and publishers. Dover used paper of good commercial quality but it suffers in comparison with the crisp feel of the handmade paper of the 1894 original.

Illustrator: WALTER CRANE. See 8.3.

Illustrations: The picture on the upper part of the front cover reproduces that which illustrates Chapter XXI, with added colours of sky-blue and brown. The decorative border alongside the pictures of Chapters VII and XXII reappears as a border to the cover picture, placed on the left side and partly above and below it, in orange-brown with some flower buds in blue.

Morris used red ink very sparingly in the Kelmscott original: even so its absence in the Dover edition emphasises the importance of its contribution to the overall decorative effect. For further comments about illustration and decoration see 11.2.

Chapter 12

Poems by the Way

Throughout his career, Morris published poems in magazines and periodicals as independent works. In 1891 he gathered these scattered pieces into a book, which he first printed at the KP. A trade edition from Reeves and Turner followed immediately. Longmans, Green, who later took over publication of Morris's works, republished the book from time to time, at least until 1920. Thereafter it went out of print for many years until the Thoemmes Press republished it in 1992. In the present century at least two publishers have issued paperback editions. None of these editions or any other has had the benefit of illustration. However, in 1992 Owen Legg printed a single poem from *Poems by the Way* at his Woodcraft Press in Tonbridge in Kent, England. He has operated this private press since 1972, at first producing ephemeral material but since 1977 finely printed books. Legg's edition commemorates a trip to Iceland he took in 1992 and reproduces Morris's poem on the same subject.

Pavilion Books later included some of the poems in their illustrated collection of Morris's poetry *The Sweet Days Die* (see 18.12). However, unlike Legg, who used his own linocut as illustration, Pavilion took illustrations from other sources for their book. The same is true of the anthology *Love Is Enough* published by Frances Lincoln in 1998 (see 18.13). Of the six poems by Morris which this book contains, two had appeared previously in *Poems by the Way*.

12.1
On/ First/ Seeing/ Iceland/
William Morris/
Woodcraft Press/ 1992

Colophon: William Morris first published this poem in 1891 in a collection of his works entitled "Poems by the Way" having written it after visiting Iceland in 1871 and 1873

This edition of 100 copies is hand set with Dante 16pt., 5pt. leaded. The handmade paper is white Wilcox 185 gsm 100 per cent cotton made at Wookey Hole Mill. The cover is Fabiano Ingres. The illustration, either of an imaginary icelandic [sic] scene or self portrait, is printed on Japanese mulberry paper.

Finished this 14th day of July 1992 at the Woodcraft Press, Tonbridge to mark my departure for Iceland with the British Schools Exploring Society. 35/100

Comment: Owen Legg wrote me that he found no market for the copies with the self-portrait, and that he replaced it with the Icelandic scene in all the copies he had.

Binding: Thick, flexible paper, grey or beige in different copies, title on upper half of front cover and author, publisher, and date in lower half, all in black. Below title a twelve-pointed star in grey, composed of three four pointed stars each rotated at thirty degrees to the next, and superimposed. The viewer can distinguish one from the others by each ray being half in outline and half in solid grey, darker than the background. Outside of back cover and inside of front cover plain. Colophon on inside of back cover.

Pagination/Size: [8] / 212 x 143 mm.

Contents: Inserted frontispiece with blank obverse, laid-in tissue guard, p. 1 title page, pp. 2-7 text, p. 8 blank.

Comment: The text begins on the obverse of the title page, on which Legg repeated the layout of the cover. He retained the deckle edges of the handmade paper.

Illustrator: OWEN LEGG. Born in London in 1935. He completed a medical degree at Guy's Hospital in London in 1959. After a year of medical work in Africa, he and his wife returned to Britain where he established a general practice, maintaining it until the end of the century. However, he pursued a simultaneous career in art, working as a printer, sculptor, and painter. Since 1999 he has devoted himself full-time to this field. He lives in Tonbridge in Kent.

OWEN LEGG
[Icelandic Landscape]
On First Seeing Iceland, frontispiece
and facing title page

Illustration: The text begins with a dropped Gothic capital, but the text is otherwise undecorated. The frontispiece linocut powerfully evokes the bleak landscape Morris describes in *The Icelandic Journals.* The upper two-thirds is a dark blue night sky with a huge full moon. A brown plain studded with semi-abstract black rocks occupies the lower third, and a range of low, stylised, bluish-green hills separates these upper and lower sections. The picture conveys the empty space and desolation of the country. It calls to mind Blatch's picture for the dust jacket of *Grettir the Strong* (see 5.2). There however one sees trees and a human figure; here the landscape is as deserted as the moon. In every respect this fine little book is a most satisfying piece of craftsmanship.

Chapter 13

The Wood beyond the World

The Wood beyond the World is the first in the group of novels which Morris scholars have lumped together as his late romances. They all have features in common: the theme of a quest; a heroine with physical resemblance to Georgiana Burne-Jones; and, if one appears in the story, a villainess physically resembling the author's wife. (See comments in the introduction to Chapter 6.) In the last thirty years, readers and writers of fantasy literature have hailed these works as the source from which the whole genre has evolved. Different publishers have therefore reissued them at intervals since, especially as paperback books. Some of these paperbacks merit special comment, since their covers illustrate the text. In particular Gervasio Gallardo provides a picture which specifically illustrates a pivotal scene for the cover of the Ballantine edition of 1969 and its reprints in 1971 and 1974. For further details see Appendix 1.

13.1
The Wood beyond the World./
By William Morris. [Half-title]

Colophon: Here ends the tale of the Wood beyond the World, made by William Morris, and printed by him at the Kelmscott Press, Upper Mall, Hammersmith. Finished the 30th day of May, 1894. Kelmscott William Morris [Decorative Kelmscott motif intervenes.]
Sold by William Morris, at the Kelmscott Press.

Limitation: [350 copies on handmade paper and 8 on vellum].

Binding: Full limp vellum with two ties, title and author in gilt on spine.

Pagination/Size: [8] [iv] 260 [6] / 208 x 141 mm.

Contents: Pp. 1-8 blank, p. i half-title, pp. ii-iii blank, p. iv frontispiece, pp. 1-260 text, p. 1 colophon, pp. 2-6 blank.

Illustrator: EDWARD BURNE-JONES. See 3.1.

Illustration and decoration: The double spread of frontispiece and first page of text has a border with a repeating pattern of flowers and curling leaves, which produces the sumptuous character usual with KP books. In this volume frontispiece and facing page of text equal each other in size, creating a most pleasing symmetry. Morris printed the chapter headings and shoulder notes in red; all else is in black. He used a large dropped capital on the first page, smaller ones at the start of subsequent chapters, and smaller ones still for the beginning of paragraphs. Most likely this reflects his perception that larger ones would be out of proportion in a book the size of this octavo. With one exception marginal decoration appears only on pages where a new chapter starts. It resembles that described in other KP books such as *The Glittering Plain* (see 11.2). The border for Chapter IX, re-used in some later chapters, is especially ornate. Morris employed the Chaucer type throughout, a suitable choice for a book which tells a story with such an archaic flavour as this one.

The illustration is one of the best-known pictures Burne-Jones did for the KP, rivalled only by such pictures as the initial illustration in the Press's edition of the works of Chaucer. It ranks among his finest, showing the Maid in full-length dress walking through the Wood, garlands at her brow and waist, the ground luscious with flowers beneath her bare feet. This picture captures well the vulnerability and beauty of the protagonist but gives no hint of the scheming and treachery which envelop her in her position of subjugation.

EDWARD BURNE-JONES
[The Maid in the Wood]
The Wood beyond the World (frontispiece)

13.2a
The Wood beyond the World/
by William Morris/
Published by the Roberts/ House, 3 Somerset Street/ Boston, 1895

Colophon: Here ends the tale of the Wood beyond the World, made by William Morris, and printed by the University Press at Cambridge, U.S.A. Finished the eleventh day of May, one thousand eight hundred and ninety-five.

Limitation: This Edition is limited to Five Hundred Copies.

Binding: Olive-green cloth-covered boards, Morris's border from the frontispiece page around edges of front cover in black. Title at top, author at bottom, a five-petalled flower at mid-level, a sword along right side, small hearts along left side, all in gilt, all within the border. Panel on spine of same border as on front cover, title at top, author at mid-level, and publisher at base, all gilt-stamped. Back cover plain. Top edge gilt, other edges untrimmed.

Pagination/Size: [2] viii, 272 [4] / 210 x 143 mm.

Comment: The publisher's Roman numeration excludes the frontispiece, even though it is printed on the same matte paper as the rest.

Contents: Pp. 1-2 blank, p. i half-title, p. ii statement of limitation, frontispiece with blank obverse and tissue guard, p. iii title page, p. iv printer's address, pp. v-vii contents, p. viii blank, pp. 1-272 text, p. 1 colophon and printer's emblem, pp. 2-4 blank.

Illustrator: EDWARD BURNE-JONES. See 3.1.

Illustration and decoration: Each page of text has shoulder notes as in the KP edition. Because of this the outer margins are quite wide, which gives a pleasing effect. The fault of this book lies in the poor quality of materials used in its production. The paper must have impressed the purchaser when new, being a thick matte, but is machine-made and starting to brown. The ink is lighter, so that one does not get the fine contrast between paper and type. For comments about the illustration see 13.1, whence came the picture used for this edition.

13.2b Note: Although printed from the same plates as 13.2a, this issue differs from it slightly in almost every aspect, making a separate description more practical.

13.2b
The Wood beyond the/ World.
By William/ Morris/
Longmans, Green, and Co./ New York, London, and Bombay/ MDCCCCII

Binding: Plain red buckram, paper label on spine, with title and author. Top edge gilt.

Pagination/Size: [2] viii, 272 / 205 x 142 mm.

Contents: Pp. 1-2 blank, p. i half-title, p. ii publication history, un-numbered frontispiece, p. iii title page, p. iv printer's address, pp. v-vii contents, p. viii blank, pp. 1-272 text.

Comment: The publication history on page ii indicates that this book is a reprint of the Roberts edition of 1895. Little Brown bought Roberts Brothers in 1898 (see Comments on Binding of 10.1a) and Longmans, Green acquired the publishing rights to Morris's works less than a year later. Longmans modified the preliminary pages as described above, slightly changed the typesetting of the title page, and dispensed with the tissue guard for the frontispiece. The book also lacks a colophon so that Longmans used two fewer sheets at the end.

Illustrator: EDWARD BURNE-JONES. See 3.1.

Illustration: See 13.1.

13.3
The Wood beyond the World/
by William Morris/
Facsimile/ of the Kelmscott Press Edition (1894)/
Dover Publications, Inc./ New York

Colophon: This Dover edition, first published in 1972, is an unabridged facsimile of the work originally published by the Kelmscott Press, Hammersmith, England, in 1894.

Binding: Thick flexible paper covers glued to sewn gatherings. Front cover and spine with black ground and border from Chapters IX and XI (pp. 52 and 76 respectively) in white on top, left side, and bottom, enclosing red panel containing title, author, and "Facsimile of the Kelmscott Press Edition" in black. Price, $3.50, top right, and title vertically on spine in yellow letters, author at top of spine and publisher at base in white. Back cover with white ground, with note by Dover about nature of the book as forerunner of the fantasy genre, and specifying material features of present edition. Front and back inside covers carry advertisements for other Dover titles. No true endpapers.

Pagination/Size: [6] [iv] 262 / 205 x 140 mm.

Contents: Pp. 1-2 blank, p. 3 Dover title page, p. 4 statement of publication and copyright, pp. 5-6 blank, p. i half-title, pp. ii-iii blank, p, iv frontispiece, pp. 1-261 text as for 13.1, p. 262 blank.

Illustrator: EDWARD BURNE-JONES. See 3.1.

Illustration: See 13.1. This facsimile conveys a better impression of the KP original than does the Roberts Brothers edition of 1895 (see 13.2a). While Roberts did not aim to produce an exact copy, they were essaying a prestigious limited edition to emulate Morris's.

13.4
The Wood beyond/ the World/
by William Morris/
Introduction by Tom Shippey/
Oxford University Press 1980

Binding: Thick flexible paper glued to gatherings. Colour reproduction of a detail from Burne-Jones's painting *Love among the Ruins* on front cover, title and author at base in yellow and red respectively. Black ground to spine and rear cover, with author and title vertically on spine in same colours as on front cover. Back cover contains a commentary on the book, its place in the fantasy genre, and some details of the format of this edition. At mid-level a colour reproduction of the entire *Love among the Ruins*. Blank sheets front and back serve as free endpapers.

Pagination/Size: xx, 168 / 196 x 127 mm.

Contents: P. i half-title, p. ii frontispiece, p. iii title page, p. iv publication information and history, pp. v-xix introduction, p. xx blank, pp. 1-168 text.

Illustrator: EDWARD BURNE-JONES. See 3.1.

Illustration and decoration: See 13.1. The publisher used the frontispiece from the KP edition, but did not include Morris's decorative border. While this omission impoverishes the picture, it does allow for its reproduction in a larger size than would have been possible with the border. Besides the frontispiece the editor also lifted the decorative dropped capitals and the colophon of the KP edition holus-bolus and incorporated them into his text at the same points. As a paperback this book cannot lay claim to distinction by virtue of the materials used in its manufacture. However, the layout is pleasing, even if it does hark back to a previous century. Both this and the Dover facsimile (13.3) offer inexpensive pleasure beyond that provided by the text.

Chapter 14

The History of Over Sea

In addition to his translations from Latin, Greek, Old English and Icelandic, Morris translated some medieval French stories in the early 1890s and published them initially at the KP. Shortly after he arranged for a trade edition, published by George Allen in 1896 under the title *Old French Romances*. Others, notably T.B. Mosher in America, published them subsequently. However, only *The History of Over Sea* ever received illustration. In his KP edition Morris issued this story and *The Tale of the Emperor Coustans* as one book. In contrast the illustrated edition described in this chapter appeared as an independent work.

Outre mer, the French term for *Over Sea,* had a particular connotation at the time the story was written not apparent in a modern English translation, but one with which Morris would have been familiar. *Outre mer* referred to the territories in the Near and Middle East occupied by the Islamic conquerors, often with particular reference to the Holy Land. The term must have had all the attraction of the exotic to readers of the time, and one can easily imagine that a story set at least in part in those surroundings would achieve popularity.

I have already commented on German editions of some of Morris's works (see introduction to Chapter 1). The anthology *Die goldene Maid* contains three of the stories which Morris translated from medieval French, including "The History of Over Sea." Peterka's illustration for this story portrays the same scene as does Rhead's frontispiece (see 14.1), in which the Lady prepares to kill her bound husband following her rape by the gang of thieves, fearing, with good reason, that he will repudiate her. Rhead's picture, while polished and assured, portrays the

Lady impeccably dressed and elegantly coiffured, needing only her carriage to go to the opera. Naked, and with her face contorted, Peterka's Lady is convincingly distraught.

14.1
The History/ of Over Sea/ Done into/ English/
by/ William Morris/
with Decorations by/ Louis Rhead/
R.H. Russell New York 1902

Binding: Paper over boards with two beige silk ties. Front and back covers have same decoration, no lettering on cover. See below and page 214.

Pagination/Size: 28 [2] / 260 x 202 mm.

Comment: Although part of the gathering, the frontispiece is not included in the pagination.

Contents: P. 1 half-title, p. 2 blank, un-numbered frontispiece, p. 3 title page, p. 4 publication information, pp. 5-28 text, pp. 1-2 blank.

Illustrator: LOUIS JOHN RHEAD. Born in England in 1857. He studied in Paris and London and became known as a portrait painter, lithographer, and poster designer. Peppin is inaccurate in saying that he did not illustrate any books except in collaboration with his two brothers, since the pictures in this Morris volume, however slight, are his alone. He died in the USA in 1926. See also 14.2.

Illustrations and decoration: The covers have a creamy background for a complex multi-coloured repeating pattern, the same front and back. A thick olive-green ruled line bordered by thin gilt ones lies 1 cm. in from all four edges of the covers. Outside this line sits a row of tiny leaves, their tips pointing outwards, their stems connected by a continuous wavy stem, all in gilt. Within the green line the repeating pattern consists of horizontal rows of semi-circles of the same green and gilt line as at the periphery. The semicircles have a 2 cm. diameter with the convexity facing upwards. Their lower ends do not quite touch the adjacent ones. Each row is set half a diameter out of phase with the one above and below it, so that the feet of each row approach the apex of the semicircles below them. A small circle enclosed by a red line bordered with gilt sits at the triple junction formed by the bases of two adjacent semicircles with the apex of the one below them. In the fan-shaped spaces enclosed by the concavity of a semicircle above and the convexity of the two quarter circles below sits a red fleur de lys bordered in gilt.

Rhead used red ink for the lettering of the title and publisher on the title page, the initial letter of the title a large dropped and decorated capital. A similar capital appears at the start of the text, which is otherwise not decorated except for the illustrations.

A decorative border in black, divided into horizontal and vertical panels, surrounds the frontispiece and another the title page. Below the frontispiece the panel extends the full width of the printed area, while

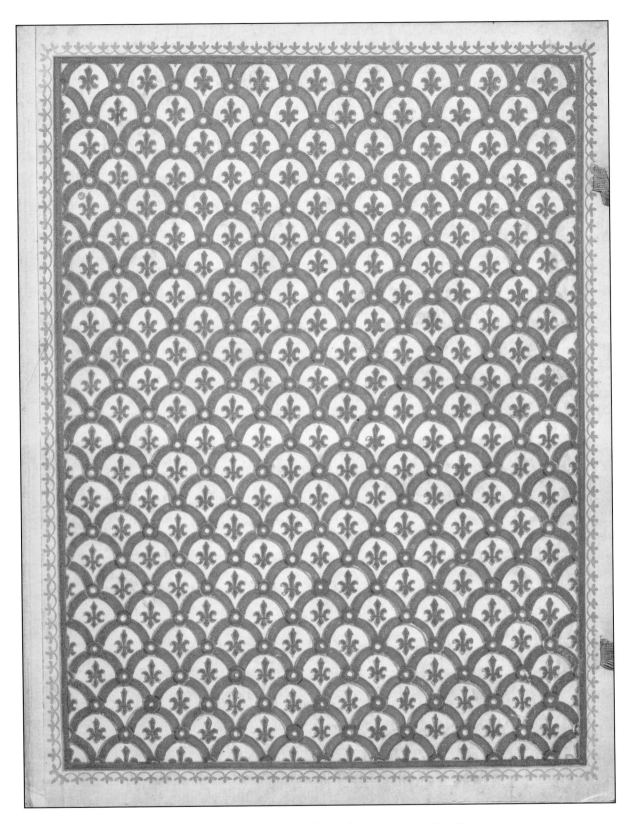

The History of Over Sea, front cover (14.1)

the vertical panels on each side of the picture rise to the top, the upper panel running between them. On the title page by contrast the panels are offset. The top one runs from the inner edge to an extension of the line formed by the outer edge of the central area which contains the lettering of title and author. The second runs from the top to the line formed by the lower edge of the lettered area, the third from the outer edge to the inner edge of the lettered area, and the last from the bottom to meet the first panel. Around the frontispiece the arrangement of these panels creates a pleasing effect. However, their design is less satisfactory. The pattern in the vertical panels forms a mirror image, one of the other, and consists of a repeating pattern of griffins. The horizontal panels differ from each other, but both have a pattern of leaves and stems with bilateral symmetry. On the title page the arrangement of panels chasing each other around the central area forms a pattern of a sort. However, it creates two major visual problems. Firstly, because the two vertical panels stand at different heights in relation to one another, the designs within them, mirror images of each other, do not face across at the same level. The discrepancy stands out due to an antlered stag at the mid-level of the panel forming a prominent part of the design. Secondly, the designer loses symmetry even further between one page and the other. Thus the two halves remain as two entities, not achieving the balance which so delights in the double spreads of KP books.

The borders around the two illustrations in the body of the text have comparable problems. Here Rhead strove for the effect of a double spread by eliminating a border from the inner part of two facing pages. Again he used panels rather than a continuous band. Again the designs in the panels differ one from another. Finally, the width of the horizontal panel on one page differs from that on the other. On the recto of one he even put two vertical panels side by side, mirror images of each other. As with the borders of frontispiece and title page, animals figure prominently in some of the designs and Rhead consistently fails to achieve the flow and grace of pattern which Morris obtains with a purely floral content.

Rhead executed the illustrations competently, though they do have a certain static quality. They focus on points of drama, the frontispiece showing the Lady about to execute her bound husband after the bandits have stripped and tethered him and raped her. He looks suitably terrified, but she, with sword held aloft, seems as composed as if she were about to carve a turkey. (See further comments in the Introduction to this chapter.) The second illustration depicts the merchant's crew retrieving the tun in which the Lady has been cooped and jettisoned, essentially the start of the second phase of her life. In the last the viewer sees the Lady cozening her Saracen husband to allow her to take a supposedly short trip with their daughter, in reality leaving to return to her former life and first husband.

14.2
The History/ of Over Sea/ Done into/ English/
by/ William Morris/
with Decorations by/ Louis Rhead/
R.H. Russell New York 1902

Date of publication: n.d. "About 1982" (Library Binding Company).

Comment: While the lettering of the title page is unchanged from that of the original, this book is actually a photographic reproduction of the 1902 edition (14.1). It lacks a new title page comparable to those which Dover supply for their facsimile reprints (see 11.4 and 13.4) which identify them as facsimiles. Copies often contain a card stuck on the front free endpaper reading "*Compliments of* Library Binding Company WACO, TEXAS." A company representative wrote me that they had put out this reproduction as a keepsake for their customers in an edition of about 500 copies. He mentioned that a leftover box of the books had got lost. Thus fewer copies may be extant.

Binding: Glossy paper over board, brown ground, printing in darker brown. Title page of 1902 edition reproduced as front cover. Title and author vertically on spine. Back cover plain with brown background colour only.

Pagination/Size: [4] 28 [4] / 248 x 194 mm.

Contents: Pp. 1-4 blank, p. 1 half-title, p. 2 frontispiece, pp. 3-28 title page and text as in 14.1, pp. 1-4 blank.

Comment: For this facsimile the printer uses brown ink throughout, losing the red colour of title and publisher on the title page in the process.

Illustrator: LOUIS J. RHEAD. See 14.1.

Illustrations: See 14.1.

LOUIS J. RHEAD
[The Lady and the Soudan]
The History of Over Sea, p. 18

Chapter 15

The Story of Child Christopher and Goldilind the Fair

The Story of Child Christopher and Goldilind the Fair came first from the KP in 1895. Like Morris's translation of *Grettir the Strong*, no illustrated edition of the original text ever appeared, though others, such as Mosher, were quick to publish non-illustrated editions. The paraphrased edition came fairly late in the flow of such adaptations, which is surprising, since *Christopher*, a tale packed with romance and adventure, seems a natural choice for the machinations of the adapter. In the 1970s Newcastle Publishers did issue an edition with the original text as a paperback with an illustrative cover (see Appendix 1).

John Martin, who wrote the paraphrase described in this chapter, wrote an introduction outlining the changes he has made, "dropping many of Morris's archaisms" and omitting "a few situations that seemed unnecessary." He means that he has bowdlerised the text. For example, in Morris's version Simon brings Christopher the severed head of Rolf. (This was a common practice up to recent times, providing both proof of death and positive identification of the victim.) Martin has Simon merely show Christopher the knife stained with Rolf's blood. However, for much of the narrative Martin adheres closely to Morris's original text. When he does change it he fails to achieve the economy of language in Morris's "archaisms," and his version is wordier.

15.1P
The Wolf's-Head/ and the Queen/
Retold by/ John Martin/ from/ "Child Christopher"/ by William Morris/
Illustrated by/ Nelson Grofe/
Charles Scribner's Sons/ New York London/ 1931

Binding: Double dust jacket, the inner smooth and plain with circular
hole cut in upper spine so as to reveal title on spine of cover beneath.
Outer jacket of glossy white paper with pictorial and decorated front
cover and spine. Title on upper front cover and spine, adapter below it
on spine and at base on front cover. Publisher at base of spine. Back
cover plain. Note about story on front flap, back flap plain. Bound in blue
buckram, plain except data on spine of jacket stamped in silver on spine
of cover. Pictorial endpapers.

Comment: The hole cut in the inner jacket to expose the title on the
spine of the cover seems pointless. One finds this feature only on removal
of the outer jacket.

Pagination/Size: xviii, 244 [2] / 224 x 157 mm.

Contents: P. i half-title, p. ii blank, inserted colour frontispiece, p. iii title
page, p. iv statement of copyright and emblem of printer, p. v dedicatory
poem by adapter, p. vi blank, pp. vii-xii introduction, pp. xiii-xiv contents,
p. xv list of illustrations, p. xvi blank, p. xvii text half-title, p. xviii blank,
pp. 1-244 text, pp. 1-2 blank.

Comment: The publisher used a good quality of materials in producing
this book. The thick matte paper shows no signs of foxing, browning or
brittleness.

Illustrator: LLOYD NELSON GROFE. Born in Pennsylvania in
1900. He was known as a craftsman in wood and as an illustrator
for periodicals, his work appearing in *Good Housekeeping* and other
magazines. He exhibited at the Philadelphia Academy of Fine Arts in
1925.

Illustrations and decoration: The book has a richness of decoration
comparable to that seen in the previous generation, such as Harrison's
Early Poems (see 2.11) or Underdown's *Gateway to Romance* (see 4.11P).
On the lower half of the front cover of the dust jacket Scribner's placed
a vignette in colour, depicting Christopher and Goldilind. Decoration on
the jacket is otherwise in black. A buttress which resembles an upright
carved table leg supports the vignette on each side. A sword overlaid
by shield adorns the mid-level of the spine. Monochrome pictures on
the endpapers have the same blue colour as the cover, and lie within a
continuous border of oak leaves, appropriate since Morris sets the story
in Oakenrealm. The pictures differ on fixed and free endpapers, but are
the same front and back. Both pictures also appear in the body of the
text.

"This!" cried Simon

L. NELSON GROFE
The Wolf's-Head and the Queen, facing p. 222

The title page carries ornate Gothic script, decorative in itself and appropriate for the story, with its setting in an early era. Just below the mid-level of the page is a decorative horizontal panel containing running wolves and curling leafy stems, emblematic of the banner of Gandolf of Brimside. A decorated shield the same height as the panel bisects it, and a larger shield, partly decorated and partly formed by letters of the page, extends above and below the panel, obscuring its central section. Decoration surrounds the heading of all the sections in the preliminary pages, and dedication and introduction also have tailpieces. Finally, the "To" with which Martin starts the first line of his address to his readers is dropped and decorated as well. An illustrative headpiece precedes the first chapter only, but every chapter starts with a dropped and decorated capital. Where space permitted, Grofe placed a tailpiece at the end of a chapter. Some of them are purely decorative, but at least two illustrate in a general fashion a character or scene in the chapter which precedes it.

Like *Golden Wings*, one of Morris's earliest stories (see 1.1), the premise of *Child Christopher* requires some suspension of disbelief, namely that a young man without influence or connections can emerge from nowhere and command the support and loyalty of powerful factions. Once past this the story, both a romance and an adventure, moves at a brisk pace. Grofe has considerable skill in composition and figure drawing. His illustrations make the reader pause at the point in the text they depict and refocus on the action, generally significant. For example he captures well the progress of the relationship between Christopher and Goldilind, from her initial disdain to their mutual attraction, and finally their triumph with Goldilind crowned and receiving the submission of their last enemy. Grofe portrays the scenes of action no less vividly, whether he shows Christopher assuming command, leading his men, preparing for battle, fighting in single combat, or defending himself against an assassin. The pictures on the endpapers balance these two aspects, one showing Christopher and Goldilind when they have discovered their mutual love, and the other before the decisive fight which determines their ultimate triumph. Altogether, this book achieves the sense of unity which is the mark of success in an illustrated work. It does not detract from it to comment that it owes much to the tradition established by Howard Pyle, in layout, decoration, and even the style of illustration found in *The Wolf's Head and the Queen*. The similarity is probably not coincidental. Scribner's republished some of Pyle's books the same year.

Chapter 16

Gossip about an Old House

This essay, in which Morris describes Kelmscott Manor, first appeared in a short-lived periodical called *The Quest*. The Birmingham Guild and their publisher G. Napier and Company established it as a literary magazine for an educated and discriminating readership. They used a high quality of materials, printing on handmade paper retaining its deckle edges, and fine press work to complete the effect. Throughout the magazine the reader finds dropped and decorated capitals, marginal decoration, and superb woodcut engravings. The number of pages in an issue varies from 48 to 52 in Numbers 1-3. In the last three issues, 4-6, pagination is continuous up to 156. The initial page, facing the inside of the front cover, repeats the title of the magazine, its number and date. Morris's essay in Number 4 follows this first page directly.

The magazine had reason to command Morris's sympathy and support on three counts. It was set up using the principles practised by Morris at his own KP. Furthermore, Morris had a connection with the Birmingham School of Art, whose staff produced the magazine, as two of the staff members, Gere (see 10.2) and Arthur Gaskin, also supplied illustrations for KP books. Finally Morris had given the address at the distribution of prizes at the Birmingham School in February, 1894. From the fourth issue onwards, the publishers of *The Quest* got help of some nature from the Boston printer Daniel B. Updike. This support enabled Updike to grant other American printers permission to bring out their own editions of *Gossip,* namely 16.3 and 16.4. In spite of Updike's help and in spite of the high standard of materials, presswork, and content the promoters ceased publication after six issues. Unlike *The Comrade* (see 10.3) and *The English Illustrated*

Magazine (see 11.1), the publishers of *The Quest* never put out multiple issues bound into volumes. Indeed, this would have been difficult in view of the stated limitation of the number of copies. However, many owners of completed sets did bind them into a single volume, and one finds the whole group as such more often than as loose copies. Nevertheless, the magazine is rare in either state. Because no standard binding exists for bound sets, the binding of the loose issues is described in this chapter.

This piece appeared for the second time as the 1895 "offprint" (16.2) from the original magazine article. In their bibliography of the Forman/Wise forgeries, Barker and Collins state, with supporting evidence, that *Gossip* in this separate form was completely fraudulent, with no connection of any kind to the Birmingham publishers of *The Quest*. Colin Franklin (1986), on the other hand, feels that the Birmingham group did supply the text, running off an extra fifty copies of the article, while Forman arranged to have the title page and colophon printed and the book bound separately. Franklin adduced the failure of the Birmingham Guild to state a limitation on issues after No. 3 as evidence for his opinion. However, this failure could have arisen for some other reason. In my copy of six bound issues the first three carry the statement "This edition is limited to 300 copies, of which this is number *60*" on the obverse of the title page, which faces the inside of the front cover. Issues IV to VI still carry "No. *60*" on the same page, but without the statement of limitation. Presumably this reflects the assignment of the same number to a regular subscriber. By contrast my loose issue of No. IV lacks a number. I suspect that the failure of the Guild to state a limitation after issue IV comes from their having printed extra copies for Updike, of which my loose copy is one.

Gossip made its third appearance, again in a magazine, in America, the first fruit of Updike's support of the Birmingham Guild. This magazine *Bradley His Book* resembles *The Quest* in that it aimed to present contemporary literature and art, including Bradley's own, to a discriminating public. The resemblance ends there. Bradley appears to have sought a wide market. He priced his magazine at ten cents a copy, less than a twelfth of the cost of *The Quest*. He achieved this by accepting advertisements for items as diverse as lawn sprinklers and handmade paper. He supplied graphic designs for some, and they do have charm. Less happily, he compromised on the quality of the materials, using machine-made paper, which is now becoming brown and brittle. Possibly to save even more on paper he adopted a small size of type which looks inconsequential on the page. Finally, he printed material from a range of sources, so that the magazine lacks unity of style overall. Aubrey Beardsley's line drawings do not share a page comfortably with the reproductions of the wood engravings of *Gossip*. On the positive side, Bradley's art work is vibrant and engaging. The magazine stands at the inception of a new era, and could symbolise through its own pages the transition from the traditional, through the decadent, to Art Nouveau. Like *The Quest* Bradley's magazine had a short life. He put out only seven issues, at monthly intervals, between May and November of 1896.

Gossip has generally appeared with the illustrations of the original edition. The exceptions comprise its publication in *The Collected Works* and an abridged version which the William Morris Society printed as a keepsake for members who participated in a visit to Kelmscott Manor in 1969.

16.1
Gossip about an Old House on the/ Upper Thames.
[In] The Quest: Number IV./ November, 1895

Colophon: Printed at the Press of the Birmingham Guild of Handicraft Limited, and published by G. Napier & Company, of 55, Newhall Street, Birmingham, by Tylston & Edwards and A.P. Marsden, of 13, Cliffords Inn, London, and by Berkley Updike, of 6, Beacon Street, Boston, U.S. America. November 1895.

Binding: Limp greenish-grey paper, title of magazine on upper front cover, above narrow, vertical, central panel containing a standing female figure in long flowing draperies, doves flying around her feet. Number of issue and date in Roman numerals to left of panel, price "Two shillings & sixpence" to right. Ruled line close to the margins. Guild's decorated monogram in centre of back cover. All lettering in olive-green. List of contents on inside of front cover, back cover blank.

Comment: The design of this cover appears here for the first time. It also appears on the covers of Numbers V and VI. The design on the covers of Numbers I-III represents men in armour riding through a wood.

Pagination/Size: pp. 3-14 / 219 x 172 mm.

Contents: P. 3 blank, p. 4 frontispiece, pp. 5-14 text. The issue has a total of forty-eight pages plus eight pages of advertisements.

Illustrators: CHARLES M. GERE. See 10.2.
    EDMUND HART NEW. Born in Evesham, England, in 1871. He studied under Edward Taylor and Arthur Gaskin at the Birmingham Municipal School of Art and exhibited in Birmingham between 1890 and 1923. He worked as an architect, landscape painter, and book illustrator, living in Oxford much of his career. He died there in 1931. See also 16.2-5.

Illustrations and decoration: The Guild decorated the text more sparingly than some of the other articles in the magazine. They used a dropped and decorated capital at the start, and further ones at intervals, about one to each double page. Other than this the text is unadorned.

The frontispiece, by Gere, originally appeared in the KP edition of *News from Nowhere* (see 10.2). In the present article it lacks the border which adds such richness to Morris's book. However this border would have been out of keeping with the rest of the decoration in the present version. New drew two pictures especially for this article which the Guild places in the body of the text. Horne has commented on the similarity of the artistic styles of Gere and New, and we see their work combined here to most happy effect. New's first illustration depicts the parlour of Kelmscott Manor. He included such intimate details as books lying on the cushioned window seat, more books, a half-full glass, plates (one with

EDWARD H. NEW
[The Interior of the House]
Gossip about an Old House, p. 10

an apple) on the Victorian equivalent of a coffee table in the foreground. The table also has inkwell, pen, and paper. A tapestry hangs on the wall to the right of a large transom window, which invites the occupant of the room to gaze through its multiple tiny panes at the sun-drenched garden beyond. Everything evokes the presence of Morris himself. The other picture, at the end of the article, occupies only a half page. It depicts the southern aspect of the house, with its dovecote and other outbuildings. Together the three pictures convey a sense of a dynamic process, in which the viewer approaches the front door, sees the interior, and then passes out through the back door and turns to look at it as he departs.

16.2
Gossip about an Old/ House on the Upper/ Thames
Written by/ William Morris/
November 1895

Colophon: Printed at the Press of the Birmingham Guild of Handicraft Limited, published in "The Quest" for November MDCCCXCV, and fifty copies done in this separate form.

Binding: Blue-grey paper over boards, title on top part of front cover in black. Linen spine with title vertically on it on paper label. Plain else.

Pagination/Size: [4] [2] 14 [8] / 219 x 173 mm.

Comment: As a supposed offprint (see introduction to this chapter), the book retains the pagination of the magazine whence it came. The version has added half- and full title pages which absorb the initial numbers.

Contents: Pp. 1-4 blank, p. 1 half-title, p. 2 blank, p. 1 title page, pp. 2-3 blank, p. 4 frontispiece, pp. 5-14 text, p. 1 colophon, pp. 2-8 blank.

Illustrators: CHARLES M. GERE. See 10.2.
    EDMUND H. NEW. See 16.1.

Illustrations: See 16.1.

16.3
Gossip about an Old House on the/ Upper Thames and Two Views of Same.
[In] Bradley/ His Book/ Vol. I. No. II. Price Ten Cents/ June 1896

Binding: Limp, peach-coloured paper covers and white paper spine. At top of front cover, title in orange letters with volume number and issue in black below. At base, month of publication in orange with year of publication in black. In centre, Art Nouveau style rose bush in black with flowers in orange. On back cover advertisement for Hartford Rubber Company in decorated black and orange lettering blocked out in elegant pattern of two rectangles with triangle between. Inside of covers printed in greenish grey with more traditional floral pattern as background to more advertisements.

Pagination/Size: pp. 27-32 / 252 x 120 mm.

Contents: See above under pagination.

Comment: Bradley placed a small reproduction of the first page of the KP edition of *Chaucer* on the page facing the start of *Gossip*.

Illustrators: CHARLES M. GERE. See 10.2.
    EDMUND H. NEW. See 16.1.

Illustrations: Bradley used the dropped and decorated capitals of the original edition, but the essay is otherwise free of decoration. As noted in the Introduction to this chapter, Bradley also used a small light type in a tall narrow format which does not enhance the appearance of Morris's text.

Like all subsequent publishers of illustrated editions of *Gossip*, Bradley used the pictures which appear in *The Quest* (see 16.1). He placed Gere's frontispiece as a head-piece above the first half page of the text and used New's picture of the southern exposure of the Manor as a tailpiece. However, he gutted the body of the text by omitting the picture of the interior. He had to reduce the size of both the pictures to fit his smaller page. He may have felt that the darker tones of the picture he left out would darken even further in a small size, and lose detail. In fact, this is not a problem in a later small edition (see 16.4).

16.4
Gossip about an/ Old House on the/ Upper Thames/
by William Morris/
Flushing Queens Borough/ New York MDCCCCI

Colophon: The illustration used as the frontispiece herein is by C.M. Gere, & was used in the Kelmscott Press edition of 'News from Nowhere.' The other illustrations are by E.H. New, & the initial letters were designed & engraved on wood by J.E. Hill.

Reprinted from 'The Quest,' by permission of the publisher, D.B. Updike, Boston, by J.E. Hill, at Flushing, Queens Borough, New York, and finished on the twenty-third day of February, 1901.

Limitation: One hundred copies of this book have been printed on Japan Vellum, seventy-five of which are for sale. This is number *47.*

Binding: Cream coloured paper lightly marbled in pale blue over boards. Title and author vertically on spine. Plain else.

Pagination/Size: [4] 26 [6] / 163 x 123 mm.

Contents: Pp. 1-4 blank, p. 1 half-title, p. 2 statement of limitation in red, p. 3 blank, p. 4 frontispiece, p. 5 title page, p. 6 blank, p. 7 foreword, p. 8 blank, pp. 9-26 text, p. 1 colophon (second paragraph in red), pp. 2-6 blank.

Comment: The foreword outlines the depth of Morris's attachment to Kelmscott Manor.

Illustrators: CHARLES M. GERE. See 10.2.
     EDMUND H. NEW. See 16.1.

Illustrations and decoration: The title page has the title and address of the publisher in red, the rest in black. At the mid-level ruled lines form an upright rectangle enclosing a stylised carnation with curling leaves and the initials of the publisher in its base. Hill used ornamented, dropped capitals for the first letter of the foreword and for almost every paragraph in the text, much more freely than did the publishers of the original edition. He printed them and a tailpiece of curling leaves in red, to very pleasing effect. He also reset the type for the caption of the frontispiece as "A view of the manor house at/ Kelmscott, in Oxfordshire, from the garden gate," and placed a decorative scroll beneath it. He reproduced both New's pictures, but placed the second in the body of the text, rather than at the end. Hill would have achieved marginally greater coherence of text and illustration had he integrated the first page of text with the frontispiece as a double spread in the manner of the Kelmscott titles. Overall, however, the publisher's layout, his pleasing and unobtrusive type, the proportions of the book, and his judicious use of red ink combine to create a most elegant and satisfying work.

16.5
William Morris/
Gossip about an Old House/ on the Upper Thames/
Pierpont Morgan Library/ 1976 [Cover]

Colophon/Limitation: 750 copies printed for the Pierpont Morgan Library as a keepsake issued during the exhibition 'William Morris and the Art of the Book', 7 September to 28 November 1976. Designed by John Dreyfus and printed in England at the University Press, Cambridge, in the Golden type designed by William Morris for his Kelmscott Press.

Binding: Thick flexible beige paper, horizontal rectangle outlined by red ruled lines just above mid-level enclosing author and title. Publisher and date at base, all lettering in black. ISBN base of back cover, plain else.

Pagination/Size: 16 / 190 x 138 mm.

Contents: P. 1 frontispiece with caption, p. 2 blank, pp. 3-4 preface, pp. 5-15 text, p. 16 illustration with caption and colophon.

Comment: The preface by John M. Crawford Jr. touches on Morris's love of nature and of old buildings. He outlines, too, the publishing history of this work, described in more detail in the present chapter.

Illustrators: CHARLES M. GERE. See 10.2.
    EDMUND H. NEW. See 16.1.

Illustrations and decoration: The text begins with a dropped and ornamented capital, the only one used in this booklet. With frontispiece and New's second picture completely separate from the text (see *Contents*), the designer shows the same disregard for placement of illustrations as do some previous editors already discussed in this chapter. However, the publisher used materials of good quality, and the edition has a pleasing look to any but the most critical. See also 16.1.

Chapter 17

The Well at the World's End

The Well at the World's End belongs in the group of the "late romances" (see Introduction to Chapter 13). Others in the group include *The Water of the Wondrous Isles* and *The Sundering Flood*. Along with *The Well*, both appeared as paperbacks with illustrative covers, first from Ballantine Books and later from other publishers (see Appendix 1). Unlike *The Well*, neither has ever received illustration beyond this. Burne-Jones provided illustration for the KP edition of *The Well*. A further edition has appeared subsequently comprising only the early part of the work. As the colophon explains, it was a student project, a practice run for future endeavours. Its truncated nature is regrettable, since the format, a large folio, gives a distinct air to the book. For this reason, its inclusion is entirely appropriate even in its incomplete state.

17.1
The Well at the World's End/
By William Morris   [Half title]

Colophon: HERE ends the Well at the World's End, written by William Morris, with four pictures designed by Sir Edward Burne-Jones. Printed by William Morris at the Kelmscott Press, 14, Upper Mall, Hammersmith, in the County of Middlesex, and finished on the 2nd day of March, 1896.
Sold by William Morris at the Kelmscott Press.

Limitation: [250 copies on hand-made paper and 6 on vellum].

Binding: Full limp vellum with three ties, title and author in gilt at top of spine.

Pagination/Size: [8] [iv] 496 [4] / 285 x 202 mm.

Contents: Pp. 1-8 blank, p. i half-title, pp. ii-iii blank, p. iv frontispiece, pp. 1-495 text, p. 496 colophon, pp. 1-4 blank.

Illustrator: EDWARD BURNE-JONES. See 3.1.

Illustrations and decoration: Morris lavished most of the decoration on the four double spreads, one at the start of each component book. Here the reader sees one of his borders around illustration and opening page. On the verso the picture occupies only the upper half; the caption sits below it in large capitals, also with surrounding decoration. On the recto Morris placed the title in small capitals immediately above the chapter heading, the latter in red. Elsewhere Morris used red only for the last sentence of the colophon. The text begins with the first word dropped and decorated. The initial "L" of the first book occupies the left half of the decoration and the remaining "ong" the right half in smaller letters. The same layout precedes each of the succeeding books which make up *The Well.* A marginal decoration accompanies each new chapter, sometimes a narrow stem twirling between the two columns of text. All chapters start with a smaller dropped and decorated capital. Even smaller ones occur at intervals in the text. Decoration is almost absent elsewhere, except for very occasional marginal decoration. Morris used Chaucer type in double columns. In this book he did not append shoulder notes.

Morris's stories move at such a pace that an artist would stand a good chance of finding a suitable subject for an illustration were he to open a page at random. In choosing his subjects Burne-Jones drew a picture at the start of each of the four books which comprise this work. He chose points of especial crisis or drama. This procedure has the virtue of focussing the reader's attention on a crucial event. However, in this book Burne-Jones has perhaps dwelt on one aspect too narrowly. All but one of his pictures show scenes of death or dying. Unquestionably, the artist rendered the scenes well. In the first Ralph solicitously clasps

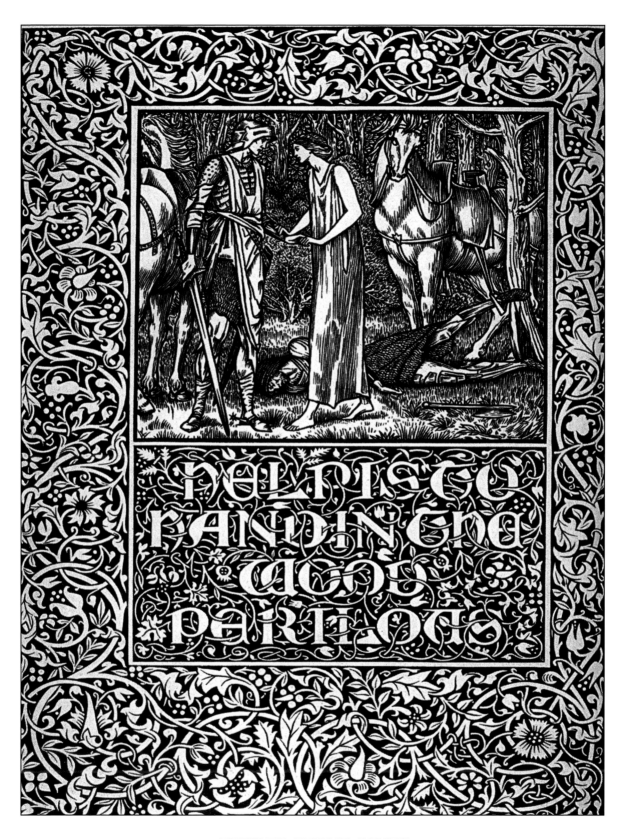

EDWARD BURNE-JONES
["Help is to hand in the Wood Perilous"]
The Well at the World's End, frontispiece

the hand of the Lady of Abundance just after he has rescued her from her two former captors, now dead at their feet, one with his foot still caught in his stirrup. The second illustration, "The Chamber of Love in the Wilderness," depicts the Knight of the Sun outside the Chamber, standing over the Lady just after he has killed her. Ralph has come upon him and has his arrow nocked, about to shoot the Knight. Once again we have a scene of death, of dynamic action, but chosen at the cost of neglecting a different dimension of the story. The third picture does move to one of these other dimensions. Entitled "Friends in Need Meet in the Wild Wood," it portrays the reunion of Ralph and Ursula as he is on his way to rescue her from thralldom from which, however, she has escaped by her own devices. Here we get a clue which the pictures have failed to provide up to this point that the story is a romance rather than pure carnage. However, the fourth picture shows Ralph leaning over a dying man to catch his last words.

17.2
An Extract from/ The Well at the World's End/
William Morris/
with Illustrations by/ Elspeth Lamb/
MCMLXXV/ Manchester Polytechnic

Colophon/Limitation: This is copy number *1* of a limited edition of twenty-five.
A joint student project between Elspeth Lamb, a post-graduate student of the Department of Fine Art who produced the original illustrations and John Campbell and Stephen Beswick, post certificate course students in the Department of Printing Technology.
The original etchings have been reproduced by Photolithography: text matter is set [in] 14pt Monotype Plantin, 3 point leaded with 36pt Plantin Italic headings.
10 copies have been printed on Strathmore Grandee Pyrenees Natural paper and bound in black buckram; in six of these, prints from the original etchings have been tipped in.
15 copies have been printed on Fortune Offset Cartridge, with litho printed illustrations and covers.
Completed December 1975 Manchester Polytechnic

Binding: Plain black buckram. No decoration or lettering. All the sheets of the book are sewn as a single gathering, the blank outermost ones serving in lieu of free endpapers.

Pagination/Size: [iv] [20] / 474 x 324 mm.

Contents: P. i half-title, p. ii blank, p. iii title page, p. iv colophon, pp. 1-19 text, p. 20 blank.

Comment: The pagination does not include Lamb's six plates with their blank obverses. Campbell and Beswick placed them after pages 2, 4, 6, 10, 12 and 14. They printed the plates on three folio sheets bound in with the rest of the pages.

Comment: Campbell and Beswick arranged the text in double columns. Given the size of the book, even these are of generous width. They do not use any adornment, but the page is pleasing in its simplicity. This extract encompasses the first ten chapters. This description applies to the first state; I have not examined any of the fifteen copies of the second state listed in the colophon.

Illustrator: ELSPETH LAMB. Born in Scotland, I believe in the early 1950s. She studied at the GSA between 1969 and 1973, then at Manchester Polytechnic for a further year and at the Ruskin School of Drawing in 1976. Beyond this she attended the Tamarind Institute of Lithography in New Mexico, where she studied printmaking. This medium has become the focus of her artistic expression and the field for which she is recognised, both by the public and by her colleagues, who elected her to the RSA and to membership of the Society of Scottish Artists. Shortly after returning to Scotland from the USA she took up a teaching position at the Edinburgh College of Art. She held this post for twenty-one years until 1999, when she left in order to devote all her time to her art. Perhaps it was the release from regular teaching responsibilities which facilitated her travel to Japan for extended periods in the early years of the present century to study Japanese printmaking. Her book *Papermaking for Printmakers*, published in 2004, resulted partly from the insights she gained there. She has exhibited in Glasgow, in Scotland generally, and outside Britain. She lives in Glasgow.

Illustrations: Lamb illustrates the nineteen pages of text with six full-page etchings. The first depicts the kingdom of Upmeads, hemmed in by mountains in the background and by a dark hill in the foreground, the viewpoint of the picture. Lamb suggests the small size of Upmeads by making the palace in the mid-ground large in proportion and the poverty of the realm by the starkness of the landscape. The mid-ground hills, between which the palace sits in its cramped valley, are dark and forbidding and devoid of vegetation. The only trees stand, or rather lean, in the foreground, bereft of leaves, seemingly dead. Everything hints at the conditions impelling the king's sons to leave their homeland.

Lamb provided two further landscapes. She and Campbell placed them toward the end of the text, closer to the point where Morris has Ralph visit the Abbey of Saint Mary. Neither picture resembles his description, both fitting better with the opening scenes at Upmeads. In the first a castle with a defensive ramp occupies the mid-ground, fields before it

ELSPETH LAMB
[The Kingdom of Upmeads]
The Well at the World's End, facing p. 2

and a woman standing among tall stalks in the foreground, possibly intended to represent Dame Katherine. Nothing in the picture hints at the ecclesiastical. In the other one sees a rider on a rearing horse outside a parapet in the foreground, fields stretching away to a river in the mid-ground, and mountains in the background. Once again the picture fits best with Ralph leaving Upmeads. Of the other three etchings, one depicts the interior of Dame Katherine's house, the second the riderless and blood-stained horse returning to Bourton Abbas, and the third the Lady of Abundance being led by her captors, a halter round her neck. Only the first of this latter group apposes the relevant text. In general, Campbell and Beswick did not place text and illustration in apposition, as discussed above in connection with the landscapes.

All the pictures have a flat appearance, with little attempt to use perspective. The viewer could interpret this as a deliberate style adopted by the artist as a pointer to the quasi-medieval setting of the story. The very flatness of the design reminds the viewer of the medieval style of illustration. Alternatively, it may represent a limitation of the medium or of the artist's technique. The last seems unlikely given the quality and irrepressible energy and exuberance of her later work. The illustrations which contain human or animal figures convey no sense of movement or vitality and evoke nothing of the drama or visual richness of the text. Lamb and Burne-Jones both drew Ralph's first encounter with the Lady of Abundance (see 17.1). The latter got movement and excitement into his rendering. Lamb portrayed three static figures. Morris's descriptions generally are so rich with detail and texture, especially that of the Abbey of Saint Mary, that they would seem to demand a response in kind from an artist.

Although this book comprises only a small part of the novel, it was an ambitious undertaking. As a large folio, it has a commanding presence, and the double columns give added dignity. The full novel in this form would have been a welcome addition to the extant versions.

Chapter 18

Collections and Anthologies

Anthologists have included works by Morris in their compilations from the time he established his literary reputation with *The Earthly Paradise* in 1870. Tauchnitz in Leipzig published *A Selection from the Poems of William Morris* in 1886, the first full-length collection devoted solely to his works. The Oxford University Press edition of *Prose and Poetry (1856-1870) by William Morris* appeared in 1913, and the Nonesuch Press edition of *William Morris: Stories in Prose, Stories in Verse, Shorter Poems* in 1934, the latter marking the centenary of Morris's birth. Particularly in recent years publishers have tended to focus on a single theme in anthologies of Morris's writings. *Selections from the Prose Works of William Morris* came from the Cambridge University Press in 1929, *Art and Socialism* from Lehmann in 1947, *William Morris: Early Romances in Prose and Verse* in 1973 (actually a revision of Dent's edition of 1907), and *Political Writings of William Morris* from Lawrence and Wishart in 1984. By 1996 specialisation had reached the point of three companion books *William Morris on Art and Design*, *William Morris on Architecture*, and *William Morris on History*, these published by the Sheffield Academic Press.

These titles contain significant collections of Morris's diverse body of writing, but by no means exhaust the list of such collections. Many others have a more limited coverage, or essentially duplicate previous titles, at least in their content of Morris's writing. All of the above books lack illustration. However, illustrated anthologies which include selections of Morris's writing appeared as early as 1877 with William Bryant's two-volume *The New Library of Poetry and Song*. Illustration does not extend to the poems by Morris. The same holds true even in

the encyclopaedic thirty-three-volume *Universal Anthology*, edited by Richard Garnett and published in 1900, and for *Through Woodland and Meadow & Other Poems*, published in 1891. Here Morris's poem has decoration, but, unlike many others in the book, no illustration.

Most anthologies which contain illustration of work by Morris have a wide scope so that their Morris content is small, often just one or two poems or a single prose work. Even some collections of Morris's writing alone have only sparse illustration. However, it is this group which makes up the majority of entries in this chapter. As noted elsewhere, Morris's popularity declined after the World War I to a low point in the 1930s, punctuated by a flurry of interest in the year of his centenary. Even in his eclipse compilers of anthologies still included one or two of his works, as did, for example, Edmund Blunden in *A Book of Narrative Verse* published in 1930. However, the loss of interest in Morris is vividly demonstrated when one notes that no illustrated anthology containing any of his work appeared in the seven decades after Hodder and Stoughton published *A Day with William Morris* about 1912 (see 18.5) until the Gramercy Press brought out *A Treasury of Fantasy* in 1981 (see 18.7).

It was not until the centenary of Morris's death that an extensive illustrated collection appeared which is devoted entirely to Morris (see 18.12). This collection, *The Sweet Days Die*, has profuse illustration, but not with pictures created for the book specifically. The reader faces again the dilemma, discussed elsewhere in these pages, of how to judge a book which represents an artificial assembly of disparate elements, where the only assessment possible centres on the skill of the design editor in making the choice of art work to pair with a particular poem. The same problem presents itself with *Love Is Enough* (18.13) in particular, and also with *A Treasury of Fantasy* (18.7) and *A William Morris Christmas Book* (18.11).

The long gap between 18.5 and 18.7 alluded to above does not take account of Collins's ill-judged hodgepodge which combines *The Defence of Guenevere* and *The Life and Death of Jason* (18.4*)*. Collins published this book about the same time as *A Day with William Morris* but may have continued to reprint it into the 1920s and beyond. Collins published this *Jason* as No. 197 of their *Illustrated Pocket Classics,* a series which eventually exceeded 350 titles. Books in the series have a standard format, with identical size, binding including endpapers, type, paper, and the same vignette on the title page, signed by Malcolm Patterson. J. Malcolm Patterson was born in 1873 in Twickenham. He did line drawing, etching, book and magazine illustration, and painting in oils, but also had regular employment as a high-school art teacher. At the time Collins put out *Jason,* their standard format included illustrations in sepia monochrome. They made an exception with *Jason,* as discussed in the entry in this chapter. The series continued into at least the 1930s, and some of the later titles also carry illustrations in colour.

A Day with William Morris also forms one of a series, Hodder and Stoughton's *Days with the Poets*. The series includes most of the major nineteenth-century British and American poets and one or two from earlier periods such as Shakespeare and Burns. The series came out in the early twentieth century, with a standard format, which includes a dust jacket of the same colour as the cover and a panel cut in it so as to expose a portrait of the poet pasted on the front cover. Early titles differ from later ones in having an unadorned linen spine of similar colour as the rest of the cover. The early titles also had different endpapers, with the same colour as the cover, a decorative border, and a triangular decoration in the otherwise plain centre. I have not seen any endpapers having these features in 18.5. Hodder did not number their titles or give a date of publication.

One can see three further entries (18.8-10) in this chapter as forming a series, though the publisher does not so classify them. The same artist, Gordon Benningfield, illustrated all of them and published them in a standard format. They are identical in pagination, size, binding, and type of content and illustration. The separate entries for 18.9 and 10 therefore document only such differences as are present. The publisher put out other books with this same format also illustrated by Benningfield, such as *Hardy Country*. However, they do not contain poems by Morris, and are therefore not included. These books have many features in common with *The Poet's Year* (see 18.2). All present a selection of poems centred on a particular theme, all are profusely illustrated, and all have a horizontal format. In the case of Benningfield's books, the layout editors, Ian Cameron and Jill Hollis, probably adopted it to accommodate the shape of the majority of the pictures.

Anthologies limited to works of Morris alone have received the letter "o," standing for "only," as a suffix to the numerical code; for books in which Morris's writing appears with that of other authors, the suffix is "p," for "partly."

The first entry in this chapter came to my attention when the process of printing the book was already started. It was impractical to renumber all the entries in this chapter, hence the expedient of using "0" for this late inclusion.

18.0a
Christmas Carols/ New and Old/
Edited by the/ Rev. Henry Ramsden Bramley, M.A.,/ Fellow of Saint
Mary Magdalen College, Oxford/ The music edited by/ John Stainer,
M. A., Mus. Doc.,/ Organist to the same College./ With Illustrations,
engraved by the Brothers Dalziel./
London:/ Novello, Ewer and Co.,/ 1, Berners Street (W.), and 38,
Poultry (E.C.)/ George Routledge and Sons,/ The Broadway, Ludgate.

18.0b
Christmas Carols/ New and Old/
Edited by the/ Rev. Henry Ramsden Bramley, M.A.,/ Fellow of Saint
Mary Magdalen College, Oxford/ The music edited by/ John Stainer,
M. A., Mus. Doc.,/ Organist to the same College./ With Illustrations,
engraved by the Brothers Dalziel./
London:/ George Routledge and Sons,/ The Broadway, Ludgate./
Novello, Ewer and Co.,/ 1, Berners Street (W.), and 38, Poultry (E.C.)

Dates of publication: None of the editions of this book carries the date
of publication. 18.0a is the first edition. The page of advertisements at
the end of the book refers to another book, *National Nursery Rhymes,* as
"just published." Novello put out that book in 1871. Furthermore, Arthur
Hughes supplied the frontispiece and two illustrations in the text of
Christmas Carols, and his biographer Leonard Roberts gives this date
for the creation of these pictures. 18.0b was probably published before
1876. In that year Novello changed their address at Poultry Lane to 80-
81 Queen Street, and this was likely to have been recorded on the title
pages of editions published after this time. The musical editor Stainer
was knighted in 1888 and later editions recorded him as "Sir John"
on the title page. However, I have not located any illustrated editions
carrying this designation. This change appears by the mid-1890s, by
which time Novello was issuing the book in a non-illustrated form and
produced editions at intervals up to the mid-twentieth century. The
appearance of the non-illustrated book sets the latest possible date for
later editions of the illustrated version in the first half of the 1890s.
I have no information about the dates of publication of other editions
between the first one of 1871 and the later date just given.

Binding: Identical in the two editions except for the colour, dull red
buckram in 18.0a and bright blue in 18.0b. Decoration on front cover
and spine both gilt stamped and in black ink. Ruled line in gilt 1 cm. in
from edges of front cover, black line directly inside it. Identical rectangles
at top and bottom enclosed by ruled line in gilt, 1 cm. from outer lines.
Broad black line inside gilt line of rectangles, with tiny decoration in gilt.
Title within this, first two words in upper rectangle, final three words in
lower. Between these two rectangles a large vertical rectangle outlined
by a border 2 cm. wide with black outer and inner lines containing stars
in gilt at intervals of a few millimeters. Complex floral design in gilt
between the lines. Each line of this border broken at its mid-point by a
circular medallion, circumference a thin line in gilt, containing a cherub

in gilt on a black background. Central picture 1 cm. in from border enclosed in double gilt lines, black background between them stamped with alternating pattern of dots and dashes in gilt. Picture has black background to standing Madonna holding child portrayed in colour of buckram. Details of dress and features outlined in black. Haloes and stars in gilt. Gilt decoration on spine similar to that in border of front cover, and similar circular medallion at mid-level. Title in gilt "Carols New and Old" horizontally, one word in each quarter of spine. Stamped pattern of front cover blind-stamped on back cover. All edges gilt. Plain chocolate-coloured endpapers.

Pagination/Size: (viii) 94 (2) / 262 x 182 mm.

Contents: P. i blank, p. ii frontispiece, p. iii title page, p. iv blank, p. v preface, p. vi blank, pp. vii-viii contents with title and artist, p. 1 blank, pp. 2-91 text, p. 92 blank, pp. 93-94 index, with title, author and composer, pp. 1-2 advertisements.

Illustrator: J. MAHONEY. Mahoney merits only a brief entry in Houfe's encyclopedia of book illustrators. Houfe records that he was active in this capacity between 1865 and 1875 and further states that he was a disagreeable man with a severe problem with alcoholism. He died in 1882 as the result of an accident related to his drinking. A check of the 1881 British census records and the register of deaths failed to identify him more precisely.

Illustrations: In addition to the frontispiece each carol has a headpiece which occupies slightly more or less than half a page from one to another. Most of the carols with their illustration cover a double spread, though two extend to three pages, one to four and one to six. The sixth page of the last in this group had space for a decorative tailpiece with a central medallion containing Madonna and Child. This same medallion reappears in smaller size as a tailpiece to the list of contents on page vi. The only other decorative feature consists of a headpiece above the list of contents on page v. In a central medallion two elderly figures hold up their hands in prayer to the Christ Child seated above them. The medallion is supported on each side by a decorative motif.

The carol by Morris is fortieth of the forty-two included, all listed using Roman numerals. It is entitled "From Far Away." In its original form the text appeared as a passage in "The Land East of the Sun and West of the Moon," one of the stories in *The Earthly Paradise.* Morris modified the wording for the purpose of the carol. Mahoney depicted a snowy scene with a man standing in the centre of the foreground close to the corner of a stone-built house, which occupies the left half of the picture. He has turned his head to a lighted window with drawn curtains, perhaps of muslin. His clothes comprise a jerkin, knee-length britches, stockings below them, and shoes with buckles, a full-length cloak and a broad-brimmed tapering hat. He has a long white beard and white hair and is playing a guitar. The background, seen only in the right-hand half of the picture, shows snow underfoot and bare trees. Mahoney's inspiration for the illustration probably came from the lines "There was an old man there beside;/ The snow in the street and the wind on the door,/ His hair was white, and his hood was wide,/ Minstrels and maids stand forth on the floor." While Morris's context makes it certain that Joseph was the old man he had in mind, Mahoney's picture does evoke the festive character of the carol, in which the second and fourth lines quoted form an incantation in each stanza.

18.1p
Illustrated/ British Ballads/ Old and New./
Selected and Edited/ by/ George Barnett Smith./
Vol. I [or Vol. II]/
Cassell, Peter, Galpin & Co:/ London, Paris & New York/ 1881/
[all rights reserved]

Comment: By 1886 the wording of the publisher's name had changed to read "Cassell and Company Limited," with an office also in Melbourne.

Limitation (Deluxe copies, printed in 1881 only): Fine paper edition, No. 30.

Comment: Cassell does not specify the number of copies in the fine paper edition. I know of the existence of No. 77, and suspect the total may be 100.

Dates of publication (Standard copies): <u>1881</u>, <u>1886</u>, 1894.

Binding (Deluxe): Quarter-bound, dark green cloth over boards, leather spine of same colour with gilt ruled line at junction. Title at top spine, volume number at mid-level, both in gilt. Plain else. Top edge gilt. Black endpapers.

Size (Deluxe): 268 x 193 mm.

Binding (Standard): Cloth over boards, background of red or bluish-green in different copies. Decorative covers, with lettering in black on front cover and in gilt on spine. The word "Illustrated" printed horizontally on inner upper part of front cover in letters 16 mm. in height, "British Ballads" in letters twice as high and sloping diagonally upwards from left to right at mid-level. Upright strokes of letters oriented parallel to sides of cover, so italicising the lettering. Similar slope to same letters on upper spine. Volume number in Roman numerals on lower part of spine and publisher at base, both in gilt. Top edge and endpapers plain.

Size (Standard): 260 x 186 mm.

Pagination: Volume I: xvi, 384. Volume II: xvi, 384.

Comment: Cassell bound in pages of advertisements at the end of these books. The content and layout of these pages vary from one edition to another, and the number of pages varies from four in 1881 to eight in 1886.

Contents: Volume I: p. i half-title, p. ii blank, inserted frontispiece, p. iii title page, p. iv statement of limitation (fine paper edition only, others blank), pp. v-vi preface, pp. vii-viii contents, pp. ix-xvi list of illustrations, pp. 1-3 introduction, pp. 4-384 text.
Volume II: p. i half-title, p. ii blank, inserted frontispiece, p. iii title page, p. iv statement of limitation (fine paper edition only, others blank), pp. v-vii contents, pp. viii-xvi list of illustrations, pp. 1-376 text, pp. 377-384 index of first lines.

Comment: Cassell were careful to supply background information. The list of illustrations includes the name of the artist who drew each picture, this not appearing with the picture itself. A short biographical sketch of the poet precedes the first ballad by him. In many instances a note precedes the ballad giving information about the event it records or other matters pertaining to it. For their fine paper edition Cassell used a smoother and better quality of paper, but the two versions are otherwise identical except for the differences in size and binding recorded above.

Illustrator: HENRY JAMES HOLLIDAY. Born in London in 1839. He entered the RA schools in 1854. During this period he came under the influence of the Pre-Raphaelites and later established friendships with Holman Hunt (see 18.12) and Burne-Jones (see 3.1). He worked as an artist, sculptor, book illustrator, and stained-glass maker. His best-known book illustrations are those for Lewis Carroll's *Hunting of the Snark,* which show his persisting affinity with the Pre-Raphaelites. He died in 1927.

Illustration and decoration: In contrast to the deluxe copies, the cover of the standard version receives ornate decoration. All lettering and decoration is in black except as noted otherwise. A thin ruled line close to the top, bottom, and outer edges of the front cover surrounds everything, and the designer placed a thicker line 1 cm. below the top line only. A diagonal ruled black line across the upper outer corner divides off a small area which contains a picture of a grand piano in gilt. An area in the bottom outer corner contains a picture in gilt of an old-fashioned settle with a carved back and a lute resting on the seat enclosed in a horizontal rectangle of three ruled lines, the inner gilt. Leaves, stems, and roses stretch across the lower part of the front cover, above a band with a geometrical pattern extending over spine and back cover. Similar leafy decoration is present on the spine and back cover, the last more open and spreading up the lowest three-quarters of the cover.

Decoration does not flag through the 800 pages of these two volumes. Starting with the preface of Volume I, ruled lines enclose the text on each page, a heavy line outside with a decorative curlicue at all four corners, and a plain, light line inside. The preface, introduction, and each ballad begin with a large dropped capital. These capitals vary greatly in form. Some have quite modest and simple decoration, others are large and more ornate, and some are illustrative of the text. Cassell inserted headpieces only occasionally, illustrative where present. One ballad follows another on the same page. Where insufficient space remains at the bottom of a page to start another ballad, they used a decorative or illustrative tailpiece. The books contain many full-page pictures, but the majority occupy part of the page, above, alongside or below the text. Only a few ballads lack illustration, and some have three or even four pictures. Longer ballads tend to have a full-page illustration, and even some shorter ones do, especially well-known pieces such as "Lochinvar."

The glory of these books lies in their layout and in their illustrations, approximately 300 in all. As suggested in the preceding paragraph, the layout editor integrates text and pictures admirably. The pictures all show a high level of technical competence and catch the spirit of the lines they seek to portray. While the illustration includes the work of many artists, there is no sense of dissonance. The only poem by Morris appears on page 176 of Volume II, "Riding Together" from *The Defence of Guenevere*. The initial dropped capital F depicts three nude boys, one standing, one sitting, and one kneeling, and all picking grapes which grow from a vine twisting up a trellis. The upright of the trellis forms the vertical stroke of the letter and extensions of the trellis the horizontal strokes. The second boy sits on the lower arm of the trellis. The picture has no obvious relevance to the poem, but adds to the overall decorative effect. The actual illustration sits on the facing page, portraying the lines "As freely we rode on together,/ With helms unlaced and bridles slack." We see two mounted knights in chain mail riding through a wood in leisurely fashion. One wears a surcoat, and both carry a lance resting on their right shoulder. The outer quarter of the picture extends nearly the length of the page, but the inner three-quarters occupies only the central section, with one stanza above and two below it. The shape of the picture thus resembles a letter T, with a broad vertical stroke, placed on its side. The sense of movement in this picture compares favourably with the static image of Hickling's illustration of the same poem (see 2.5). The poem ends with a decorative tailpiece on page 178.

18.2p
The Poets' Year/ Original and Selected/ Poems Embodying the Spirit of the Seasons/
Edited by/ Oscar Fay Adams/
Including Poems by/ Longfellow, Tennyson, Whittier, Lowell, Browning,/ Morris, Bryant and Others/
Fully Illustrated/
Boston/ D. Lothrop Company. Publishers/ Washington Street Opposite Bromfield

Date of publication: 1890.

Binding: Buckram, orange or brown in different copies. Decorated front cover and leafy decoration on spine with title vertically in gilt. Back cover plain. All edges gilt.

Pagination/Size: [viii] [308] [2] / 220 x 327 mm.

Contents: Pp. i-iii blank, p. iv frontispiece, p. v title page, p. vi statement of copyright, p. vii preface, p. viii blank, pp. 1-262 text, pp. 1-2 blank.

Comment: Adams edited a series of twelve anthologies for Lothrop in 1885 called *Through the Year with the Poets*, each containing poems related to a separate month. He selected the poems in *The Poet's Year* from these earlier books, using rather less than half of them. His editing of this earlier series is much better, including not only a list of contents but separate lists of authors, first lines and even subjects. The composite illustrated edition has none of these features, but does contain illustrations. The publisher printed the book on glossy, fairly heavy paper, which allows printing of illustrations and their inclusion as part of the gatherings. It has the additional virtue of resisting foxing. However, its weight makes the book vulnerable to separation of binding from gatherings and the latter from each other.

Illustrator: Not identified.

Illustration and decoration: On the front cover the title occupies most of the centre, the word "Poet's" surrounded by a laurel wreath with a ribbon trailing below it. "Poet's" is superimposed on a gilt-stamped rising sun with shooting rays. The lettering and decoration elsewhere on the front cover is stamped in dark brown except for a landscape in gilt which depicts coniferous trees and a lake. Ruled lines in brown partly surround the picture. A wavy line lies around the top and sides of the title, ending in a curlicue at inner end. Curlicues also appear at the left lower corner with wavy lines extending from them, one vertically half the height of the cover and the other rather more than half its breadth. Internally the book lacks decoration as such, and relies on its illustrations for its decorative effect. A picture emblematic of the month, with a few lines of poetry headed by the name of the month, precedes each of the twelve sections. The obverse remains blank. Most of the sections contain 26 pages. February has 28 and December 20. The editor laid out the text in three columns, reflecting the horizontal format of the book as a whole. Every second or third page a picture with a caption from an adjacent poem replaces text, most often in the central column, sometimes in one of the flanking columns, and sometimes in two of them. In addition, each section has a full-page illustration with a blank obverse, either page 13 or 15 of the section, also with a caption from an adjacent poem. All the illustrations are in black and white. Some artists sign their pictures but most do not, and the publisher gives no list of illustrators.

Adams included from one to three poems by Morris in the sections between January and September but failed to select any Morris poems for the last three months. The large number of poems overall precludes illustration of the majority, even though Lothrop illustrated the book generously. As one would expect on a statistical basis, only one of Morris's poems receives an illustration. We find this poem on the penultimate page of the section for June, a lyrical excerpt from *The Earthly Paradise*, which the editor entitled "A Night in June." The caption "Through their half-opened casements now there blew / A sweet fresh air, that of the flowers and sea..." comes from near the end, and actually refers to the dawn. The artist rendered his subject evocatively and with competence, equally true for almost all the art work in this book. Predictably, one sees a large window giving a view of trellised flowers and a stone balustrade with the sea in the background. A young woman in a white, full-length dress sits in a chair with wooden arms and a high, upholstered back gazing out at the scene. What one sees of the room suggests opulence, with a heavy curtain tied back, and a rich carpet underfoot. The only inconsistency with the text lies in the impression of full bright daylight created by the contrast between the exterior and the darkness of the room. Nevertheless, the artist seems to have executed his picture specifically for this poem, since the correspondence between text and picture is so close.

18.3pa
Guin-/evere/
Tennyson/ & Morris/
George G. Harrap/ and Company/ London

18.3pb
Guinevere/.
Poems by/ Lord Tennyson/ and W. Morris/
Thomas Y Crowell/ & Co. New York

Note: The two editions differ in the layout and wording of the title page. Harrap and Crowell seem to have had an agreement to publish jointly; they collaborated on another title described in this book (see 4.9P).

Date of publication: n.d. "1900" (UBC).

Binding 18.3pa (Deluxe): Flexible brown suede, yapped edges, plain except for dark brown square outlined by ruled line in gilt on upper front cover. Square contains title and authors in gilt.

Binding 18.3pa (Standard): Dark brown paper over boards, patterned to create the impression of leather. Cover design as in deluxe version.

Binding 18.3pb (Deluxe): Flexible brown suede with yapped edges. Title on upper front cover in horizontal rectangle with background in gilt. Rose bush with long stem rising from rose leaves at base of cover extends to below title. Matching lines, beginning as Celtic knot below leaves at base, curve outwards towards edges of cover, then upwards. On each side they split at mid-level, one of the new lines merging into each side of rose bush, the other into base of rectangle. Gilt rose flower below centre of rectangle and two more flanking leaves at base, all else in brown. Covers plain else. Top edge gilt. Endpapers a lacework pattern of curly green lines and dots.

Binding 18.3pb (Standard): No copy located. I am unaware whether Crowell published this form.

Comment: Multiple copies with the same binding give assurance that the description above for 18.3ap applies to the original binding. That for 18.3pb, based on examination of a single copy, is not certainly original, though it appears to be so. Its appearance is reminiscent of the cover designed by Will Bradley for *Bradley His Book*, Volume I, No. 2 some four years earlier (see 16.3).

Pagination/Size: 48 / 169 x 116 mm.

Contents: Inserted frontispiece and title page with tissue guard, p. 1 half-title of "Sir Lancelot and Queen Guinevere," p. 2 blank, pp. 3-4 text, p. 5 half-title of "Guinevere," p. 6 blank, pp. 7-32 text, p. 33 half-title of "The Defence of Guenevere," p. 34 blank, pp. 35-48 text.

Comment: The description of contents derives from copies of 18.3pa. In my copy of 18.3pb, page 1 of 18.3pa appears between the front free endpaper and the obverse of the frontispiece. This probably results from incorrect insertion of frontispiece and title page, rather than representing a feature of the edition as a whole. The placement of page 1 after the title page is more consistent with that of other half-titles, all preceding their own poem. The text comprises Tennyson's poems "Sir Lancelot and Queen Guinevere" and "Guinevere," and Morris's "The Defence of Guenevere." Each half-title appears in Gothic script, and the title of the poem sits, also in Gothic script, at the top of each page of text.

Illustrator: DANTE G. ROSSETTI. See 2.4.

Illustration and decoration: The publisher lavished almost all the decoration in the book on the title page, which has a cream-coloured ground unlike the paper of the rest of the book. The lettering, in Gothic script, occupies a fairly small vertical rectangle centred slightly above the mid-level. The initial letter of the title is dropped, and it, the publisher's first and last names, the C of "Company," and the initial[s] of the city appear in bright red, the rest of the lettering in green. The rectangle is outlined in red. A broad border surrounds it. The inner part of the border, roughly 1 cm. across, has a brown background, overlaid with twining green stems and small red flowers. The stems and flowers extend outside the brown part of the border for about another centimetre. The printer obtained the brown colour by overprinting the green and red. The remaining decoration comprises a dropped capital at the start of each poem.

The only picture in the book is the frontispiece, an unfinished sketch Rossetti did in 1858 of Guinevere as modelled by Jane Burden, who later married William Morris. It was reproduced photographically by Frederick Hollyer. The choice of picture is more apt than the editor might have known. The adulterous relationship between Rossetti and Morris's wife, now common knowledge among those familiar with Morris's life, was not widely known then. Writers on Morris delight in casting Rossetti as Lancelot, however unconvincing his appearance and behaviour for that role by the time of the affair in the late 1860s (see Introduction to Chapter 6). The drawing depicts head and torso of its subject, but only the head and neck are finished, emphasising Jane's luxuriant black hair, her large eyes, and long neck. Her dress appears only in a few preliminary lines.

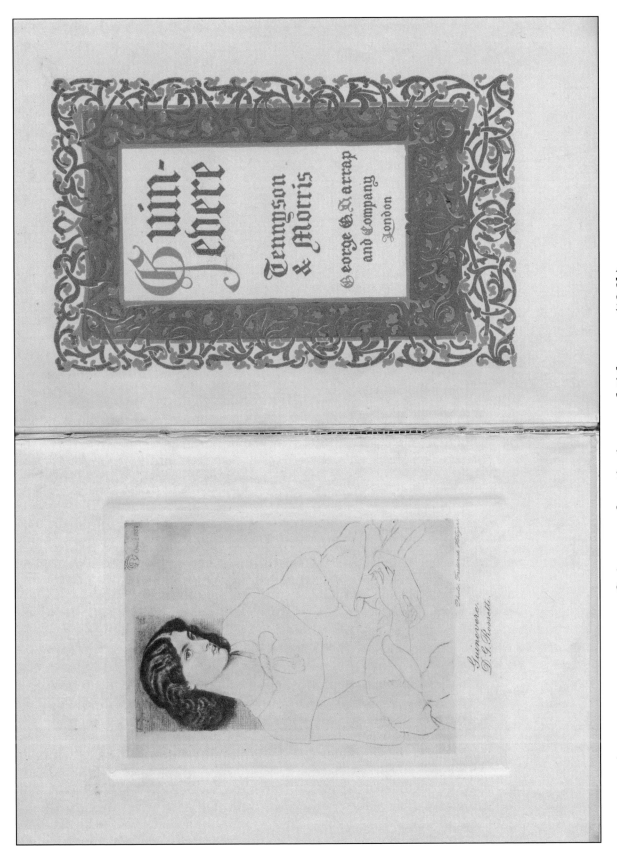

Guinevere, frontispiece and title page (18.3b)

18.4o
The Life and Death/ of Jason/
W. Morris/
Illustrated by P. B. Hickling./
London & Glasgow/ Collins' Clear-Type Press

Date of publication: May 1912 (LeMire).

Comment: Collins probably issued reprints at later dates. See below.

Binding (Deluxe): Embossed maroon leather, Morris's signature reproduced in gilt, centre of front cover. Title and author at top of spine, publisher at base, leafy and floral decoration between, all in gilt. Back cover plain. All edges gilt, maroon endpapers, obverses of free endpapers white, silk bookmark.

Binding (Standard): Bright red cloth over boards, plain except for same design on spine as for deluxe version. Some reprints, probably later ones, lack decoration on spine. Edges plain, maroon endpapers as in deluxe version, no bookmark.

Pagination/Size: [2] 474 [4] / 150 x 101 mm.

Contents: P. 1 half-title, p. 2 blank, inserted frontispiece and title page on glossy paper, obverses blank, p. 3 contents, p. 4 blank, pp. 5-470 text, p. 471 half-title to index, p. 472 blank, pp. 473-474 index, pp. 1-4 advertisements.

Illustrator: PERCY B. HICKLING. See 2.5.

Illustrations and decoration: The title page is printed in monochrome sepia. In the top half, ruled lines decorated with two small wreaths above, and a hanging garland on each side, enclose title, author and illustrator. A vignette occupies the lower half and depicts an elderly man reading a book while sitting in an armchair before an escritoire with a glass-fronted bookcase above it. In front of him is a tall stand on three legs surmounted by a vertically oriented circular object seen at an acute angle, possibly a mirror or a small work of art. His dress suggests the Regency period, with knee-length stockings and breeches buckled above them. More books lie scattered on the floor by his side. A smooth pillar with a Corinthian capital and a winged cherub clutching the base flanks the picture on each side.

Hickling drew four illustrations for this edition of *Jason*, including the frontispiece, all in a sepia monochrome in conformity with the publisher's practice for the series (see introduction to this chapter). The second half of the book consists of all the poems in *The Defence of Guenevere*, with the same illustrations as those Collins used in their edition of this work (see 2.5). Collins did not, however, reproduce the head- or tailpieces seen in that edition. The pictures which originally appeared in *Guenevere* remain in colour in this edition of *Jason*. The monochrome pictures illustrating the *Jason* section do not sit well with Hickling's previous colour pictures for *Guenevere*, and destroy any pretension to artistic unity.

Morris packed *Jason* with incident and adventure, so an illustrator has a daunting task in choosing the best subjects, especially if limited to four pictures. Hickling tends to portray figures rather than incident in illustrating this book. The last picture shows Jason seated by the beached wreck of the Argo, contemplating the beached wreck of his own life, fated to end in a few seconds as the rotting timbers of the ship collapse and crush him. The scene we see in the picture itself is placid, even static. All the drama comes from the reader's knowledge of what is about to happen. The other pictures seek to catch the drama of the instant more overtly. The frontispiece shows the moment when Hylas encounters the nymph who encompasses his death by enticing him into her watery domain. This is the most successful of Hickling's illustrations, catching the seductive power of the nymph and the doomed virility and prowess of the youth. In the second illustration Hickling uses only a single figure, Medea, as she guides Jason to the lair of the dragon guarding the Golden Fleece. Hickling seeks to convey Medea's fear, as expressed in the line quoted in the Illustrations section of 3.1, which begins "If I give the word / Then know that all is lost . . . ." Hickling's portrayal does not convince the viewer. It suggests the timidity of a schoolgirl leaving the house on her first date, rather than the wary but resolute heroism of a powerful sorceress whose actions dominate the story and determine its direction. The third illustration depicts the daughters of Pelias as they come to witness the witchcraft which Medea has duped them into believing will restore their father's youthful vigour. Hickling catches their mixed fear and hope. However, his rendering falls far short of the same scene painted on an Attic vase nearly two and a half thousand years earlier (see 3.3).

18.50a
A Day with/ William/ Morris/
by M.C. Gillington/
London/ Hodder & Stoughton

18.50b
A Day with/ William/ Morris/
by M.C. Gillington/
New York/ Hodder & Stoughton

Date of publication: n.d. "1912" (BL).

Comment: The picture of Morris on the front cover is signed "Michael, 1911." Thus the British Library attribution of 1912 seems plausible.

Binding: Dust jacket not examined. Grey paper over boards, colour portrait of Morris chest length pasted on centre of front cover, framed by black ruled line. Name above portrait, series title below, decoration of single leaf on each side. All lettering and decoration in black outlined in gilt. Title vertically on spine in gilt. Laurel wreath enclosing publisher's monogram on centre of back cover all in gilt. Covers plain else. Endpapers plain in some copies, pictorial in others.

Comment: The pictorial endpapers are a feature of both the London and New York editions. Thus the plain endpapers of some copies probably represent different impressions. Hodder and Stoughton provide no information on this point.

Pagination/Size: [iv] [44] / 201 x 143 mm.

Comment: The numeration excludes the illustrations, printed on glossy paper, but does include the separate pages with the captions, on the same matte paper as the rest of the text.

Contents: P. i portrait of Morris, p. ii caption of frontispiece, inserted frontispiece facing title page, obverse blank, p. iii title page, p. iv list of other titles in series, pp. 1-44 text with four inserted illustrations.

Comment: A line drawing of a younger and more vibrant-looking Morris replaces a half-title page. The text is a rather fanciful description of a typical day in Morris's life, set at Kelmscott House on June 21, 1879. It seeks to delineate Morris's personality by a portrayal of his physique, work habits, and activity generally, and by quotations from his works and conversation. It provides a sympathetic but rather one-dimensional picture of the man. Gillington included among the quotations lengthy excerpts from several of Morris's poems, and Frampton illustrated five, of which three come from *The Defence of Guenevere*. The publisher used a thick matte paper, still in good condition in copies I have examined.

A · DAY · WITH
WILLIAM
MORRIS
BY M · C · GILLINGTON

LONDON
HODDER & STOUGHTON

E. REGINALD FRAMPTON

O, russet brown and scarlet bright,
When the Sword went out to sea,
My sisters wore: I wore but white:
Red, brown and white, all three;
Three damozels; each had a knight,
When the Sword went out to sea.

"The Sailing of the Sword"
A Day with William Morris, frontispiece
and title page

Illustrator: EDWARD REGINALD FRAMPTON. Born in 1872. He studied in France and Italy. He is best known as a mural artist, especially of religious subjects, and as an art educator. He died in 1923. See also 18.6p.

Illustrations and decoration: Hodder used decoration sparingly. In copies with pictorial endpapers the viewer sees an orange-brown monochrome illustration of a tranquil landscape with a pond and trees in the foreground and a castle perched on top of a hill in the background. On the title page decoration is limited to the publisher's monogram in red at the mid-level. The initial letter of the text is a large dropped and decorated capital, reminiscent of Morris's own designs. The cover picture, signed and dated (see *Date of publication* above) portrays Morris late in life with bags under his sunken eyes, and a suggestion of fatigue and despondency about him. Its honesty puts one in mind of the later self-portraits by Rembrandt. The artist may have worked from a photograph in his depiction of Morris. However, a photograph resembling this picture is not in the public domain, as far as I know. Most likely the artist was Arthur C. Michael, a book illustrator active at this time. All the pictures have a wide margin, and each one in the body of the text is a recto and has its caption on the recto preceding it. The verso facing the picture is left completely blank. The pictures are printed on glossy white paper, mainly in bright blues and reds, and have a decorative quality reminiscent of the illustrations of Jessie King (see 2.1). Without exception, they portray static human forms, mainly soulful-looking women, rather than any of the action which fills the poems. One can easily imagine a heavenly host of similar figures in Frampton's religious paintings. The best illustration is the frontispiece, which depicts yet again the three sisters watching the sailing of the Sword (see 2.5 and 2.11). Frampton illustrates the departure of the three knights and catches well the desolation on the face of Ursula, whose man, however, does return to her. Perhaps naively, Frampton interprets the "Sword" as the name of the ship and therefore writes the word on the stern of the departing vessel, rather than seeing "Sword" as symbolic of the armed men.

Comment: According to Houfe, Frampton illustrated a book called *The Poems of William Morris*. Possibly Hodder draws on this book for the pictures in 18.5 and 18.6. However, I have never seen a copy, nor even any other reference to it.

18.6 Note: The following entry and a companion volume, *Days with the English Poets*, share a common format, including size, similar binding, and title page of the same design. Lund printed the latter, the whole series *Days with the Poets* (see 18.5) and presumably 18.6 as well. The type on the page is identical in both 18.5 and 18.6.

18.6p
Days/ with the/ Victorian/ Poets/ Rossetti/ Morris/ Mrs. Browning/
Hodder &/ Stoughton

Date of publication: n.d. 1912-1914.

Comment: An inscription on the endpaper of my copy reads in part "Christmas 1914." Thus this title came out at the same time or soon after the preceding book (18.5o), which contains the same text about Morris and the same illustrations.

Binding: Dull green buckram, title on upper quadrant of front cover within double ruled lines. Remaining quadrants with medallion portraits, the same as those on *Days with the Poets* series, Rossetti upper right, Morris lower left, Barrett Browning lower right. A swirling pattern of stems, leaves, and berries around portraits, all decoration and letters in gilt with single ruled line in gilt around all. Title on top of spine, laurel wreath just above mid-level, poets' names halfway from there to base, publisher at base, all in gilt. Back cover plain. Endpapers dull brown.

Pagination/Size: [iv] [132] [2] / 195 x 144 mm.

Comment: The section on Morris occupies pages 45-88.

Contents: P. i half-title of Rossetti section, p. ii caption facing blank obverse of inserted frontispiece, p. iii title page, p. iv blank, pp. 1-44 text, p. 45 half-title of Morris section, p. 46 caption facing blank obverse of inserted illustration, pp. 47-88 text, p. 89 half-title of Barrett Browning section, p. 90 caption facing blank obverse of illustration, pp. 91-132 text, pp. 1-2 blank.

Comment: The text is the same as that already described as a separate book under 18.5o, and the pictures appear on the same glossy paper. Unlike the inserted form they take in 18.5o, they are tipped in on inserted sheets of the same paper as Hodder used for the endpapers. The same good quality of matte paper was used in both books for the text generally.

Illustrator: E. REGINALD FRAMPTON. See 18.5o.

Illustrations and decoration: The cover portraits of the three artists reproduce the heads only of the pictures on the cover of the separate edition, in Morris's case 18.5. The internal illustrations are the same as in the separate book. The printing on the title page of the present volume is in red, between two pillars supporting a semicircular arch. On both sides, outside the pillars, are line drawings, each a mirror image of the other, showing a castle on a cliff with trees at its base, shrubs in the foreground, and cumulus clouds above. The half-title which precedes each section has the section title in red, surrounded by a spray of roses and their stems, in black.

Stories from/ William Morris/ Retold from/ "The Earthly Paradise"/ by/ Emily Underdown/
Thomas Nelson & Sons, Ltd./ London, Edinburgh and New York

This book contains material from *The Earthly Paradise* and from *The Life and Death of Jason*. However, it appears in Chapter 4, listed as 4.13P, for reasons enunciated there.

18.7pa
A Treasury of/ Fantasy/
Edited by/ Cary Wilkins/
Illustrated/
Gramercy Books/ New York. Avenel

Date of publication: 1981.

Binding: Dust jacket with pictorial cover. Title upper front cover, large letters in white, list of authors mid-right in black, editor at base in small white letters. Title vertically on spine, publisher at base, both in white. Laudatory comments about contents printed in black on back of jacket. Flaps carry information in heated prose about book. Bound in red buckram, title vertically on spine, publisher at base, both in gilt, cover plain else.

Pagination/Size: viii, 504 / 228 x 153 mm.

Contents: P. i half-title, p. ii list of other titles, p. iii title page, p iv statement of copyright and acknowledgements, p. v contents, p. vi illustration, pp. vii-viii foreword, p. 1 half-title of "The Story of Sigurd from *The Volsunga Saga*," p. 2 illustration, pp. 3-47 text, p. 48 tailpiece, pp. 49-258 half-titles and texts by authors other than Morris, p. 259 half-title of "The Wood beyond the World," p. 260 illustration, pp. 261-343 text, p. 344 tailpiece, pp. 345-504 half-titles and texts by authors other than Morris.

Comment: The anthology contains eleven stories by several nineteenth- and twentieth-century writers in this genre, including the two by Morris. "The Story of Sigurd" is a truncated version of the *Volsunga Saga*; it contains Chapters 13 to 32 of the Morris version. This section encompasses the birth, life, and death of Sigurd.

18.7pb
A Treasury of/ Fantasy/ Heroic Adventures in Imaginary Lands/
Revised Edition/
Edited by Cary Wilkins/
Illustrated/
Chatham River Press/ New York

Date of publication: 1984.

Binding: Paperback with pictorial cover on light brown background. Title at top front cover, authors at base, both in black. Editor's name horizontally at top of spine, title vertically below it, publisher at base, all in black on green ground. Beige ground back cover, contents there in black.

Pagination/Size: viii, 472 / 228 x 153 mm.

Contents: P. i half-title, p. ii frontispiece, p. iii title page, p. iv statement of copyright and acknowledgements, p. v contents, p. vi illustration, pp. vii-viii foreword (somewhat shortened from that in 18.7a), p. 1 half-title of "The Story of Sigurd from The Volsunga Saga," p. 2 illustration, pp. 3-47 text, p. 48 tailpiece, pp. 49-258 half-titles and texts by authors other than Morris, p. 259 half-title of "The Wood beyond the World," p. 260 illustration, pp. 261-343 text, p. 344 tailpiece, pp. 345-472 half-titles and texts by authors other than Morris.

Comment: Except as noted, the layout of the two editions is identical, but for the substitution of a short story by Frank Baum for a longer one by Lord Dunsany. This accounts for the shorter length of 18.7pb.

18.7pa & b Illustrators: AUBREY VINCENT BEARDSLEY. Shortly after his marriage, Beardsley's father lost the source of his independent income. Beardsley, who was born in 1872 in Brighton, therefore grew up in genteel poverty. His family saw him as a delicate child, and by the age of seven his doctor had diagnosed him as having pulmonary tuberculosis. His wealthy maternal family arranged that he leave the unhealthy conditions of his home, by then in London, to live in the country. Eventually they moved him back to Brighton to stay with a great-aunt. He attended the Brighton Grammar School, where his artistic talents became manifest. He also displayed exceptional gifts in other directions. He was a voracious reader with a retentive memory. He had skill as an actor. He was a fine pianist with an intense appreciation of music, who even composed some juvenile pieces. He could write well, and later showed promise in both prose and poetry. However, the family's financial problems dictated that he get a job when he left school in 1888, and he obtained work as a clerk in London. To satisfy his ravenous intellectual and artistic cravings, any spare money he had at this time went on books, music, or the theatre. However, his poor home and working conditions precipitated a recurrence of tuberculosis late in 1889. The enforced idleness required for recovery allowed him even more time for reading, and it was during this period that he began to find self-expression in drawing. By 1891 he had made a serious commitment to art, and he received encouragement from Burne-Jones (see 3.1), whom he met in July of that year. At Burne-Jones's suggestion he enrolled that autumn in the Westminster School of Art, where he received a good grounding in graphic art. However, he was largely self-taught through the extraordinary range and depth of his study of previous artists and artistic styles. His abilities were quickly recognised. Admirers drew him to the attention of the publisher J.M. Dent, from whom he received a major commission in 1892, to illustrate a new edition of *Le Morte d'Arthur* published the following year. He achieved a wider audience in 1894 with his work done for the new periodical *The Yellow Book*, and other commissions followed. He fell out with the publisher of *The Yellow Book*, but in early 1896 his work appeared in a similar periodical, *The Savoy*. Since the recurrence of tuberculosis in 1889 he had been having periodic relapses, necessitating convalescence of various lengths. He had driven himself in his work, and had not neglected the charms of the London prostitutes nor the offerings of the vintners. I am not the first to see in Beardsley the inspiration for the character of Dubedat in Bernard Shaw's play *The Doctor's Dilemma*. By 1897, Beardsley's style of life had contributed to an alarming deterioration of his health. He went to convalesce, first to the south coast of England and then in May to France. He continued to draw, but his artistic output declined due to progressive debility. He died in southern France in early 1898. (See Sturgis.)

LANCELOT SPEED. Born in London in 1860. He came from a privileged background, being educated at Rugby and Clare College,

Cambridge. He was known mainly for his illustrations for books and magazines. He lived at Barnet and at Southend-on-Sea, and died in the latter town in 1931.

Illustrations and decoration: The picture on the dust jacket of 18.7pa features a brown monochrome scene which extends over both covers and spine. It depicts a lake with distorted pillars of rock rearing from the water and two onlookers in the foreground gazing across the expanse. The nearer onlooker stands by another rocky pillar, holding a root which twines up it. Behind her, on the back cover, a paved floor extends backwards to an arch, through which one gains another view onto the lurid background. The cover illustration of 18.7pb does not repeat that on the dust jacket. On the paperback the reader sees a picture done in white, green and brown by Russ Hoover. An over-muscled man, a huge broadsword in one hand, clutching with the other the hand of a bored-looking princess, is leaping from among the coils of an enormous dragon which rears behind them, its head and outstretched wing forming a backdrop. The woman is standing stock-still, not leaping with him. The broad-minded would take Hoover's picture as a portrayal of Sigurd and Fafnir, but it is so general and so little related to the text that the notion is not sustainable. For one thing Brynhild is not even present when Sigurd encounters Fafnir.

Five swords, one vertical, and the rest placed diagonally, adorn the mid-level of the title page of both editions. The diagonally placed swords sit as two crossed pairs, each weapon in a pair parallel to its fellow, and the pairs symmetrically sitting to either side of the vertical one. The five blades intersect in their mid-sections. This decoration appears later as the frontispiece for one of the stories. Tailpieces appear on the obverse of the last page whenever the text finishes on a recto. They are representational but not necessarily illustrative of the text. For example, the tailpiece in 18.7pa following *The Wood beyond the World* depicts a unicorn, not present in the story itself. In 18.7pb the designer substitutes a different tailpiece. As noted above, the publisher of 18.7pb replaced the story which follows *The Wood* and in doing so supplied different illustrations for the new story. They consist entirely of head- and tailpieces for almost all the chapters. Other than this the two editions have the same textual illustrations. The new tailpiece for *The Wood beyond the World* shows an androgynous figure standing on the right, arms folded across the chest, and an enormous gossamer wing which occupies most of the picture. Once again the picture bears no relation to Morris's text. Indeed, this tailpiece has features in common with pictures illustrating the next story, subtitled *An Electrical Fairy Tale*, and may have come from that source.

The relevance of illustration to text varies. The illustration on page vii of both editions and the one on page ii of 18.7pb only do not illustrate the text of any story in these books. Those accompanying the text purport to do so. Speed drew the pictures used to illustrate "The Story of Sigurd" for a condensed version of this story which appeared originally in *The Red Fairy Book* in 1890. The editor of the present work has reproduced

all of his five pictures. They show considerable technical skill and catch
the drama. Since they were done for the same story, they are entirely
appropriate. Beardsley's illustration for the other story, "The Wood
beyond the World," is limited to a frontispiece which originally appeared
in *Le Morte d'Arthur*, the verso of a double spread between pages 308-
309 of the edition of 1907. The picture shows a figure half reclining in
a meadow, with the caption "And when he awoke it was broad day, calm
and bright and cloudless." Thus the picture is apposite, but does not
highlight a significant point in the story. It therefore adds nothing to the
text or the book as a whole.

18.8pa
Poems of the Countryside/
Pictures by Gordon Benningfield/
Viking

Dates of publication: 1987 (twice) 1988 (twice).

18.8pb
Poems of the Countryside/
Pictures by Gordon Benningfield
[Devizes: Selectabook]

Date of publication: n.d.

Comment: Selectabook published this book in 1998 or later, since the
statement of copyright reads "The Estate of Gordon Benningfield." The
artist died that year.

18.8pa & b Binding: Pictorial dust jacket, different illustrations on front
and back covers, both also in body of text. Title on upper front cover;
artist's name at base; artist, title and publisher on spine; all lettering
in black. In 18.8pa publisher's name appears vertically and in 18.8pb
horizontally. 18.8pa bound in grey buckram, artist, title, and publisher
vertically on spine in gilt, plain else. 18.8pb bound in paper over
boards duplicating pictures on jacket. Identical front and back pictorial
"endpapers."

Comment: Online descriptions refer to the existence of a paperback version of 18.8pa. This appears to be the result of computer error, as two such copies when ordered both proved to be the hardback version.

18.8p Pagination/Size: 128 / 165 x 246 mm.

Comment: In his list of pictures the publisher included illustrations on the "endpapers." These so-called endpapers comprise the outermost two sheets of the first and last gatherings, and Viking included them in the pagination, so that pages 1 and 128 are pasted to the covers. I treat these two sheets as normal endpapers in describing the binding.

Contents: P. 4 frontispiece, p. 5 title page, p. 6 publication information, p. 7 list of illustrations, pp. 8-9 contents, pp. 10-125 text.

Comment: The list of illustrations identifies the locations of the pictures, none of which has a caption in the text. Most pages form a double spread, with text on one side and illustration on the facing page. The designers set short poems in a single column. Many others appear in two columns, and two in triple columns. Occasionally they placed a part-page picture alongside its poem, sometimes with two such pictures and their poems facing each other as a double spread.

Illustrator: GORDON BENNINGFIELD. Benningfield started as an ecclesiastical artist but in the 1960s became known for his depiction of the English countryside. By the 1980s he reached a wide audience through television appearances and his illustration of books about the country life, including the three anthologies of poetry here described. He was a committed environmentalist with a special interest in butterflies, which provided the focus for his first book. The Post Office commissioned him to design postage stamps illustrating butterflies and other insects. His environmental convictions prompted him to act as a co-founder of the Countryside Restoration Trust, and he served as President of the Butterfly Conservation organisation. He was married with two daughters. He died in 1998.

Illustrations and decoration: Benningfield was an artist of great technical competence, who excelled in all the subjects he chose. The appearance of the illustrations in this book and its companion volumes suggests that most of the originals are watercolours with a few in pencil. Landscapes predominate, but he also did close-up studies of flowers, birds and insects, always with meticulous accuracy. For someone attracted by modern art, his pictures may lack excitement: his style owes little to the twentieth century. However, they do have great charm, and his art and these books must have found a ready market. Indeed, he made book illustration a large part of his career, to judge by the number of books of this type which he produced in the 1980s and 1990s.

In this book and in its companion volumes, poem and picture match with great fidelity, both in detail and in overall conception. Where poem and picture share the same page both fit precisely together, suggesting the

GORDON BENNINGFIELD
"February"
Poems of the Countryside, p. 86

artist drew the illustration to fill the area left empty. Benningfield must have worked closely with the designers to achieve this harmony. Looking at the books one would find it impossible to say whether the artist sought subjects already having a text in mind, or whether the compiler made inspired choices of poems facing pictures previously created by the artist. Most likely both procedures operated at different times. A companion volume (see 18.10p) assigns Hollis sole credit for the selection, and she may have done most or all of it in this book as well. Benningfield does assert copyright dating from 1980, probably well before his collaboration with Cameron and Hollis began.

All decoration is illustrative and dazzles with its profusion and variety. The endpapers have an identical white ground, a ruled black border close to all edges, and a large circular illustration in the centre of the page depicting butterflies on stalks of grass, each picture a mirror image of the other. A spray of honeysuckle adorns the title page and a poppy the following one. Beyond this one finds purely textual illustration. The poems by Morris comprise extracts from the sections in *The Earthly Paradise* eulogising the months of February and August, and the early poem "Fair Weather and Foul." Full-page illustrations accompany all three. For February Benningfield renders the monochrome vista of a flooding stream and snow-covered meadow in the appropriate monochrome of a pencil drawing. In the picture for August the artist paints a glowing scene with a field of golden wheat being harvested with a team of two horses, the tall elms of the poem rising in the background. The last illustration catches fair weather and foul in the fleeting transition from storm to sunshine which one finds in any climate subject to rapid change, in this case the uplands of Dorset. We see a flock of sheep grazing in the foreground, low grey hills in the background, and a turbulent orange sky louring over all.

18.9pa
Green and Pleasant Land/ Poetry of the English Countryside/
Pictures by Gordon Benningfield/
Viking

Date of publication: 1989.

18.9pb
Green and Pleasant Land/ Poetry of the English Countryside/
Pictures by Gordon Benningfield
[Devizes: Selectabook]

Date of publication: n.d.

Comment: See comments under 18.8. In this book, the statement of copyright refers to "Gordon Benningfield" rather than to his "Estate." Thus the Selectabook edition may predate Benningfield's death in 1998.

Binding, Pagination, Size, and *Contents:* See 18.8.

Illustrator: GORDON BENNINGFIELD. See 18.8.

Illustrations: As in 18.8 the endpapers have the same illustration front and back, again the one on the pastedown a mirror image of that on the free endpaper. In this book they depict thistle and bindweed. For the title page the artist drew a meadow with a farm in the background, while poppyseed heads appear on the following page. This book contains only one poem by Morris, part of "Summer Dawn" from *The Defence of Guenevere.* Benningfield illustrated it with a full-page picture in colour which shows an indistinct succession of breaking waves surging towards an equally indistinct beach in the foreground, all bathed in diffuse pink light. The colour tones are identical to those Govey uses in her illustration of the same poem (see 2.16), but the overall effect puts one in mind of late works by Turner. For further comments on Benningfield's illustration see 18.8.

18.10pa
Poems of the Seasons/
Pictures by/ Gordon Benningfield/
Viking

Date of publication: 1992.

18.10pb
Poems of the Seasons/
Pictures by/ Gordon Benningfield
[Devizes: Selectabook]

Date of publication: n.d.

Comment: After 1998. The statement of copyright reads in part "The Estate of Gordon Benningfield." See 18.8.

Binding, Pagination, Size, and *Contents:* See 18.8.

Illustrator: GORDON BENNINGFIELD. See 18.8p.

Illustration and decoration: As in previous titles in this group the pictures on the free and fixed endpapers are mirror images of each other. They depict a rich clump of kingcups in full colour. The title page carries a picture of a spray of blackberries, while the following page has a thistle in colour. This book also has just one extract by Morris, a few lines from "Autumn," from *The Earthly Paradise.* Poem and picture sit alongside each other on the same page. On an autumnal light-brown background the artist painted a spray of black bryony berries and leaves, the latter with their autumn colouring. The picture is no more than symbolic.

18.11 Note: The Heritage Press seems to be a small commercial venture publishing ephemeral items with an orientation to the Arts and Crafts movement. Malvern is an English market town near the Welsh border.

18.11p
A William Morris/ Christmas Book/
The Christmas Story in Stained Glass/
by William Morris and Burne-Jones/
and in Verses by Morris and Others./
Ann S. Dean/
Heritage Press, Malvern/ ISBN 1 873089 02 3

Date of publication: 1990.

Binding: Paperback with flexible thick cover decorated with Morris's chintz, *Brer Rabbit.* Title on centre, front cover in white rectangle enclosed by two black lines. ISBN similarly on back cover. Inside of covers blank.

Pagination/Size: [16] / 211 x 149 mm.

Contents: P. 1 title page, p. 2 frontispiece, pp. 3-5 introduction, pp. 6-15 text, p. 16 advertisements and acknowledgements.

Comment: The introduction describes the source of the illustrations employed in the book and gives general background information on Morris's firm.

Illustrators: EDWARD BURNE-JONES. See 3.1.
    WILLIAM MORRIS. See Introduction. See also 18.13p.

Illustrations and decoration: The Morris design on the cover is in Christmas red and has a strong vertical orientation, with the focus of the pattern running top to bottom in the midline of front and back covers. The title page has a detail from a stained glass window produced by Morris and Company. The textual illustrations come from similar designs for stained glass windows. Around the poems the book's designer placed marginal decorations which originally appeared in KP books, some at the sides, some at the base, and one at both locations.

All the illustrations depict a scene from the Nativity legend, and each carries a caption which identifies the location of the church window whence it came. The frontispiece is a pasted-in colour photograph of a window depicting the Virgin and Child. The rest of the illustrations are in black outline. Each occupies a verso, with the carol it illustrates on the facing recto. The designer, Ann Dean, tried to select scenes from the windows which match the subject-matter of the carol. She is not entirely successful with this. For "The Shepherds' Carol," the only text by Morris which she included, she used a scene which depicts the Presentation in the Temple. Nevertheless this small booklet is well laid out, the black outlines of the pictures lending themselves to the format.

18.12o
The/ Sweet Days/ Die/
Poems by William Morris/
Selected and with an Introduction by Pamela Todd/
Pavilion

Colophon (in part): First published in Great Britain in 1996 by/ Pavilion Books Limited/ 26 Upper Ground, London SE1 9PD . . . Compilation and design …David Fordham and Pamela Todd/ Typeset in Helvetica Bold and Garamond Light by SX Composing Ltd. Rayleigh/ Printed and bound in Italy by Graphicom

Comment: Online listings of this book sometimes refer to Trafalgar Square as the publisher. Trafalgar Square is a distributor for other publishers and does not publish under its own imprint. As far as I know, no other publisher has issued an edition of this book.

Binding: Dust jacket with pictorial front cover. Title and author in gilt in black rectangle surrounded by two gilt ruled lines on upper left. Title and author vertically on spine, publisher at base, all in gilt on black ground. Back cover with deep cerise ground and central grey panel containing first two stanzas of Morris's Prologue to *The Earthly Paradise.* Flaps with information about Morris, the book, and the editor. Book bound in blue buckram with data on spine of jacket repeated on spine in gilt. Plain else. Grey endpapers.

Pagination/Size: 96 / 181 x 181 mm.

Contents: P. 1 half-title, p. 2 frontispiece, p. 3 title page, p. 4 dedication and publication information, p. 5 contents, p. 6 illustration, pp. 7-11 introduction, pp. 12-95 text, p. 96 acknowledgements.

Comment: A large number of the poems face a picture by a Pre-Raphaelite painter. Many pages, particularly those with no facing illustration, have Morris's signature in grey and greatly enlarged, as a background. The selection of poems ranges from the verses in "The Hollow Land" of the *Oxford and Cambridge Magazine,* through some from *The Defence of Guenevere, The Earthly Paradise,* and *Love Is Enough,* to those published at intervals in magazines and gathered up in *Poems by the Way.* The text is placed in one or two columns depending on the length of the line and of the overall poem.

Illustrators: FORD MADOX BROWN. Born in Calais in 1821. He studied in Belgium, Antwerp and Italy, and married in Paris in 1841. However, he spent his professional career in London. Although he was not a formal member, his precepts and practice were the foundations on which the group who formed the PRB built their theory of art. He especially influenced Rossetti (see 2.4), who was his pupil for a time. Brown was active as a teacher of art, especially in the 1850s, when he lectured at two art schools for working men. While he was known mainly as a painter, he did book illustration and some design work for Morris's company in its early years. Indeed, he was a founding member of the company in 1861 and by virtue of this later created difficulty for Morris. He insisted on recompense out of proportion to his input when Morris assumed sole control in 1874 of what was by then a thriving enterprise. However, this seems out of character; William Rossetti records him as unselfish and possessed of a strong social conscience. Indeed, like Morris he was active in the socialist movement, especially during the 1880s at a time when he was in Manchester engaged in decorating its new town hall, a huge Victorian Gothic structure, which still dominates the centre of the city. He was also noted for his hospitality and conversational powers. He died in London in 1893. His grandson was the writer Ford Madox Ford.

EDWARD BURNE-JONES. See 3.1.

EVELYN DE MORGAN. Born Mary Evelyn Pickering in 1855 into an affluent and conventional family which, on her mother's side, embarrassed itself by producing talented artists from time to time. The black sheep of the Pickering flock in the mid-nineteenth century was the painter Roddam Spencer-Stanhope (see below), Evelyn's mother's brother. Evelyn showed early her passion for art and her determination to pursue it as a career in the teeth of her family's opposition. In the early to mid 1870s she studied at the Slade School of Art, where her talent was recognised by first prizes in painting from antiques and from life and by the award of the Slade Scholarship. She also received instruction from her uncle. By the mid-1870s, she was selling enough of her work to afford a lengthy stay in Italy to further her study of art. She established herself as a successful painter in the 1880s, exhibiting regularly at the Grosvenor and later at the New Galleries. In 1887 she married the potter William de Morgan, who did tile work for Morris's company. They had a supremely happy marriage, clouded in its first half by the failure of de Morgan to match his genius as a potter with an ability to make money from this craft. He eventually had to close his business, but then embarked on a successful career as a novelist. Meanwhile Evelyn, whose painting had supported them in the early years, continued her own work. She was an allegorical painter whose paintings show the influence of Burne-Jones. By the early twentieth century, the revolutions in artistic practice, Cubism and like movements, made Evelyn reluctant to exhibit. She may have felt that the public would see her style as out of artistic fashion. At the same time, her husband's financial security based on his writing relieved her of the necessity to earn money herself. Thus she still painted, but made little attempt to sell this later work. She died in London in 1919, two years after her husband. (See Stirling.)

CHARLES M. GERE. See 10.2.

ARTHUR HUGHES. Born in London in 1832. He showed early artistic talent and enrolled in the Government School of Design in 1846, transferring to the RA schools a year later. His ability was recognised there by the award of a silver medal for drawing in 1849. About this time he became aware of the PRB, and over the next few years gravitated into their circle, adopting their style of painting for his own work. Indeed, he was one of the Pre-Raphaelites gathered by Rossetti to paint the murals on the ceiling of the Oxford Debating Hall in 1857-58. He had begun to sell his paintings by 1854, and also became known for his illustration of books. However, in neither of these fields did he attain the success which the quality of his work merited. As a result, his financial situation was precarious at intervals, necessitating repeated moves from houses occupied in more affluent times to more humble surroundings. His paintings depict in particular religious themes, the Arthurian legends, and scenes of romantic love. His early marriage to Tryphena Foord in 1855 and their subsequent large family may have given him special insight into the last subject. Morris so admired *April Love*, one of Hughes' romantic paintings, that he bought it in 1856. Hughes's many friends valued him for his kindness, good nature and modesty. However, these qualities accompanied a diffidence which may have made it difficult for him to assert himself sufficiently to promote his career. He did start to achieve more recognition late in life, especially as a book illustrator in the early twentieth century. He was awarded a Civil List Pension in 1912. He died in London in 1915. See also 18.13p. (See Roberts.)

WILLIAM HOLMAN HUNT. Born in London in 1827. He did not come from an artistic background; his father was employed in commerce, and Hunt himself worked for a short time as a clerk. He entered the RA schools in 1844 and also studied under H. Rogers. He was a founding member of the PRB, an association which influenced his artistic style thereafter. While he became known primarily as a painter, both in oils and watercolour, he also received acclaim for his illustration of Moxon's 1857 edition of Tennyson's poems. Hunt was a religious man; this found expression in his paintings with religious themes, and also in his visits to the Middle East and the Holy Land for extended periods in the 1850s to the 1870s. He also travelled and lived in Continental Europe for long periods during this time. En route to the Middle East in 1866, and recently married, he and his wife stopped in Florence, where she contracted cholera and died. He himself died in London in 1910.

SIDNEY HAROLD METEYARD. Born in Birmingham in 1868. He studied at the Birmingham School of Art under Edward Taylor and worked in Birmingham throughout his life. He did also exhibit at the RA. He died in 1947. See also Appendix 2.

SIR JOHN EVERETT MILLAIS. Born in Southampton in 1829. He came of a wealthy family and displayed a precocious artistic talent which received encouragement from his parents. He entered the RA schools as early as eleven years of age. Here he met Holman Hunt (see above) and got caught up in the swirl of new ideas about art which found expression in the PRB, of which he became a founding member. For most of the following decade, he adopted a Pre-Raphaelite style, in which he produced his finest paintings. John Ruskin championed his work early, and they became friends to the point that they went on a painting holiday to Scotland in 1853, accompanied by Ruskin's wife Effie Gray. The trip had momentous consequences: Gray left her husband, secured an annulment, and married Millais in 1855. Millais's illustrations of this period, both in content and subject matter, reflect his emotional turmoil. He was elected RA in 1856, a date which signalled his shift to a conservative artistic expression. He retained his remarkable facility and increased his popularity with the public at the cost of suppressing any innovative tendency, genius descending to talent. Throughout the rest of his life, he remained a prolific painter, creator of book illustrations, and producer of prints and etchings. He received a knighthood in 1885 and was elected President of the RA in the year of his death, 1896. See also 18.13p.

SIR JOSEPH NOEL PATON. Born in Dunfermline, Scotland, in 1821. He studied at the RA schools and was influenced by the PRB. While he spent his working life in Scotland, he maintained a presence in London, exhibiting at the RA between 1856 and 1883. However, his main activities centred on Edinburgh; he was elected to the RSA in 1850, and received the appointment as the Queen's Limner for Scotland in 1860 and a knighthood in 1867. He painted scenes of Scottish history and legend but achieved more recognition as a genre painter of fairies and of religious subjects. He undertook book illustration from the 1840s onwards. He died in Edinburgh in 1901.

MARY F. RAPHAEL. She was active 1889-1915 and known as a landscape and genre painter. She lived in London.

BRITON RIVIERE. Born in London in 1840, the son of a drawing teacher. He showed an early talent in the drawing of animals, which remained one of his major artistic activities. He also did some illustrations for magazines. He died in London in 1920.

DANTE G. ROSSETTI. See 2.4.

FREDERICK SMALLFIELD. Born in Homerton, England, in 1829. He studied at the RA schools and exhibited at the RA between 1849 and 1886. However, he was especially known as a watercolourist. He exhibited much of this work at the Royal Institute of Painters in Watercolour. He lived in London, dying in 1915. See also 18.13p.

JOHN RODDAM SPENCER-STANHOPE. Born in 1829 in Yorkshire. He studied under G.F. Watts, but was more associated with the PRB and influenced by them. Indeed, he was one of the group whose members cooperated in painting the ceiling of the Oxford Union Hall in 1857-58 (see Introduction). He moved with his wife to Italy in 1872 for relief of long-standing asthma and became an active member of the expatriate English community, lending his artistic talents to the decoration of the Anglican church there, for example. He died in Florence in 1908.

JOHN MELHUISH STRUDWICK. Born in Surrey, England, in 1849 (ECR). He studied at the RA schools and in South Kensington, I believe at the NATS. He worked as a studio assistant to Spencer-Stanhope (see above) and Burne-Jones (see 3.1) at different times, and was influenced by them. He exhibited at the RA, the Grosvenor, and the New Galleries.

JOHN WILLIAM WATERHOUSE. Born in 1849 in Rome to parents who were both artists. The family lived in Rome until 1853, when they returned to London. Trippi claims that Waterhouse had life-long fluency in Italian stemming from his early exposure to the language. Waterhouse's mother died in 1857, and his father re-married in 1860, and in 1861 sent his son to school in Leeds, whence the family had originated. Here Waterhouse acquired a command of Latin and a love for the Classical authors, reflected in his choice of subjects for his paintings for much of his career. He had returned to London by 1868, and lived with his father and step-mother until 1883. In this year he married Esther Kenworthy, another artist. The couple moved into rented rooms, rather than buying a house. This implies that their permanent childless state was a choice made at the outset of their marriage.

When Waterhouse returned to London from Leeds, he showed his interest in art by registering for privileged access to the art department of the British Museum, and by successfully applying for admission to the RA Schools in 1870. He studied there for only a year or two but did also receive training from his father. He sold his first painting in 1872 and sent his work to several London galleries from this time on, including the RA exhibitions, which became a major outlet for his paintings. His increasing productivity necessitated the rental of his own studio at Primrose Hill in 1878. He was elected an Associate of the RA in 1883. Waterhouse's wife particularly enjoyed the theatre. Trippi suggests that the couple's attendance at theatrical performances contributed to the heightened sense of drama in Waterhouse's pictures from this point. Another influence which would have tended in the same direction stemmed from his interest in occultism and the supernatural. Possibly hints of these features in his work helped to secure his election as a full Royal Academician in 1895. Certainly, he achieved increasing recognition through the 1890s, which may have influenced his decision to buy a combined house and studio at St John's Wood in 1900.

Ironically, 1900 saw the peak of the artist's career. He was held in high esteem by his fellow Academicians, taught regularly at the RA Schools, saw his work acclaimed and commanding high prices, and moved in the most privileged social circles, including the Athenaeum Club, to which he was elected in 1899. Beyond this point his paintings, with a few exceptions, never achieved the intensity of his earlier work, his popularity faded, he relinquished his teaching at the RA, and he lapsed into comparative obscurity. We can attribute part of this decline to the same winds that blew so unfavourably for Evelyn de Morgan (see above). Indeed, one can see other, intertwined parallels between these two artists: the similar influences which affected both, their artistic style, their love of Italy (Waterhouse visited there repeatedly throughout his life), and the curve of their careers. Unlike de Morgan, Waterhouse had some patrons who continued to buy his work, and he turned to the reliable market of portrait paintings to a greater extent. In general, however, he did not seem to possess a strong business sense: he never entered the profitable market of book illustration or decorative commissions, nor did he arrange for mass editions of prints of his work. His financial situation must have been precarious. The strain it caused may have contributed to the prematurely aged and frail appearance seen in photographs taken during the last three years of his life. He died in London in 1917. See also 18.13p. (Trippi.)

WILLIAM J. WEBB[E]. He lived in London and worked as a landscape and genre painter. He is known to have travelled in the Middle East and Europe, and to have studied in Dusseldorf. He exhibited at the RA between 1853 and 1878.

"CHW." Not identified.

Illustrations and decoration: The picture on the front of the dust jacket occupies its whole surface and reproduces in colour part of *Saint Cecilia* by Waterhouse. The frontispiece and a third picture which faces the initial page of the introduction also serve a decorative function; the designers Fordham and Todd do not link them to any poem in the text. Apart from this the book lacks decoration.

The selection, as the title implies it will, draws mainly on Morris's lyrical and love poetry. I believe it is the first with this particular emphasis. Lovers of Morris's poetry therefore owe a debt of gratitude to those who conceived and saw the book through to its finished state. In contemplating illustration the designers may have thought that pictures contemporary with the poems would complement them better in spite of the absence of the artists' direct response to the text. In fact, in one or two instances, we do have an interaction between poet and artist, though in the opposite direction. Burne-Jones's *Briar Rose* series of paintings inspired Morris's verse. Both appear in this collection. One would expect Fordham and Todd could find a match more easily for lyrical and love poems than for narrative poetry. This proves to be the case, especially with the poems eulogising the various months. Madox Brown's *The Pretty Baa-Lambs* sits well with Morris's "March," as does Burne-Jones's *Summer Green* with "July," and Millais' *Autumn Leaves* with "September." Others, such as Rossetti's *Venus Verti Cordia* with "Pomona," seem equally felicitous. A few come close to matching the poem, but do not quite catch its mood. Two examples suffice. Holman hunt's *Straying Sheep*, with its emphasis on the animals, does not mesh seamlessly with "From the Uplands to the Sea," even though one sees both of these geographical features in the picture. In similar fashion Strudwick's picture of an orchard in the full richness of its crop fails to suggest the tone of Morris's lines in which the last fruits hanging on the trees await the onslaught of winter.

Too many pairings go wildly astray, particularly those accompanying narrative poems. *Laus Veneris*, which faces "Two Red Roses across the Moon," bears only the most tangential relationship to the text. The picture which faces the first lines of "The Haystack in the Floods" does show a knight and a lady, but far from the dogged brunette riding in mud and rain through open country we see a drooping blonde standing in dry woodland. The second picture does not retrieve the situation. The climactic scene in the poem demands illustration, and Todd uses Paton's *The Bluidie Tryst*. This melodramatic painting depicts a woman distraught with anguish, standing over her murdered lover. She is alone. Godmar's sentence, black as thunderclouds, "Take note, my lady, that your way / Lies backward to the Chatelet!" needs his presence for the picture to drive home the full force of the lines. One has only to compare Harrison's rendition of the same scene (see illustration accompanying 2.11) to realize how short Todd's selection falls. Similar mis-matches occur with some of the lyrical poems. Madox Brown's *The Hayfield* does not incarnate the spirit of a poem which begins, "Pray but one prayer for me twixt thy closed lips." When one compares this picture with those done specifically for "Summer Dawn" (2.16 and 18.8), the shortcoming of the pairing becomes plain. Similarly in "Tapestry Trees" and "The Lion" Morris focuses on the subject of the title. However, the illustrations in this book focus on the female figure which dominates the picture. Two further examples serve in closing. Evelyn de Morgan's *The Garden of Autumn*, with the abundance of harvest therein, sits poorly with the pessimism of Morris's lines to Autumn on the opposite page. Since the compiler includes Morris's eulogies to all four seasons, Fairfax Murray's pictures for "The Lapse of the Year" in *A Book of Verse* (6.1) would seem a better choice, to name only one example. Lastly, Fordham and Todd use Waterhouse's *Miranda, The Tempest* to illustrate "Fair Weather and Foul." Perhaps they saw Miranda as an allegory for the fair weather. Even so the poem gives no licence for the presence of the ship which figures so prominently in the picture. Compared with the treatment of the same subject by Benningfield (18.8), this choice too fails in its aim.

18.13pa
Love/ Is Enough/ Pre-Raphaelite Paintings and Poems/
With an Introduction by Clive Wilmer/
Frances Lincoln

Colophon: Love is Enough: Pre-Raphaelite Paintings and Poems ©
Frances Lincoln Limited 1998.
First published in Great Britain by Frances Lincoln Limited, 4 Torriano Mews Torriano Avenue, London NW5 2RZ.

18.13pb
Love/ is Enough/ Pre-Raphaelite Paintings and Poems/
With an Introduction by Clive Wilmer/
Past Times

Colophon (in part): Love is Enough: Pre-Raphaelite Paintings and Poems Special Edition for PAST TIMES ®, Oxford, England First published in Great Britain in 1998 by Frances Lincoln Limited, 4 Torriano Mews Torriano Avenue, London NW5 2RZ . . . Set by MATS, Southend-on-Sea, Essex Designed by David Fordham

18.13pc
Love/ Is Enough/
Poems and Paintings Celebrating Love/
CB/ Contemporary Books

Colophon (in part): Cover and interior design by David Fordham. Set by MATS , Southend-on-Sea, Essex. First published in Great Britain in 1998 by Frances Lincoln Limited, 4 Torriano Mews Torriano Avenue, London NW5 2RZ. This edition first published in 2000 by Contemporary Books. A Division of NTC/Contemporary Publications Group, Inc.

Binding: Front and back of dust jacket have detail from *Love among the Ruins* by Burne-Jones in colour over whole surface, title in gilt lower left. Title and publisher vertically on spine in panel with cream-coloured ground. Front flap with brief notes, PRB poets in book, back flap with biographical details of author of introduction. Bound in blue buckram, pictorial endpapers.

Pagination/Size: 96 / 185 x 117 mm.

Comment: As in 18.8-10, the outermost two sheets of first and last gatherings serve as endpapers.

Contents: Pp. 1-3 endpapers, p. 4 colophon and publication information, p. 5 title page, pp. 6-7 introduction by Wilmer (18.13pa & b), p. 6 preface, p. 7 epigraph from "The Flight of Love" by Shelley (18.13pc), pp. 8-85 text, pp. 86-91 index of artists and paintings, pp. 92-93 index of poems, pp. 94-96 endpapers.

Comment: The layout editor, David Fordham, pays his readership the compliment of assuming they all have a detailed knowledge of the poets he includes, since the index lists them by date of birth, Wordsworth first born in 1770, Swinburne last in 1837. He includes six poems by Morris, drawn from a variety of his works. Most of the poets included lived before the PRB movement, Wordsworth, Shelley, Byron, and Keats, for example. However, some of their poems served as inspiration for the Pre-Raphaelite painters.

Illustrators: EDWARD BURNE-JONES. See 3.1.
    ARTHUR HUGHES. See 18.12.
    JOHN E. MILLAIS. See 18.12.
    WILLIAM MORRIS. See Introduction.
    DANTE G. ROSSETTI. See 2.4.
    FREDERICK SMALLFIELD. See 18.12.
    JOHN W. WATERHOUSE. See 18.12.

Illustration and decoration: David Fordham, one of the designers of *The Sweet Days Die*, also designed this book. Thus the reader finds a strong resemblance between the two. In this book Fordham selected verses dealing with love by a range of nineteenth century poets, and paired them with reproductions of works by Pre-Raphaelite painters. *Love Is Enough* suffers by the comparison in that it is barely half the size of the earlier book. Furthermore its upright shape does not lend itself to the reproduction of paintings whose shape is most often a horizontal rectangle. Thus Fordham frequently resorted to providing only part of a painting with consequent loss of the artist's conception of the subject. The extent of the loss is particularly severe where the poems and the picture deal with the same subject, as in Waterhouse's paintings *La Belle Dame sans Merci* and *Hylas and the Nymphs* facing poems with the same title. More often Fordham betrays a deficiency in selecting specific matches between poem and verse. In several instances a painting he pairs with a poem by Morris in *The Sweet Days Die* reappears in *Love Is Enough* paired with a work by a different poet. Among others, Burne-Jones's *The March Marigold* and his *Green Summer* now resurface with Wordsworth's "The Lost Love" and Clare's "Evening" respectively, while Smallfield's *Early Lovers* reappears with Hood's "Time of Roses." More appropriately, Fordham reunites Rossetti's painting *Venus Verti Cordia* with his poem of the same name. The last pairing also exemplifies Fordham's attempt to match poem and painting by drawing heavily on the works of Rossetti, who clearly had some of his own poems in mind when choosing a subject to paint. In this instance and in others where the artists executed their paintings to illustrate a particular poem, the two complement each other well. For other poems, the editor's search for a match had varying success.

All the decoration comprises pictures by Burne-Jones, and like the textual illustration all is in full colour. The dust jacket carries his *Love among the Ruins*, and the endpapers a detail from *Laus Veneris*. Both also appear as part of the textual illustration. On the title page Fordham completes the decoration with *The Soul Attains* from the *Pygmalion Series*. The colour of the last excels over the black and white reproduction of the same picture in *Pygmalion and the Image* (4.4).

The publisher borrowed the title for this anthology from Morris's play and used its refrain in the selection. The book has six poems by Morris in all, four of which had already appeared in *The Sweet Days Die*, paired with the same pictures as in that book. Two are *The Briar Rose* and *Another for the Briar Rose,* with its group of elegant sleeping women in one, and a tangled thorn hedge in the other, both evoking images of *The Sleeping Beauty*. Morris makes the parallel even more explicit in his poem. One of the new entries is an extract from *Praise of My Lady* coupled with Morris's portrait of his future wife, the subject of the poem. The other matches an extract from *Cupid and Psyche* with a painting by Burne-Jones of the same subject.

Appendix 1

Paperback Editions with Covers Illustrating the Text

Paperback editions of works by Morris have a long history. Writing of the first English edition of *News from Nowhere*, Buxton Forman records that "the main issue was but a thick trimmed pamphlet in a paper wrapper." The paper of the wrapper for this book is no thicker than that used for the rest of the book, and is not illustrated. Paperback books with an illustrated cover became commonplace as early as the mid-nineteenth century with the introduction of the so-called yellowbacks. The term denotes inexpensively produced books which catered to the mass market of travellers that resulted from the development of the railway system in Britain However, I am unaware of any of Morris's works in this format. Paperbacks published after the mid-twentieth century include numerous republications of works by Morris. Those with internal illustration appear in the main text. However, many have no relevance in the context of the present book. In some the picture bears no relationship to the contents. Some are anthologies in which the cover may have a similar irrelevance to the content or illustrate a story by a different contributor.

In the 1970s two publishers, Ballantine and Newcastle, produced most of Morris's prose fiction in paperbacks which have a cover illustrating the text. Ballantine Books probably had more financial resources and they certainly achieved greater uniformity and interest in the four titles they issued. They employed a fantasy writer, Lin Carter, as editor for all four, and indeed for several works of fantasy by other authors which they published during this period. The covers which Ballantine commissioned from Gervasio Gallardo provide the dramatic impact of these editions. Newcastle Publishing put out their Morris titles and translations in their *Forgotten*

Fantasy series. They did so without duplicating the Ballantine titles. The Newcastle editions are rather larger than those of Ballantine, necessarily so because they photo-reproduced early octavo editions. Ballantine, on the other hand, did a new printing for the books they published, working with traditional galley proofs. Newcastle's covers tend to the decorative rather than the illustrative. However, they did use original art work for most of their covers, though we cannot hail the fidelity of the picture to the story. The list below includes the titles with a reasonable claim to illustrate the text.

The start of the twenty-first century has seen a plethora of paperback editions of almost all of Morris's works from his writings on art, social matters, politics, and architecture, to his poems, translations and fiction. Many of these books lack an illustrative cover. Some that have one, such as the titles from the Aegypan Press, do not warrant inclusion, since the pictures are so clearly anachronistic or irrelevant to the text. A few examples suffice. On the cover of *The House of the Wolfings* the viewer sees a nineteenth-century scene of a punt on a tranquil river with a university-like building in the background. The picture fails to convey the appropriate support for a tale of a Germanic people repelling Roman incursions. (Presumably Morris set his story early in the first century of the Christian era when the Germanic tribes effectively destroyed Roman ambitions in Germania at the battle of Teutonburg Forest.) In *The Roots of the Mountains* the viewer sees a row of nineteenth-century cottages by the side of a rushing stream with cliffs rising on the opposite bank. The cover picture of *The Water of the Wondrous Isles* aims at an impression of mist with the sun about to break through. At the base are indistinct darker forms. The image puts one in mind of Turner's late work, and may be reproduced from one of his paintings. In summary, the general nature of these pictures precludes them from further consideration as illustration relating in any way to the text.

A minority of these recent editions do have illustrative covers, notably those from the Wildside Press. This publisher even seems to have commissioned some of the pictures especially for their book.

I have arranged the list which follows chronologically by date of publication.

Longmans, Green

News from Nowhere. London. Longmans, Green. 1936. The cover carries Gere's picture of Kelmscott Manor (see 10.1). This edition appeared as #14 in the Swan Library series, the hardcover version of which is not illustrated. The first hardcover edition came out in 1933, but I do not know if a paperback edition appeared contemporaneously.

Collier

The Volsunga Saga. New York: Collier Books, 1962, reprinted 1967 and 1971. The cover shows a Viking warrior and his ship, reproduced from Culver Pictures. The cover portrays a man of the period and culture of the Volsungs, and we can accept the picture as illustrative of the text, though scarcely depicting a particular scene.

Ballantine

The Wood beyond the World. First US edition July 1969, reprinted January 1974. UK edition August 1971. The cover art portrays the scene in Chapter 10 in which Walter first meets the Maid as she sits dabbling in the stream by the grey rock. The artist Gervasio Gallardo depicts the scene with fidelity to the details of Morris's description. His picture extends over front and back cover.

The Well at the World's End. 2 volumes. First US edition August 1970 (Vol. 1) September 1970 (Vol. 2), reprinted December 1972 and September 1973. Re-issued as a single volume July 1975 and May 1977. The two volumes of this edition have an illustration which extends over front and back covers. If one thinks of front and back cover as each forming one panel of the picture, there are three panels between the two volumes. One panel is common to each volume, namely the front cover of volume 1 and the back cover of volume 2. Thus the back cover of volume 1 and the front cover of volume 2 form the supporting sides of a triptych. The picture shows the scene in Chapter 18 of Book III, in which Ralph and Ursula stand under the Dry Tree by the edge of the poisonous pool and see the crow about to drink its water and then die. In the one-volume edition the publisher uses only the central and right-hand panels, and places them in reverse order to that found in the two-volume set.

The Water of the Wondrous Isles. US edition November 1971. UK edition 1972. There are some differences in the typography of the covers of these two editions, but the cover art is the same. Unlike the two titles described above, the picture on the cover of this book seems symbolic in part. It portrays Birdalone sitting with her back to the viewer on a flower-covered bank with small woodland animals around her, a large tree trunk immediately to her left. This foreground resembles a spot described in Chapter 9 of Part 1. She is naked, though covered by her

waist-long hair. She is gazing out over a wide bay in which sits the Sending Ship. Atop each of the two headlands enclosing the bay is a castle, and through the open mouth of the bay small islands appear, faint in the haze of distance. The whole scene suggests Birdalone on the verge of starting on her Quest, looking out at the way she will go in pursuing it.

The Sundering Flood. US edition May 1973. I am unaware of a UK edition. The front cover reproduces fairly closely the picture of the City of the Sundering Flood inset in the map which faces the first page of text in the first trade edition and on the front fixed endpaper of the KP edition. The picture extends over the back cover as a fanciful representation of mountains in the background, forest in front of them, and a flower-covered headland with a unicorn standing on it in the foreground.

Unicorn

The Sundering Flood. British and US editions published in 1973, in Brighton and Seattle respectively. The picture extends over the front and half of the back covers. It portrays a procession in medieval dress entering the gate of a walled city. Its appearance suggests that it comes from a book of hours. The publishers presumably intended it to represent the City of the Sundering Flood.

Newcastle Publishing Company, Hollywood, California

Golden Wings and Other Stories. March 1976. Newcastle reprinted an introduction which Alfred Noyes wrote originally for *The Early Romances of William Morris,* published by J.M. Dent in 1907. They re-used the decorated border of the title page, done by Reginald Knowles, substituting their own title and publisher's name within it. The actual text is a photo-reproduction of the prose section of the Dent edition, somewhat enlarged. For the cover illustration they adapted a picture by Patten Wilson from *Hero-Myths and Legends of the British Race,* published in 1915 by George G. Harrap. The designer achieved a fairly convincing rendering of the protagonist of the title story. (I am indebted to Douglas Menville of Newcastle Publishing for the information about the origin of the picture.)

Child Christopher and Goldilind the Fair. April 1977. This book has an original introduction by Richard B. Mathews, but otherwise the text consists of a photographic reproduction of the Mosher Press edition of 1900, which came out in an edition of 450 copies. Robert Kline did an illustration which extends over the front and back covers and the spine, a spirited rendering of Christopher, sword in hand and Goldilind on his other arm, facing a mounted knight across a ditch. Possibly the artist sought to depict the eve of the battle on the holm.

The Roots of the Mountains. April 1979. This book lacks the promised introduction by Mathews. The publisher states that the text reproduces the Longmans, Green edition of 1896. However, that is itself identical to the first trade edition of 1890, published by Reeves and Turner. The artist, Riley K. Smith, drew a cover design competently executed but static, showing Face of God and the Bride rather than a scene or action.

One of the Newcastle titles, *The Glittering Plain,* does have a frontispiece, and therefore appears in the main text (see 11.3).

Alan Sutton Publishing Limited, Stroud, Gloucestershire, UK

The Well at the World's End. 1996. The cover reproduces a detail from Burne-Jones's painting *Temperantia,* and depicts a woman in a loose-fitting full-length dress pouring water from a large vase. Possibly the publisher selected this image as representative of Ursula during her time in thralldom.

Oxford University Press

News from Nowhere. 2003. For the cover the publisher reproduced a photograph taken from an open upstairs window of Kelmscott Manor in 1898. The viewer sees outhouses and trees in the background. The window in both size and its multiple small panes resembles the one drawn by New to illustrate *Gossip about an Old House* (see 16.1).

Dover

News from Nowhere. 2004. Dover reproduced in brown the picture of Kelmscott Manor by C.M. Gere (see 10.2) which Morris first used in the KP edition of this same work. Dover also included Morris's essay "How I Became a Socialist" as an introduction.

Wildside Press, Gillette, New Jersey

The Well at the World's End. 2 volumes. 2000. Both volumes have the same cover, a woodland scene of moss-covered tree trunks and rocks, with what seems to be the entrance to a grotto in the foreground, possibly intended to represent the Chamber of Love. Wildside claim copyright for the cover, which they presumably commissioned specially for this edition.

The Wood beyond the World. 2001. The cover illustration portrays an open woodland scene of a general nature, with a hill in the background seen through the trees, and a lurid sunset above it. It depicts the text

only in the most non-specific way – a wood in the story, a wood in the picture.

The Sundering Flood. 2001. The cover depicts a precipitous bush-covered slope rising from a bay, with a castle and houses perched at the top. The picture has a nineteenth-century style. However, the publisher did not identify the source, nor name the artist, if it was commissioned for this edition. Possibly the publisher intended the castle and houses to portray the town at the mouth of the Sundering Flood.

The Glittering Plain. 2001. The publisher reproduced the title page of the Newcastle edition of 1976 (see 11.3) as the cover of this edition, using garish colours and re-setting the lettering. This book is slightly larger than its predecessor, but identical in most other respects, with the same introduction, glossary, and layout of text. The difference in size stems from larger margins, so great at the top that the layout looks odd. Wildside does not, however, use the picture by Pyle found in the earlier book. Illustration is limited to the ship described under 11.3.

It seems clear that Wildside acquired the rights to the Newcastle titles. They also published the following works:

Art and Architecture: Essays 1870-1884. 2003. The cover illustration depicts the sort of medieval cross seen in the square of some English towns such as Banbury, houses of similar period in the background. Probably the publisher sought to hark back to Morris's preoccupation with the architecture of this time with this picture. It carries an indecipherable signature in its bottom left corner.

Early Romances. 2003. This book is a facsimile reprint of the Newcastle Publishing Company edition of *Golden Wings* (see above). Indeed, it carries the words "The Newcastle Forgotten Fantasy Library Volume VIII" on the half-title page. The cover depicts a mounted knight blowing a horn, a lady behind him on the same horse, and a Neuschwanstein-like castle on a high cliff in the background. The picture has an indistinct signature which looks like "Donn Crane." The style is very much that of Walter Crane.

The Water of the Wondrous Isles. 2004. The cover has what appears to be original art work. It depicts Birdalone as a child, fancily dressed and wearing a necklace with large beads and multiple chains, stepping over the threshold of a door, her head barely the height of the latch. Behind her lie some paving stones and what may be an abandoned wheel, while the background is a misty blur. Presumably the artist sought to depict the point in the story when Birdalone is living with the Witch Wife.

Inkling Press

The Roots of the Mountains: A Book that Inspired J.R.R. Tolkien. 2003. The cover illustration appears to be original with the Inkling Press. It depicts a woman in a long dress and cape standing by a large tree in a sparsely treed and rocky landscape. She holds her forearm over her forehead in an attitude of grief or despair, the whole in an orange monochrome. The subject is of a general nature, and does not relate to an obvious event in the story. Indeed, it seems unlikely to do so; the same cover appears on two companion titles published by Inkling, *The House of the Wolfings: A Book That Inspired J.R.R. Tolkien* and a book which combines these two works of Morris, *More to William Morris: Two Books That Inspired J.R.R. Tolkien: The Roots of the Mountains and The House of the Wolfings.*

On the Lines of Morris' Romances: Two Books That Inspired J.R.R. Tolkien: The Wood beyond the World and The Well at the World's End. 2003. The cover illustration, in a yellow monochrome, depicts a young woman sitting on a rocky ledge which falls away behind her. She wears a full-length dress, her attention given to braiding her waist-long hair. The trunk and lower branches of a tree rear behind her, and a range of dark mountains stretches across the far background. The publisher does not supply information about the source of the picture, but it is in sympathy with the spirit of the two novels, being in the Pre-Raphaelite style. This book is rather larger than most paperbacks, with the text in double columns.

THE·DEFENCE·OF·GVENEVERE

NEVERTHELESS·YOV·O·SIR·GAVWAINE
LIE
WHATEVER·HAPPENED·ON·THROVGH
ALL·THOSE·YEARS·
GOD·KNOWS·I·SPEAK·TRVTH·SAYING
THAT·YOV·LIE·

SIDNEY H. METEYARD
The Quest, No. 3, p. 15

Appendix 2

Orphan Pictures

From time to time artists have drawn pictures which illustrate one or another of Morris's works but which were never published as part of the work. One artist did this to provide editorial copy, another as an exercise in technique, and a third for use in a projected edition which did not come to fruition. In general I have come across these "orphan pictures" by chance; there may be many more. The list below gives the name of the artist, the work which contains the scene, and the book or magazine which published the picture.

1. A picture by Sidney H. Meteyard (see 18.12) illustrating the three-line stanza beginning "Nevertheless, you, O Sir Gawaine, lie" from *The Defence of Guenevere*. In *The Quest*, No. 3, page 15 (The Birmingham Guild, Birmingham, July 1895).

2. Three pictures by Jessie M. King (see 2.1) illustrating scenes from *The Wood beyond the World*. In *The Studio*, Volume 17, November 1899. In his biography of King, White writes that "a group of them" was awarded the Silver Medal in the National Competition for art students, and "three of them [were] reproduced in *The Studio*." The phrasing suggests there might be other pictures in the series which were not published. However, White wrote in response to my query that he did not know of any others.

3. A series of pictures by Charles M. Gere (see 10.2) drawn for a projected edition of *The House of the Wolfings*. Reproduced in Peter Stansky's *Another Book that Never Was* (San Francisco: The Book Club of California, 1998).

In addition there is a painting in the collection of the Birmingham Art Gallery which illustrates *The Man Born to Be King.* However, as far as I know it has never been reproduced.

"Parent pictures" also exist. For example, Morris drew his inspiration for "The Tune of Seven Towers" and "The Blue Closet," both poems in *The Defence of Guenevere,* from watercolours with those titles by Rossetti. Morris bought the pictures from the artist in 1857.

Appendix 3

Unique Copies with Illustration

A unique book can acquire its status from either of two procedures. It can be created from writing on blank paper and binding the completed text, or it can arise from embellishment of a copy of an existing edition. In one sense an author renders a book unique by inscribing it. However, this discussion deals only with books unique by virtue of their content. By their nature such copies lie beyond the scope of a book dealing with published editions. However, Morris and others did create such copies, some of which also contain illustration. Anyone seeking information about illustration of Morris's work needs some awareness of unique copies, if only because of the possibility that a publisher may print a facsimile edition, as happened with *A Book of Verse* (see 6.1).

The earliest unique copies originated with Morris himself. For nearly a decade starting in the late 1860s he found a passion for calligraphy, and wrote several of his works in his own fine script, besides the works of others, such as *The Rubaiyat of Omar Khayam* and an unfinished *Aeneid*. Both these have achieved a level of public awareness, the first from a facsimile edition by the Phaidon Press in 1981, and the latter from its description in a private press book *A Pre-Raphaelite Aeneid* published by Ward Ritchie in 1934. Most of Morris's own writings in his calligraphic script remain in manuscript form. Fairbank documents their locations, but his references hold good only for those in public institutions. Inevitably those in private collections will change hands if they have not already done so in the period since his book appeared in 1970. Some of the manuscripts have decoration, but few contain illustration, the *Volsunga Saga* in the Bodleian Library at Oxford being in this minority.

The illustration comprises several female figures on the title page, most drawn in outline only, and two fine miniatures by Fairfax Murray surrounding the dropped capitals of Chapters 1 and 10. The first depicts Sigi in the act of slaying Bredi, and the second Borghild holding the cup of poison with which she kills Sinfiotli, both these episodes being crucial points in the story. The manuscript has a permanent form, in stiff vellum covers by the Doves bindery. However, George Wardle, who supplied decoration for the title page and chapter headings, did not complete this work, and decoration peters out in the later part. This failure to finish either text or decoration occurs elsewhere among Morris's manuscripts, such as some others held by the Bodleian Library and also his *Aeneid* already mentioned.

The incomplete nature of some manuscripts makes finished ones the more noteworthy. Between 1871 and 1873 Morris wrote out the text for one of his own works, combining his calligraphy with illustration by Fairfax Murray. This book, *The Story of Frithioff the Bold*, appeared at auction in 1987. Christie's catalogue of the sale provides an excellent description with illustrations. Like *The Volsunga Saga* described above, the book is of quarto size, bound by Cobden-Sanderson in turquoise morocco with the title, author, and decoration vertically in gilt on the spine. Morris wrote on handmade paper using brown-black ink, in double columns. The first page is decorated with an opulent border, and other pages have marginal decorations. Fairfax Murray's two exquisite miniatures catch the essentials of the story admirably. The first, at the start of the text, shows Frithiof and Ingibiorg dallying in Ingibiorg's bower on Baldur's Mead. Frithiof's loss of Ingibiorg to King Ring is passed over, and in the second picture, halfway down column 40, at the start of Chapter 14, one sees the aged king on his deathbed, Ingibiorg lying beside him, and Frithiof in attendance at the foot of the bed. This book has always been in private hands, going from one collector to another. Morris owned it initially, but it passed from him to Fairfax Murray some time during Morris's lifetime. It sold at Sotheby's sale of Fairfax Murray's collection in 1919, and again in an American auction in 1934. It last appeared at the auction of the Doheny collection in New York in 1989 alluded to above.

Other calligraphers have created manuscripts of texts by Morris. However, documentation comparable to that provided by Fairbank for Morris's calligraphy does not exist. Experts in the field acknowledge Graily Hewitt among the foremost British calligraphers in the first half of the twentieth century, and he executed two Morris texts of which I am aware. He had a particular regard for Morris, and read one of the three papers delivered before the Double Crown Club in 1934, which marked the centenary of Morris's birth. These proceedings appeared as *Three Papers on Morris* published by the Sherval Press. Given this interest it seems altogether possible that Hewitt may have executed more than just two Morris manuscripts.

Hewitt created one of the manuscripts of which I have knowledge in collaboration with Allan Vigers as artist. Between them they produced

an exquisite piece of work which would have delighted Morris. Beginning in 1907 and finishing in May 1908, they wrote and decorated the title poem from *The Defence of Guenevere,* on vellum, bound by Katherine Adams in full royal-blue morocco with gilt decoration. It measures 201 x 146 mm. The initial decoration, a heraldic shield, appears in lieu of a half-title page on the verso of the first sheet after three blank pages. The next verso and its facing recto carry a double spread, with the title on the left and the first stanza on the right. The lettering is in gilt, and the initial capital of the title and first word of the poem are large and dropped. A border, predominantly of red and blue flowers and leaves, surrounds the letters. Within this border Vigers placed some small heraldic shields ascribed to Knights of the Round Table. He also included Guenevere in a long white dress and green cloak in the lower left corner, and her antagonist Sir Gawain in the corresponding corner on the right. At the base of each of the following seventeen pages of text Vigers drew a heraldic shield surrounded by decoration similar to that of the border of the title page. Hewitt supplied a list of the knights with whom he and Vigers associated the shields on the page after the end of the text. This book now forms part of the collection of the Huntington Library in San Marino, California. Hewitt decorated but did not illustrate the other Morris manuscript, *The Day Is Coming.* He may have written this manuscript late in his life, since it seems to have passed directly into private hands after his death in 1952.

Anyone who embellishes a copy of a published book creates a unique copy, whether or not he or she set out with this intention. He faces a constraint not encountered by a calligrapher starting with pen and blank paper, namely where to place his contemplated decoration or illustration. The improvers adopt one or both of two strategies. Some add colour to what originally appeared in black and white, some fill in the free space available, mainly on title page and margins of the text, while others combine the two procedures. Perhaps not surprisingly, Morris also produced the most noteworthy example of a unique book created from a copy of a published edition.

Parenthetically, one can trace Morris's interest in book design from the 1860s when he and Burne-Jones contemplated a fine illustrated edition of *The Earthly Paradise,* through the following decades when he arranged for large paper copies as a part of editions of his works, and on to the final phase of the KP. Before this final period this interest found more overt expression in 1888, when Morris published the Superior Edition of *The Roots of the Mountains* limited to 250 copies. This book relies on the quality of its materials and the elegance of its layout for its effect. However, Morris sought to go further, and found the opportunity to do so when he attended the Arts and Crafts Exhibition in 1889 and saw there some illuminated manuscripts by Edmund Reuter. Reuter was a Swiss artist living in London at the time whose main occupation was the decoration of pottery ware. He later returned to Switzerland where he achieved a measure of recognition and success. The quality of Reuter's manuscript illumination impressed Morris. On the basis of it he

commissioned Reuter to enhance a copy of the Superior Edition beyond its original austere elegance, to convert Gothic to Rococo.

Reuter took five years, from 1889 to 1894, to fulfil Morris's expectations. Morris then rebound the book in limp vellum with vellum endpapers, and placed the title on the top of the spine and the date at the base. Reuter's work begins on the title page which he decorated profusely with ornamental leaves and flowers, picked out in gold and brilliant colours. He treated the chapter headings similarly, but did also insert some marginal decoration on other pages of the text. The overall effect is stunning and invites comparison with the decorated manuscripts of the medieval era. Reuter placed the only textual illustration on the last page. A miniature painting there portrays a medieval town with a river in the foreground, and houses on each bank connected by a bridge with towers. Snow-capped mountains rear in the background. The illustration matches well the description of Burgstead given in the opening chapter.

Like *The Story of Frithiof* this book has passed from one private collector to another. It became part of William Foyle's vast collection in 1934 when he bought it at auction. Christie's dispersed the collection in their auction of 2000. The sale catalogue provides a description and excellent reproductions of the decoration and illustration. Maggs Brothers listed the book in their catalogue #1296 in early 2001, when it presumably sold to another private collector.

Reuter's illustration of *The Roots of the Mountains* is exceptional only in the quality of the work. Examples of hand-embellished copies of a standard edition appear from time to time, and are probably more common than one might suppose. In the period up to 1914 a wealthy leisured class existed in Britain and North America, some of whose members, especially women, had limited opportunity for the expression of their talents. Some found an outlet in the decoration of published books. Many such books would remain in the family as heirlooms, and are therefore impossible to locate and document. Books of this kind appear for sale from time to time. An example comes from the 1870s when Julia Pocock illustrated "The Doom of King Acrisius," one of the stories from *The Earthly Paradise*, with line drawings done in black ink. Pocock was a trained artist who lived in London, where she was recognised as an illustrator and miniaturist and also worked in other artistic media. This equipped her well for the work being discussed. She obtained a copy of the first volume of the ten-volume edition of *The Earthly Paradise* published in 1872, disbound it, and drew marginal illustrations throughout the text.

Pocock's thirty-eight illustrations are all original ink drawings, done in the margin of the text. She executed them with considerable skill, using a very fine nib. The ink matches the print so exactly that at first glance the pictures look printed too. Even with some overlap onto the text itself in some drawings, the narrow space available limited the artist's room for manoeuvre. Thus all the drawings depict the human figure, the one exception being Perseus in the act of slaying the monster,

As down the beach he ran to meet the foe.
  But he, beholding Jove's son drawing near,
A great black fold against him did uprear,
Maned with grey tufts of hair, as some old tree
Hung round with moss, in lands where vapours be;
From his bare skull his red eyes glowed like flame,
And from his open mouth a sound there came,
Strident and hideous, that still louder grew
As that rare sight of one in arms he knew:
But godlike, fearless, burning with desire,
The adamant jaws and lidless eyes of fire
Did Perseus mock, and lightly leapt aside
As forward did the torture-chamber glide
Of his huge head, and ere the beast could turn,
One moment bright did blue-edged Herpe burn,
The next was quenched in the black flow of blood;
Then in confusèd folds the hero stood,
His bright face shadowed by the jaws of death,
His hair blown backward by the poisonous breath;
But all that passed, like lightning-lighted street
In the dark night, as the blue blade did meet
The wrinkled neck, and with no faltering stroke,
Like a god's hand the fell enchantment broke,
And then again in place of crash and roar,
He heard the shallow breakers on the shore,
And o'er his head the sea-gull's plaintive cry,
Careless as gods for who might live or die.

  Then Perseus from the slimy loathsome coil

JULIA POCOCK
[Persius Slaying the Monster]
The Doom of King Acrisius, **p. 274**

where a crocodile-like creature appears as well, drawn across the bottom of the page, while the figure of Perseus occupies the outer border. All the drawings illustrate a character or characters in the story at that point. The book finishes with a tailpiece depicting a fern, executed with the same delicacy as the rest. While the illustrations do not have a great dramatic impact, they are a charming embellishment which adds distinction to an otherwise pedestrian edition. Pocock inscribed the book to M.M. Holloway and dated it 1872. One has to assume Pocock gave it to a friend rather than a relative, where one would expect her to have used a first name. A later inscription sees the book pass from a grandfather, perhaps the same Holloway, to his granddaughter. The volume whence this text comes contains three of the stories in *The Earthly Paradise.* This begs the question whether Pocock illustrated the other two stories in the volume in a similar fashion.

When an artist adds only decoration to a book, as distinct from illustration, the task becomes easier. He or she can adapt decoration to the space available, in margins and even between lines. By contrast an illustration requires more space. All the examples of decoration of published books by Morris of which I am aware come from the nineteenth century. The first edition of *Love Is Enough,* published in 1873, includes twenty-five large-paper copies. In 1886-87 Beatrice Pagden decorated one of them. It is now in the Pierpont Morgan Library in New York (catalogue # PML77075). Pagden produced an exquisite effect, filling the margins with wonderful watercolour renditions of leafy sprays and British garden and wild flowers, scarcely repeating herself in regard to species, and each picture unique in itself. If one were to extend the concept of illustration to see flowers as allegorical of love, one could regard this book too as illustrated.

A book published about the same time with similar adornment can lay better claim to be illustrative, with decoration of equally high calibre. In the early 1870s Morris had his books published by Ellis and White. These books include the second edition of *The Defence of Guenevere* in 1875. Ellis owned one of the twenty-five large-paper copies, and had it decorated, possibly also by Beatrice Pagden. Ellis rebound this copy in full limp vellum. The artist depicted wild flowers almost exclusively, though in a variety equal to that seen in the book described in the previous paragraph. Lacking the brilliance and showiness of cultivated flowers, the decoration does not have the immediate impact of Pagden's *Love Is Enough.* However, the decorative scheme possesses more unity and gives greater satisfaction from its very restraint. The lettering of half-title and title pages is enclosed in gilt ruled lines and the rest of these two pages filled with leafy sprays and flowers. The artist used a similar pattern for subsidiary half-titles of individual poems and the first page of all the longer poems and for many of the shorter ones, sometimes using ink-ruled lines around the lettering and sometimes none at all. The case for an illustrative dimension in the pictures comes from the choice of flowers accompanying particular poems. The subtitle of *Sir Galahad, A Christmas Mystery,* suggested holly leaves and berries to the artist. Around the first page of *Two Red Roses across the Moon* the reader finds red roses in pairs and rose leaves in abundance. By contrast leaves reminiscent of yew appear on the first page of *King Arthur's Tomb*, and so on with carnation leaves for *The Gilliflower of Gold*. Maggs Brothers advertised this book in one of their catalogues in the mid-1990s, and it now resides in a private collection.

The addition of colour to existing letters, decoration or illustration is the simplest route for an improver to take to create a unique copy, and the hardest to find, for reasons already discussed. For example, the collection in the libraries at the University of British Columbia has one on its open shelves, not even recorded as out of the ordinary. Their copy of *Illustrated British Ballads, Old and New* (see 18.1) has had some of its originally black and white illustrations coloured with watercolour, presumably by a former private owner.

A Kelmscott copy of *The Sundering Flood* has added colouration of the inset map on the front fixed endpaper. Apart from this, I know of only one other instance in which illumination has been added to a book from the Kelmscott Press. Morris inscribed a copy of *The Tale of Emperor Coustans and Over Sea* for his engraver at the Press, W.H. Hooper. Hooper applied glowing colours to the double spread of the title pages of both stories and to all the dropped and decorated capitals throughout the text. He achieved the effect noted in some of the other illuminated copies of a medieval manuscript. Nevertheless this appendix must close with the reiteration that books described here represent only the few known to the writer, almost certainly do not come close to the total which exist, and may not even be representative of that total.

Bibliography

Aho, Gary. *William Morris: A Reference Guide.* Boston: G.K. Hall, 1985.

Allegemeines Künstlerlexicon: bio-bibliographischer Index A-Z. Munich-Leipzig: K.G. Saur Verlag, 1992-2000.

Ash, Russell. *Dante Gabriel Rossetti.* New York: Abrams, 1995.

Baile de Laperriere, Charles. *The Society of Women Artists Exhibitors 1855-1996.* Calne, Wilts., UK: Hillman Manor Press, 1996.

Barker, Nicolas, and John Collins. *A Sequel to an Enquiry into the Nature of Certain Nineteenth Century Pamphlets by John Carter and Graham Pollard: The Forgeries of H. Buxton Forman and T.J. Wise.* Aldershot, UK: Scolar Press, 1983.

Benezi, E. *Dictionnaire critique et documentaire des Peinteurs, Sculpteurs et Graveurs (de tous les temps).* Paris: Libraire Grund, 1976.

Bishop, Philip R. *Thomas Bird Mosher, Piratical Prince of Publishers: A Comprehensive Bibliography & Source Guide to the Mosher Books, Reflecting England's National Literature & Design.* New Castle, DE, and London: Oak Knoll Press and The British Library, 1998.

Buckman, David. *Dictionary of Artists in Britain since 1945.* Bristol: Art Dictionaries, 1998.

Bowers, Fredson. *Principles of Bibliographical Description.* Princeton, NJ: Princeton UP, 1949. Rpt. New Castle, DE: Oak Knoll, 1994.

Buxton Forman, H. *The Books of William Morris Described with Some Account of His Doings in Literature and the Allied Crafts.* London: Hollings, 1897.

Carter, J.W., and G. Pollard. *An Enquiry into the Nature of Certain Nineteenth Century Pamphlets.* London: Constable, 1934.

Castagno, John. *Artists as Illustrators: An International Directory with Signatures and Monograms 1800-Present.* Metuchen, NJ: Scarecrow Press, 1989.

Cave, Roderick, et al. *Private Press Books, 1969.* Pinner, Middlesex, UK: Private Press Libraries Association, 1970.

Christie's Auction Catalogue. *The Estelle Doheny Collection: Part VI. Printed Books and Manuscripts Concerning William Morris and His Circle.* New York: Christie, Manson and Wood, 1989.

Cope, Dawn, and Peter. *Postcards from the Nursery: The Illustrators of Children's Books and Postcards 1900-1950.* London: New Cavendish, 2000.

Darton, F.J. *Modern Book Illustrators in Great Britain and America.* London: The Studio, 1914.

de Freitas, Leo. *Charles Robinson.* London: Academy Editions, 1976.

Duncan, Bob. *James Leatham 1865-1945.* Aberdeen: Aberdeen People's Press, 1978.

Elliott, David B. *Charles Fairfax Murray: The Unknown Pre-Raphaelite.* Lewes, UK: Book Guild, 2000.

Engen, Rodney K. *Walter Crane as a Book Illustrator.* London: Academy Editions, 1975.

Fairbank, Alfred. See Morris, William, and Eirikr Magnusson.

Falk, Peter, et al., eds. *Who Was Who in American Art 1564-1975: 400 Years of Artists in America.* 3 vols. Madison, CN: Sound View Press, 1999.

Felmingham, Michael. *The Illustrated Gift Book, 1880-1930.* Aldershot, UK: Scolar Press, 1988.

Fitzgerald, Penelope. *Edward Burne-Jones: A Biography.* London: Michael Joseph, 1975.

Franklin, Colin. *The Private Presses.* London: Studio Vista, 1969.

Franklin, Colin. *Printing and the Mind of Morris.* Cambridge, UK: Rampant Lions Press, 1986.

Gaunt, William. *The Restless Century: Painting in Britain 1800-1900.* London: Phaidon Press, 1972.

Golden, Catherine J., ed. *Book Illustrated: Text, Image, and Culture 1770-1930.* New Castle, DE: Oak Knoll, 2000.

"Hans Gabriel Jentzsch." *Wikipedia, der freien Enzyklopädie.* <http.// de.wikipedia.org/wiki/Hans_Gabriel_Jentzsch>. 29 Dec. 2005.

Harris, Martin, et al. *Burne-Jones.* London: Barrie and Jenkins, 1973.

Horne, Alan. *The Dictionary of 20th Century British Book Illustrators.* Woodbridge, Suffolk, UK: Antique Collectors' Club, 1994.

Houfe, Simon. *The Dictionary of 19th Century British Book Illustrators.* Woodbridge, Suffolk, UK: Antique Collectors' Club, 1996.

Johnson, Fridolf. *Treasury of American Pen-and-Ink Illustration 1881-1938: 236 Drawings by 103 Artists.* New York: Dover, 1982.

Johnson, Jane, et al. *The Dictionary of British Artists 1880-1940: An Antique Collectors' Club Research Project Listing 41,000 Artists.* Woodbridge, Suffolk, UK: Antique Collectors' Club, 1976.

Kelvin, Norman. *The Collected Letters of William Morris.* 4 vols. Princeton: Princeton UP, 1984-1996.

LeMire, Eugene D. *A Bibliography of William Morris.* New Castle, DE: Oak Knoll, 2006.

Mahoney, Bertha F., et al. *Illustrators of Children's Books.* Boston: Horn, 1947.

Mallalier, Huon L. *The Dictionary of British Watercolour Artists up to 1920.* 2nd ed. Vol. 1, *The Text.* Woodbridge, Suffolk, UK: Antique Collectors' Club, 1986.

Masse, Gertrude C.E. *A Bibliography of First Editions of Books Illustrated by Walter Crane.* London: Chelsea, 1923.

Mather, Frank. *America's Great Illustrators.* New York: Abrams, 1978.

Morris, William, and Eirikr Magnusson. *The Story of Kormak the Son of Ogmund.* London: William Morris Society, 1970. [Contains Alfred Fairbank's bibliography of the Morris manuscripts.]

Morris, William. *The Juvenilia of William Morris.* Ed. Florence S. Boos. London: William Morris Society, 1983.

Opitz, Glenn B. *Mantle Fielding's Dictionary of American Painters, Sculptors and Engravers.* Poughskeepie, NY: Apollo, 1983.

Parry, Linda, ed. *William Morris.* London: Philip Wilson, 1996.

Peppin, Brigitte, et al. *Book Illustrators of the Twentieth Century.* New York: Arco, 1984.

Peterson, William S. ed. *The Ideal Book: Essays and Lectures on the Arts of the Book by William Morris.* Berkeley: University of California, 1982.

Peterson, William S. *A Bibliography of the Kelmscott Press.* Oxford: Clarendon, 1984.

Peterson, William S. *The Kelmscott Press: A History of William Morris's Typographical Adventure.* Oxford: Clarendon, 1991.

Pitz, Henry. *Howard Pyle: Writer, Illustrator, Founder of the Brandywine School.* New York: Clarkson Potter, 1975.

Pye, John W. *A Bibliography of American Editions of William Morris Published by Roberts Brothers, Boston 1867-1898.* Brockton, MA: John William Pye Rare Books, 1990.

Ransom, William. *Private Presses and their Books.* New York: Bowker, 1929.

Roberts, Leonard. *Arthur Hughes: His Life and Work. A Catalogue Raisonné with a Biographical Introduction by Stephen Wildman.* Woodbridge, Suffolk, UK: Antique Collectors' Club, 1997.

Schreiner, Berenice. "The Collaboration of G.F. Bodley and J.R. Spencer Stanhope in Florence 1892-1904." *J. William Morris Society* 14.2 (Spring 2001): 90-95.

Scott, Temple [J.H. Isaacs]. *A Bibliography of the Works of William Morris.* London: Bell and Sons, 1897.

Spencer, Isobel. *Walter Crane.* New York: Macmillan, 1975.

Stirling, Anna M.W. *William de Morgan and His Wife.* London: Thornton Butterworth, 1922.

Sturgis, Matthew. *Aubrey Beardsley: A Biography.* London: Harper Collins, 1999.

Suriano, Gregory R. *The Pre-Raphaelite Illustrators: The Published Graphic Art of the English Pre-Raphaelites and Their Associates.* New Castle, DE: Oak Knoll, 2000.

Thompson, Susan O. *American Book Design and William Morris.* London: British Library, 1996.

Trippi, Peter. *J.W. Waterhouse.* London: Phaidon, 2002.

Walsdorf, John J. *William Morris in Private Press and Limited Editions.* Phoenix, AZ: Oryx Press, 1983.

Waters, Grant M. *Dictionary of British Artists 1900-1950.* Eastbourne, UK: Eastbourne Fine Art, 1975.

White, Colin. *The Enchanted World of Jessie M. King.* Edinburgh: Canongate, 1989.

Williamson, George C. *Bryant's Dictionary of Painters and Engravers.* Port Washington, NY: Kenikat Press, 1964.

Wills, Hilary. *Sheffield Artists 1840-1940.* Sheffield: privately printed, 1996.

Wood, Christopher. *The Pre-Raphaelites.* New York: Viking, 1981.

Wood, Christopher. *Dictionary of British Art.* 3rd ed. Vol. 4, *Victorian Painters.* Woodbridge, Suffolk, UK: Antique Collectors' Club, 1995.

Index of Artists

Underlined items are illustrated in the text.

Artists Identified Only by Their Initials

ACB. *5.1P*

EHG. *4.3*

FLS. *11.1*

?RI. *8.4-5*

CHW. *18.12o*

Notes Added in Press

Facsimile editions of *The Collected Works of William Morris* appeared in 1966 and in 2000. Russell and Russell of New York published the earlier one, maintaining the same size as Longmans and binding it in black buckram, plain except for the title, volume number and publisher in gilt on the spine and mustard coloured endpapers. Russell supplied an additional title page, but the text is otherwise identical to the Longmans edition. The photo-reproduced illustrations lack the clarity of the originals of 1910-15, and Russell used machine-made paper for the text as a whole. Volume 4 of this edition would appear appropriately in Chapter 4 after 4.6. Volume 11 would appear appropriately in Chapter 7 after 7.1.

Adamant Media Corporation put out a later facsimile as a paperback, smaller in size and with the frontispieces displaced, to follow the title page. Volumes 4 and 11 would appear appropriately after entries for the Russell edition above. The covers of all 24 volumes have an identical design overall, but an inset panel on the front cover contains an illustration more or less appropriate for its contents.